ALEXANDER THE GREAT

ALEXANDER THE GREAT

J. R. Hamilton

Associate Professor of Classics
in the University of Auckland

HUTCHINSON UNIVERSITY LIBRARY

LONDON

HUTCHINSON & CO (*Publishers*) LTD
3 *Fitzroy Square, London W1*

London Melbourne Sydney Auckland
Wellington Johannesburg Cape Town
and agencies throughout the world

First published 1973

This book has been set in Times type,
printed in Great Britain on smooth wove paper
by the Camelot Press Ltd, London and Southampton,
and bound by Wm. Brendon of Tiptree, Essex

ISBN 0 09 115450 2 (cased)
0 09 115451 0 (paper)

To Claire, John and Neil

CONTENTS

MAPS

PREFACE

Alexander was a controversial figure in his lifetime. He remains controversial today. One major reason for this is the conflicting nature of our evidence, which I have tried to sketch in the opening chapter. Few of those who have written on Alexander have questioned his military genius—some indeed have considered him (mistakenly) to be no more than a great conqueror—but each inevitably stresses different aspects of his character and intentions. Tarn and Wilcken have stressed the effect of his Greek education on his thinking, and Wilcken has credited him with a missionary zeal to promote Hellenism in the lands he conquered. To me his heredity and his background are more important; he remained, essentially, Macedonian. This explains his hard drinking (denied, significantly, by Tarn) and, where circumstances called for it, the ruthless elimination of rivals. On the other hand, I find Alexander less cunning and calculating than Badian and others have done.

It is commonplace that the reign of Alexander marked a turning-point in the history of the Greek world, and Alexander's conquests, it is clear, opened up a vast new field to Greek and Macedonian settlers and traders. Nevertheless, while the Seleucid rulers, who inherited much of Alexander's empire, continued to found cities, to develop trade, and to promote exploration, Alexander's direct influence on succeeding centuries appears to have been slight. His vision of a ruling race of Macedonians and Persians and the measures to promote his 'policy of fusion' did not survive him. I have, therefore, ended this book with Alexander's death or, to be more exact, with the rejection of his plans by the Macedonian army. The best Introduction to the Hellenistic Age that followed is still Tarn and Griffith, *Hellenistic Civilisation*.

I should point out to readers that the location of the many Alexandrias which Alexander founded and the routes which he followed are not certainly known and that they will doubtless find other identifications in other books. We do not know, for example, which passes Alexander used in crossing and recrossing the Hindu-Kush; the Khawak pass favoured by others is just as likely (or unlikely) as the Khushan pass shown on my map. Sir Mortimer Wheeler, in fact, has reminded us that archaeology has revealed no trace of Alexander's presence east of Persepolis.

In a general way my obligations extend over many years, during which I have profited greatly from the advice of Mr G. T. Griffith, Professor Ernst Badian, and Professor Gerhard Wirth. More immediately, my great debt is to Professor Badian, who read the manuscript of the book and made a large number of suggestions, the vast majority of which I have been happy to accept. I am grateful also to my wife, who performed the task of the 'general reader' and suggested various stylistic improvements, and to Miss Ann Douglas and her staff for agreeing so readily to numerous changes and additions to my original manuscript.

Auckland
December 1972   J. R. HAMILTON

I

THE SOURCES

In the Preface to his *Anabasis of Alexander* Arrian claimed that accounts of Alexander were more numerous and more conflicting than those of any other historical figure. This may no longer be so, but in the last fifty years we have had many very different portraits of Alexander. Sir William Tarn and Fritz Schachermeyr have contributed two of the most notable, which differ widely from each other. To Tarn Alexander is essentially a Greek gentleman, chivalrous and in the main self-controlled, drinking only to keep his friends company, for the sake of the conversation; he is a man with a mission, seeking to realize his conception of the 'Brotherhood of Man'. Schachermeyr, on the other hand, sees Alexander as ruthless, indeed cruel, indulging in deceit and treachery to gain his ends, as a 'Titanic' figure aiming at the conquest of the world.

Without doubt the very different experience and background of the two historians go some way towards explaining their different interpretations of the evidence. Tarn[1] lived the life of a Scottish gentleman, and his values were those of his age and class, while his *Alexander the Great*, although not published until 1948, is not essentially altered from the chapters which he contributed to the sixth volume of the *Cambridge Ancient History* more than twenty years earlier. *Alexander der Grosse* appeared only a year after Tarn's book, but its background is the rise and fall of the Third Reich. Its author had seen at close quarters the nature of despotic power, and his Alexander in some respects resembles Hitler. Yet the historian is not a novelist, free to invent his characters, and much of the difficulty in arriving at a true picture of Alexander undoubtedly lies in the nature of the sources of our information. In many periods of history the historian can call upon the evidence of inscriptions, coinage, and

[1] Superior figures refer to Notes, pp. 171–83.

archaeology to control or supplement the literary sources. The reign of Alexander is no exception, but their evidence makes a smaller contribution than one would have hoped, and the student of Alexander relies essentially, as Arrian did, on written accounts of Alexander, whose purposes and prejudices he must attempt to assess. However, the situation confronting the modern historian is quite different from that which faced Arrian. Instead of a mass of contemporary or near-contemporary writings, he has precisely five complete or substantially complete narratives, none earlier than the reign of the emperor Augustus, some three hundred years after the death of Alexander.

The primary sources[2]

Behind these narratives lie the accounts of the so-called primary sources, whose 'fragments' have been assembled from citations in the extant historians and in other writers, notably the geographer Strabo and Athenaeus, the collector of anecdotes. Most of these early writers, unfortunately, are little more than names to us. There are only about half-a-dozen of whose work enough survives for us to form some judgement of its scope and tendency, even assuming, what is by no means certain, that the 'fragments' (seldom quoted verbatim) are representative of the work as a whole. It is some compensation that occasionally we have the assistance of the comments of later writers who had the opportunity, denied to us, of reading the complete work.

The term 'Alexander-historian', which we often use to describe these early writers, may perhaps mislead. It suggests a literary man; but of the writers whose 'fragments' permit analysis, only Callisthenes and perhaps Cleitarchus could properly be described as such. Of the remainder, Nearchus and Onesicritus were experienced sailors (and Thucydides reminds us that the art of sailing is not quickly learned), Chares was Alexander's chamberlain, Ptolemy a general and later king of Egypt, while Aristobulus appears to have been an engineer or an architect. All but Ptolemy were Greeks, and all but Cleitarchus accompanied Alexander on his expedition. Each illuminated different aspects of Alexander, reflecting their various opportunities for obtaining information, their differing relationships to the king, their individual backgrounds and aims.

Callisthenes[3] was certainly the earliest historian of Alexander. Unlike the others, he had an established reputation as a writer when he joined Alexander at the start of the campaign, although the fact that he was Aristotle's nephew doubtless influenced the king to invite him. He became what we may fairly call Alexander's official historian or 'press agent', a position which gave him exceptional

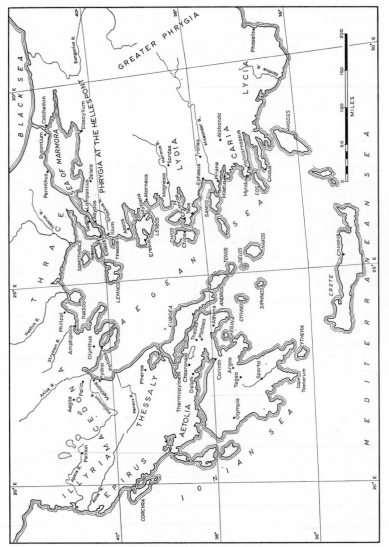

Greece and the Aegean

opportunities but at the same time imposed on him the restriction that he could relate, surely, only what Alexander approved. His task was evidently to produce for Greek consumption an account of Alexander's achievements that would stimulate the reluctant enthusiasm of the Greeks for the 'crusade' against the Persians. It would be naïve to suppose that such an account contained anything derogatory of Alexander and nothing in the extant fragments suggests that it did. Indeed, it appears certain that Callisthenes cast Alexander in 'heroic' mould in such a way as to recall his ancestor Achilles. Divine approval in the shape of thunder and lightning salutes his cutting (or untying) of the Gordian knot and the selection of a site for Zeus' temple at Sardes, divine assistance permits his passage along the Pamphylian coast and his journey through the desert to Ammon's shrine at Siwah. There the priest explicitly addresses the king as 'son of Zeus', while the oracle of Apollo among the Branchidae prophesies in like terms. Before the battle of Gaugamela, Alexander prays to the gods to help the Greeks, if he really is 'son of Zeus'. But to be the son of a god is not the same thing as being a god, and Callisthenes did not, as is often asserted, take the further step of proclaiming that Alexander was divine. Still, the tendency of Callisthenes' narrative is clear and it is scarcely surprising to find that later writers called him a 'flatterer' (*kolax*). His influence was doubtless considerable, even if we cannot trace it in detail. Nevertheless, his account failed to establish itself as *the* history of Alexander. Perhaps it was felt to be too partial or perhaps, since it was cut short by the author's arrest, other versions were preferred simply because they were complete.

Unlike Callisthenes neither Onesicritus nor Chares seems to have written a detailed account of Alexander's progress, and the influence of Chares at least was negligible. Nevertheless, his official position ensured his presence at Alexander's attempt to introduce the ceremony of *proskynesis* or prostration, at the mass marriages at Susa, and (probably) at the banquet when Cleitus was murdered. For these important events his testimony as an eye-witness is invaluable, particularly in view of the reticence of the 'official' account. Onesicritus[4] may have begun his book during the expedition and completed it within two or three years of Alexander's death. Certainly he wrote before Nearchus, who refuted his claim to be the leader, not the second-in-command, of the naval expedition from the Indus to the Euphrates. So far as we can judge, Onesicritus seems to have written a historical romance in which Alexander occupied the place which Cyrus the Great had done in the *Cyropaideia* of Xenophon. It is not perhaps surprising that Onesicritus as a pupil of Diogenes the Cynic should have depicted Alexander as the 'philosopher in arms' and exaggerated the king's philosophical qualities which, so Onesicritus would persuade us, were of greater assistance to him than his slender material resources. What is more reprehensible, and more dangerous, is his habit of blending fact with fiction, a habit of which Strabo, who made extensive use of Onesicritus' account of India, complains with feeling. Fortunately, among the extant writers on Alexander only Plutarch seems to have made much use of his book, although the schools of philosophy may have taken him more seriously.

4.   Alexander's admiral Nearchus wrote an account in the Herodotean manner of his voyage from the Indus to the Persian gulf. This forms the basis of Arrian's *Indica* and was used extensively by Strabo and the elder Pliny; otherwise it was neglected. In view of his close friendship with the king (which led to his exile under Philip) and the few details which he has given us, we must regret that Nearchus did not seek to draw a detailed portrait of Alexander. Still, the discussions which he held with Alexander before the voyage about the choice of a commander gave him the opportunity to describe the king's concern for the safety of the fleet (and for Nearchus himself!), while his meeting with Alexander at Gulashkird enabled him to bring out the king's swift and violent reactions to good and bad news. It is to Nearchus that we owe the interesting (and neglected) fact that Alexander sought by the foundation of cities to lead the Cossaeans and their neighbours to forsake their nomadic existence and settle down to cultivate the soil.[5]

The remaining three writers are more important. Arrian avowedly based his *Anabasis* on Ptolemy and Aristobulus, while the so-called 'vulgate'—Diodorus, Curtius, and Trogus (extant only in Justin's third-century epitome)—made extensive use, directly or indirectly, of Cleitarchus. The order in which they wrote and their motives for writing are controversial and likely to remain so.

5.   It has generally been thought that Ptolemy wrote his *History of Alexander* towards the end of his life, perhaps after 285 when, on his son becoming joint ruler of Egypt with him, he presumably enjoyed greater leisure. This assumption has recently been challenged.[6] Ptolemy gave, clearly, no ungenerous account of his own part in the expedition and, more important, he omitted or occasionally misrepresented the achievements of some of the Macedonian leaders, notably Perdiccas, who were his opponents in the wars of the Successors. This last fact, it is suggested, makes it likely that Ptolemy wrote, perhaps soon after 320, to conceal the leading position which Perdiccas had enjoyed at Alexander's death and to stress the favour with which he himself had been regarded. This attractive theory provides a more compelling motive for Ptolemy's attitude to Perdiccas and the other leaders than does the traditional date, but

involves placing the appearance of his book before any date yet
suggested for Cleitarchus. This appears questionable for the reasons
given below, although a date earlier than the traditional one may well
be correct. In any case, whenever Ptolemy wrote and whatever his
motives were, it seems certain that he was extremely reticent about the
more controversial episodes in the career of Alexander, either out of a
disinterested reverence for his former leader or, more probably, as
part of his cult of Alexander.

By contrast with the personal part of his book, Ptolemy's account
of military operations is invaluable, particularly after he was
appointed to the staff in 330 and began to hold independent commands.[7] Although his accounts of the major battles, as we see them
through Arrian's eyes, present many problems, it is his preservation
of the details of units and their commanders that alone renders their
solution possible. In fact, the amount of detail which Arrian provides
has suggested to many that Ptolemy must have had access to official
documents, in particular the *Diary* from which Plutarch and Arrian
quote. But, while it is perfectly possible that Ptolemy possessed some
documentary evidence, it is perhaps more likely, especially if he
wrote soon after Alexander's death, that he relied mainly upon an
excellent memory. At any rate, it seems to have been established that
the *Diary* from which Arrian and Plutarch quote was either a forgery
or that, if genuine, it dealt only with events at Babylon towards the
end of Alexander's life.[8]

Whatever may be the case with Ptolemy, Aristobulus was undoubtedly an old man when he came to write about Alexander.
Indeed, he is said to have been eighty-four when he began to write, a
statement supported to some extent by the reference in his work to
the battle of Ipsus fought in 301. The 'apologetic' nature of some of
the 'fragments'—like Callisthenes, he was termed a 'flatterer'—
suggests that he wrote to defend Alexander's memory from his
detractors. Cleitus, he maintained, was entirely to blame for the
brawl that led to his death, and Philotas and Callisthenes were guilty
of plotting against the king. He denied that Alexander was a heavy
drinker and appears to have sought to refute the view that towards
the end of his life he became a prey to excessive superstitition. On the
other hand, we owe to Aristobulus much of the geographical information in Arrian, including a valuable description of the march
through Gedrosia. But perhaps his most important contribution is his
account of Alexander's activity in the last year of his life—his
measures to improve the canal system of Babylonia and navigation
on the Tigris, his plans to explore the Caspian sea, the expeditions
sent to explore the coastline of Arabia and his preparations for the
conquest of the country.

Probably most scholars would place the appearance of Cleitarchus' book between 310 and 300, but Tarn and others have argued for a date after 280. There is no decisive piece of evidence, and the arguments on either side cannot be discussed here, but on balance the earlier date seems to me more probable.[9] In particular, it is hard to credit that Cleitarchus writing in Alexandria after the publication of Ptolemy's book would have contradicted his former ruler. Yet, while Ptolemy explicitly stated that he was not present when Alexander was almost fatally wounded among the Malli in India, Cleitarchus stated that Ptolemy was one of those who saved the king's life. It seems altogether more plausible to suppose that Ptolemy was correcting Cleitarchus. Again, if Ptolemy's book had appeared, would it not be a strange kind of compliment for Cleitarchus to pay Ptolemy—and he surely praised the king's character—to offer an account of the major battles that was utterly at variance with Ptolemy's? Yet Arrian's version, based on Ptolemy, conflicts in many important respects with that given by Diodorus, and Diodorus, it seems likely, depends on Cleitarchus.[10]

Whenever he wrote, Cleitarchus produced the most popular account of Alexander's expedition. What probably gained him his many readers was the attention he paid to the personal element and the sensational treatment of the subject-matter—Thais inciting a drunken Alexander to fire the palace at Persepolis, the week-long Bacchanalian revel through Carmania, the story that Alexander was poisoned by Antipater's son. But an incident may be treated sensationally and still be true, and there is no indication, if we may take Diodorus' narrative to be a tolerably accurate reflection of Cleitarchus' book, that he sought to denigrate Alexander. Indeed, Cleitarchus, like Callisthenes, seems to have portrayed Alexander as a 'hero'. That the king was responsible for a number of massacres and that he maintained a harem may well be the simple truth. In Greek as in Roman times massacres of 'barbarians' were unlikely to reflect adversely upon their author's character, while Alexander had good reason to adopt the trappings of the Persian monarchy.

It was not only the 'primary sources' of which the extant writers on Alexander had to take account. As we can see most clearly in Plutarch's two youthful essays, *Concerning the good fortune or good qualities of Alexander*, rhetoricians found in his career a fruitful source of topics for discussion and the reasons for his extraordinary success, in particular, were hotly debated.[11] Philosophers, too, discoursing on the evils of passion and drink, found no lack of horrible examples to hold up to their pupils. Individual Peripatetics, such as Theophrastus, were doubtless moved by the execution of Callisthenes to maintain that Alexander's character suffered from his success and his exposure to oriental luxury, but the school as a whole does not seem to have condemned him. This was left for the Stoics. For them Alexander became the classic example of the man who owed his success not to his character but to Fortune. In particular, they pointed to his delusions of grandeur which led him to adopt the luxurious garb of the east and to aspire to become a god. The murder of Cleitus, too, was a favourite theme, combining as it did Alexander's failure to master his anger and his addiction to drink.

The extant historians

The writers whose works have survived did not simply reproduce what their sources told them; they, too, had their own predilections and prejudices. Diodorus,[12] who dealt with Alexander's reign in Book 17 of his *Universal History*, is probably the least individual of these writers, although an extensive lacuna in the manuscripts deprives us of his narrative of events in Bactria, Sogdiana, and the extreme west of India, and we have consequently little idea how he treated a whole series of incidents of vital importance for Alexander's relations with his Macedonians. We do know, however, from the extant Table of Contents, that in the missing portion Diodorus related a whole series of massacres. Clearly his account was not 'apologetic'; yet, as I have said, a list of massacres need not indicate hostility, since those killed were 'barbarians'. On a number of occasions Diodorus supplies information lacking in the other historians, notably the detailed figures for Alexander's forces, or a version of events that conflicts with theirs; but his most individual contribution is the stress which he lays upon the influence and particularly the fickleness of Fortune. His comparatively favourable picture of Alexander may reflect the light and shade of the Cleitarchean portrait; it agrees, however, with his own view that successful statesmen are righteous, as Drews has pointed out. The attribution to Alexander of the typical virtues of the Hellenistic monarch, magnanimity, kindness, and love for his subjects, are doubtless due to Diodorus himself.

The loss of the first two books of Quintus Curtius Rufus' *History of Alexander* has deprived us of information about his date and his purpose in writing, which he doubtless made clear in his preface.[13] Consequently scholars have dated his work as early as Augustus and as late as Severus Alexander. But only the reigns of Claudius and Vespasian deserve serious consideration and the former seems clearly preferable. Indeed, it is probable that the writer is the same person as the Curtius Rufus, mentioned by Pliny and Tacitus, who governed Upper Germany and Africa in the reign of Claudius, and he may be the rhetorician of the same name contained in Suetonius' list.

Certainly the writer of the *History of Alexander* was steeped in rhetoric.

The numerous instances when Curtius' narrative closely corresponds with that of Diodorus show them to have drawn on a common source, and the similarity between several passages in both authors and the scanty 'fragments' of Cleitarchus strongly suggests that he was that source. But Curtius was clearly a more independent writer than Diodorus and his work reflects to a greater degree his own experience. His gruesome description of the torture of Philotas and the malice of his enemies surely argues acquaintance with treason trials. The most striking feature of Curtius' portrait of Alexander, apart from the emphasis on the king's constant good fortune, is the sudden deterioration in his character after the death of Darius. Examples of Alexander's rage and cruelty certainly occur earlier, but it is at this time that he turns to feasting, drinking, and women, adopts Persian pomp and luxury, and seeks recognition of his divinity. Curtius' attitude is a compound of hostility towards 'barbarians' and hatred of the ruler cult, for he believed, as others have done, that by seeking to introduce *proskynesis* Alexander aimed at divinity. Arrian had the same prejudices, but he was altogether a more sensible and a more charitable man, and doubtless had less reason to hate autocratic rule. That Alexander changed as the expedition progressed, few would deny; but Curtius exaggerates, perhaps less because he was swept along on a flood of rhetoric than because his feelings were deeply involved. Not only did Curtius treat Cleitarchus more independently than Diodorus—the Persepolis episode, for example, illustrates in Curtius the drunkenness of Alexander, while in Diodorus the part played by Thais and the revenge motive are stressed—but he made use of Ptolemy and perhaps also of Trogus. His narrative of military operations, as a comparison with Arrian shows, is based to some extent on Ptolemy, but despite his (conjectured) experience as an imperial legate his knowledge of military affairs seems meagre. The speeches which are a prominent feature of his book may also owe something to Ptolemy but they are in the main the product of his own imagination.

In the first or second decade of the second century A.D. the Greek biographer Plutarch composed *Lives* of Alexander and Julius Caesar as part of his series of *Parallel Lives*.[14] For the *Alexander* he consulted a variety of primary sources, particularly Aristobulus and Chares, and a collection or collections of letters written by or to Alexander. The scope of the *Life* was limited. For Plutarch expressly states that he was a biographer, not a historian. Further, he was concerned with the character of Alexander, neglecting the larger issues, his military achievements, the administration of his empire,

his plans for exploration or conquest. But within its limits the *Life* is
valuable. For Plutarch refers to, or quotes from, over thirty letters
written or received by Alexander; a few of these are certainly
authentic, and others may be.[15] Again, most of what we know about
Alexander's early life (little enough, to be sure) we owe to Plutarch,
who also reveals something of the personal feuds in the entourage of
Alexander. Plutarch was perhaps too civilized to appreciate fully the
rugged and, at times, savage Macedonians, and too prone to seek to
explain away Alexander's failings. He recognized that Alexander
changed for the worse, that he could be cruel and implacable, but he
maintained that this cruelty was the king's reaction to the unjust
criticism of his 'friends'; for Alexander, he judged, valued his
reputation more than life itself. The slanders of his 'friends' led him
to execute Philotas and Callisthenes; they, not Alexander, indulged
in luxurious living; if Alexander was rash, it was to encourage them.
Plutarch naturally welcomes Aristobulus' statement that Alexander
drank seldom and then only to be companionable, he praises his
generosity and chivalry, and perhaps exaggerates his interest in
philosophy. But the *Life*, unlike the early speeches, is not devoid of
criticism. Alexander gave way too often to anger—it was the dominating feature of his character—while his grief at Hephaestion's death
was excessive, and his massacre of the mercenaries at Massaga was a
blot on his otherwise unblemished record.

 The best of the extant writers on Alexander is Arrian,[16] a native of
Nicomedia in Bithynia, who attended the lectures of the Stoic
philosopher Epictetus and preserved his master's teachings for
posterity. When he came to write his *Anabasis*, perhaps between A.D.
140 and 150, he was already a practised writer with several lesser works
to his credit and he had behind him a distinguished career in the
Roman imperial service, culminating in the governorship of the
important frontier province of Cappadocia. He based his book, he
tells us, on Ptolemy and Aristobulus, supplementing their accounts
with the 'stories' of other writers where these seemed 'worth relating
and reasonably reliable'. Clearly he made good use of Ptolemy in
military matters, for his experience enabled him to understand warfare whose essentials had changed little in almost five hundred years.
The *Anabasis* provides the basis of our knowledge of Alexander's
campaigns, although it is perhaps to be regretted that he chose to
concentrate on Alexander's exploits and to tell us little of Persian
plans until the Persians came into contact with Alexander.[17] The
qualities of Alexander as a leader are everywhere apparent—his dash,
his persistence, his courage and resource when things went wrong. It
is greatly to Arrian's credit that, a Stoic himself, he avoided the
doctrinaire condemnation of Alexander popular in Stoic circles. His

criticism of the king for his excessive ambition, in which he found the dominant motive for his conquests, and for the lack of self-control that led to Cleitus' murder is not unjustified, and his judgement on Alexander is in general understanding and humane. But there are times, one feels, when he is not critical enough of Alexander and too much influenced by the attitude of his sources. According to Ptolemy and Aristobulus the burning of the palace at Persepolis was a deliberate act of policy; we should not guess from Arrian's account that others explained the incident differently. Philotas, again, is briefly dismissed as guilty of treason, although Arrian does seem to have had his doubts about Callisthenes. The destruction of Thebes and the massacre of the Greek mercenaries at the Granicus evoke no hint of criticism from Arrian, although even the amiable Plutarch suggests that Alexander was responsible for the Theban tragedy. Occasionally Arrian's prejudices, I believe, mislead him. He shared with Curtius and Plutarch, and doubtless many others, hostility to the cult of the ruler. Hence Alexander's claim to be the son of Zeus was for him a mere 'device', and the arrival of sacred envoys (*theoroi*) at Babylon in 323 acknowledging Alexander's divinity provoked him to sarcasm. Again, Arrian shared the widespread contempt for 'barbarians' and thought Alexander's adoption of Persian dress and ceremonial simply another 'device', to render him less alien to the Persians. He seems not to have realized how seriously Alexander intended his 'policy of fusion', the creation of a single ruling race of Persians and Macedonians.

Finally, we have Justin's third-century epitome of the *Philippic Histories* of Pompeius Trogus, a Romanized Gaul writing in the age of Augustus. His account of Alexander, contained in Books 11 and 12, has obvious affinities with Diodorus and Curtius in its attitude to his divinity and his adoption of Persian practices, but goes beyond them in accepting the story that Olympias conceived Alexander after mating with the god Ammon in the form of a great snake. If Justin is less prone to moralizing than Curtius, this is probably due to the brevity of the epitome; he is no less critical of Alexander. Tarn finds in Justin 'not much bread to an intolerable deal of sack', and in the books dealing with Alexander's reign this is undoubtedly true. On the other hand, in Book 9, which recounts the events of Philip's last years, he provides us with some valuable information. For it is Justin alone who tells us that in 339 Alexander campaigned with his father against the Scythians, and that Philip walked to his death between the two Alexanders, his son and his son-in-law.

The ancient writers on Alexander tended, in general, to concentrate on the person of Alexander and to neglect the wider aspects of his reign. We should gladly know more, for example, about the administration of his empire or his financial arrangements or his motives in founding cities. But it is, for the most part, not lack of evidence that renders the modern historian's task difficult so much as the problem of deciding between the merits of conflicting versions of the same incident, in particular between the testimony of what may fairly be called 'the official version' and that of 'the vulgate'. It is certain that Alexander set fire to the royal palace at Persepolis. But should we believe Arrian when he tells us that the king set it alight deliberately, as a matter of policy, or should we credit the authors of 'the vulgate' who relate that the conflagration was the result of a suggestion made to the drunken Alexander by the Athenian courtesan Thais? Again, when Alexander massacred the Greek mercenaries at Massaga, should we follow Diodorus in thinking that Alexander 'nursed an implacable hatred towards them', or accept Arrian's statement that the mercenaries were preparing to desert? Was Arrian (or Ptolemy) falsifying the record, or was Diodorus (or his source) seeking to blacken the king's reputation?

Alexander's relationship to Ammon, his 'orientalizing policy', the deaths of Cleitus, Philotas, Parmenio, and Callisthenes made him a controversial figure in his lifetime, and Arrian's expectation that he had written a masterpiece which would set the record straight was not fulfilled—or deserved. There is no definitive history of Alexander.

2

THE MACEDONIAN HOMELAND

Demosthenes, the implacable enemy of Macedon, was fond of describing Philip as a 'barbarian' and once at least referred to his marshals as 'slaves'.[1] Vulgar abuse, of course, was the stock-in-trade of the Athenian politician; yet such abuse would have been pointless had there been no difference between Greeks and Macedonians, and important cultural and political differences did, in fact, divide them.

That the Macedonians were of Greek stock seems certain.[2] The claim made by the Argead dynasty to be of Argive descent may be no more than a generally accepted myth, but Macedonian proper names, such as Ptolemaios or Philippos, are good Greek names, and the names of the Macedonian months, although they differed from those in use in Athens or Sparta, were also Greek. The language spoken by the Macedonians, which Greeks of the classical period found unintelligible, appears to have been a primitive north-west Greek dialect, much influenced by the languages of the neighbouring barbarians. The nobility, however, spoke Greek as well and by the end of the fifth century had become partially Hellenized. Alexander I (c. 495–450) had been recognized as a Greek by the officials at Olympia and allowed to compete in the Olympic Games, while Archelaus (c. 413–399) had attracted to his new capital, Pella, a string of artists, including the painter Zeuxis and the tragedians Agathon and Euripides, whose *Bacchae* was written there.

Yet the extent of this cultural development should not be exaggerated. The Macedonian nobles were less interested in the theatre and in intellectual argument than in hunting and fighting, while their capacity for unmixed wine was notorious. They thought of themselves as Macedonians, different from and doubtless superior to their Greek cousins, who clearly reciprocated these feelings.

For the political differences between Macedon and the Greek

states the geographical situation of Macedonia was largely responsible.[3] Lying between Greece and the Balkans, Macedonia acted as a
barrier, shielding the Greek states from the incursions of the restless
northern peoples, Illyrians, Paeonians, and Thracians, and enabling
them to develop politically from monarchy to aristocracy or democracy. Such development the Macedonians themselves could not
afford; to survive they needed strong leadership. Hence Macedon
remained a monarchy, not very different from the monarchies of the
Homeric poems.

The constitution of Macedon was uncomplicated, embodying the
monarchy and the people in assembly, which, as in early Rome, was
the army, but possessing no important magistrates or formal Council.
The people elected, or at any rate acclaimed, a new king, a member
of the Argead dynasty, though not necessarily the eldest son, and
probably took an oath of allegiance to him. Whether the monarch
then took a reciprocal oath is doubtful, and his responsibility to his
people may have been moral rather than constitutional. The second
function of the assembly, as we can see in the trial of Philotas, was to
judge in cases of treason. Subject to the limitation that he could not
lawfully put a *noble* Macedonian to death without trial, the king was,
constitutionally, an absolute monarch, possessing full powers in war
and diplomacy.[4]

But the nobles, although they might possess no official recognition,
nevertheless played an important part in the state. They were the
great landowners who in return for a grant of land—all land was the
property of the crown—were bound to serve their king in peace and
war. Originally, as the 'Companions' (*Hetairoi*) of the king, they
guarded his person in battle, and when this duty was transferred to
the Royal Squadron of the Companion cavalry they retained the
title of 'Companions' and provided his generals and administrators.[5]
Although Philip bestowed much of the land gained by conquest
upon lesser landowners and immigrant Greeks, the greater nobles
must have continued to form the nucleus of the Companions, who
acted as an unofficial Council.[6] To them the king might submit
matters for discussion and, although he was in no way bound by
their opinions, it would be a bold, or foolhardy, monarch who would
follow Agamemnon's example and disregard the unanimous decision of his Council.

The relationship between the king and the nobles was very close.
They wore the same dress as he did, the purple mantle (*chlamys*)
and the broad-brimmed hat (*kausia*), and they did not hesitate, as we
can see from the accounts of Alexander's reign, to speak their mind
to their ruler. Unlike the Persian monarch, the king of Macedon was,
in practice, *primus inter pares*. It was this fact which, in part at least,

made Alexander's adoption of Persian dress and Persian court
ceremonial so hard for the Macedonian leaders to accept.

Macedonia was potentially a great power. The fertile lowland
plains, built up by alluvial deposits, were capable of supporting vast
numbers of sheep, horses, and cattle, while on the mountains
extensive forests yielded an abundance of excellent timber. This
timber and the other necessity for shipbuilding, pitch, were in the fifth
and early fourth centuries exported in great quantities to Athens and
the Chalcidian League.[7] The foothills contained substantial deposits
of gold and silver. According to Herodotus (5.17), the mines on
Mount Dysorus returned Alexander I a talent a day, while the gold
mines in the region of Mount Pangaeum, which Philip acquired early
in his reign, were said to have contributed one thousand talents per
annum to the Macedonian exchequer.[8]

But three factors had hindered the development of the Macedonian
kingdom before Philip came to the throne—the attacks of the
neighbouring tribes, the hostility of the Chalcidian League and of
Athens, and, most of all, the weakness of its own central government.
This weakness was due particularly to the strife within the royal
family and to the efforts of the outlying cantons to assert their
independence. The Argead dynasty, with its capital at Aegae and
later at Pella, ruled the Macedonian homeland in the fertile plains
round the lower valleys of the rivers Axius (Vardar) and Haliacmon.
They also claimed suzerainty over the cantons in the plateau and hill
country to the west and north. But the rulers of these districts,
Lyncestis, Orestis, and Elimiotis, were themselves kings or princes
and commanded the loyalty of their followers in much the same way
as did the northern barons under the Tudors or the Highland chiefs
in Scotland until the failure of the Jacobite rebellion of A.D. 1745;
when, as frequently happened, the central power was weak, this
suzerainty was more nominal than real.

The expedition which Alexander led against Persia in 334 was
ostensibly a 'crusade' undertaken to avenge Xerxes' invasion of
Greece and the burning of Greek temples. But the Macedonian units
were the backbone of the expeditionary force and the enterprise was
essentially Macedonian. Twenty-five years earlier this would have
been inconceivable. In 359 Perdiccas III, the eighth king to rule
Macedon since the death of Archelaus in 399, had died in battle with
the Illyrians, together with 4000 of his followers, leaving an infant
son, Amyntas, to succeed him. At least two of the western cantons
were lost to the victorious Illyrians, the Paeonians in the north
threatened invasion, and no fewer than five pretenders, one supported
by Athens, another by the Thracians, asserted their claims to the
throne of Macedon. It seems little less than a miracle that

Perdiccas' brother Philip, first as regent and then as king, by his resolution, leadership, and diplomatic skill repelled all these dangers and within a generation made Macedon the leading power on the Greek mainland.

Addressing his mutinous troops at Opis in 324, Alexander reminded them of his father's achievements:

Philip found you a tribe of impoverished vagabonds, most of you dressed in skins, feeding a few sheep on the hills and fighting, feebly enough, to keep them from your neighbours—Thracians and Triballians and Illyrians. He gave you cloaks to wear instead of skins; he brought you down from the hills into the plains; he taught you to fight on equal terms with the enemy on your borders, till you knew that your safety lay not, as once, in your mountain strongholds, but in your own valour. He made you city-dwellers; he brought you law; he civilized you. He rescued you from subjection and slavery, and made you masters of the wild tribes who harried and plundered you; he annexed the greater part of Thrace, and by seizing the best places on the coast opened your country to trade, and enabled you to work your mines without fear of attack. Thessaly, so long your bugbear and your dread, he subjected to your rule. . . . (Arrian *Anabasis* 7.9, trans. de Selincourt)

The speech is Arrian's own composition, but the substance may go back, if not to Alexander, at least to Ptolemy. Rhetorical it undoubtedly is, but a solid basis of fact underlies it. The Paeonians and Agrianians became dependent on Macedon, while the Thracians occupied a position between that of a Roman province and a client kingdom, keeping their own kings but subject to a Macedonian governor. Thessaly was not conquered and did not become a province, but Philip was elected *archon* and given control of its harbour and market dues.[9]

But it appears very doubtful whether the Macedonians were as poor at the start of Philip's reign as 'Alexander' maintains. For the Macedonian phalanx came into existence when it was decided to call the infantry 'Foot Companions' (*pezhetairoi*) on the analogy of the cavalry 'Companions', a decision which is attributed to 'Alexander' by the fourth-century historian, Anaximenes of Lampsacus. If Anaximenes is correct, this can only be Alexander II, who ruled from 369 to 368.[10] We must conclude, therefore, that ten years before Philip gained control of Macedon a considerable number of Macedonians were well enough off to provide their own equipment.[11]

Nevertheless, Philip's reign was the turning-point in the history of Macedon. His conquests provided the country not only with an increase in territory but, more important, with continued security. The result was a great increase in population and doubtless in prosperity. While Philip could muster only 10,000 men in 359,

Alexander had about three times that number of Macedonians available to him at the start of his expedition in 334. The conquest of the Greek cities in the Chalcidian peninsula and on the coast of Macedonia which had denied the Macedonians access to the sea must have resulted in an upsurge of trade and in the development of urban centres. But these did not become cities in the Greek sense of the word, for they played no part in the political life of the country. Macedon remained essentially a nation of farmers and herdsmen, the same sort of men who made up the armies of ancient Rome.

The army with which Alexander conquered the Persian empire was in essence Philip's creation. His years as a hostage in Thebes, probably between 368 and 365, coincided with the Theban hegemony over Greece, and it was then that he was introduced to military science. Epaminondas in 371 had won the battle of Leuctra for Thebes by holding back his weaker troops of the centre and right, while his Theban hoplites, massed fifty deep on his left, routed the Spartans opposing them. Philip modified Epaminondas' strategy of the oblique approach and gave pride of place to the cavalry. The Companions, greatly increased in number, were formed into squadrons on a district basis and became the striking force.[12] The Foot Companions had a less spectacular but equally vital role: to pin down part of the enemy line while the cavalry struck in flank or rear. They were divided by tribes into battalions large enough to operate independently and together formed the invincible phalanx, armed with a longer weapon than the Greek hoplite and relying on a steady advance rather than on a charge. While the phalanx probably existed before Philip's accession, the *Hypaspists*, or Guards, were introduced by Philip to protect the flank of the phalanx and to maintain contact with the cavalry.[13] They were not organized on a tribal basis, but were crack troops drawn from all the districts of Macedonia and owing allegiance directly to the king. Later Philip was to add to the army light-armed troops from the conquered territories, notably Paeonia and Thrace. Again, although he failed to capture Perinthus and Byzantium, Philip's use of siege engines and the newly developed torsion catapult[14] foreshadowed the sieges of Tyre and Gaza. Not only did constant training and campaigning forge the disparate elements into a military machine unmatched in Greek warfare but its almost unbroken success must have assisted materially in creating a feeling of unity and patriotism in Macedonia. The army was Philip's greatest legacy to his son.

Philip well knew that the greatest weakness of the kingdom was the centrifugal tendency of its outlying cantons. To counteract this he sought to attach the nobility to his person. According to the contemporary historian Theopompus, he created 800 new 'Companions', some of these certainly immigrant Greeks of distinction, but others undoubtedly Macedonians.[15] These new 'Companions' were granted estates in the territory taken from the conquered Greek cities. A similar motive surely underlies Philip's creation of a corps of Royal Pages.[16] These noble youths were closely attached to his person and were allowed to sit at his table. He alone had the right to flog them for breaches of discipline, and they attended him when he hunted and in battle and kept guard over him while he slept. From their ranks were to come generals and administrators, and under Alexander at least their training was not confined to military matters but included literature and philosophy.

Although Philip was not the first Macedonian monarch to encourage Greeks to take up residence at his court, during his reign Hellenization proceeded faster than ever before. Greek became the official language of the army and the administration, and we know that Eumenes, Nearchus, and many other Greeks settled in Macedonia at this time. But it is easy to exaggerate the extent to which the Macedonians became Hellenized. The great mass of the population was largely untouched by outside influences and even at court the older Macedonians were probably little affected. Philip's policy, it seems likely, was aimed primarily at securing the advancement of Macedon and for this he found Greeks useful, perhaps essential. Alexander and his contemporaries received a good Greek education and in them Greek culture was more securely rooted. But admiration for Greek culture need not imply a desire to secure the welfare of Greece, as the Romans of the late Republic were to demonstrate, and we are under no compulsion to believe that Alexander's attitude to the Greeks differed essentially from Philip's.

Under Philip Macedon grew strong militarily and economically, stronger than she had ever been, and more united; yet such unity as she possessed was recent, and precarious. Macedon had been strong before and had dissipated her resources by internal feuds. At Philip's death there was no guarantee that she would not do so again. Her enemies clearly thought, perhaps even expected, that she would. But they underestimated Philip's work, and Alexander.

3

THE YOUNG ALEXANDER

Philip had good cause to remember the year 356. Militarily it was a year of unbroken success, mainly at the expense of Athens. Pydna, a Greek foundation on Macedonian soil and an ally of Athens, was betrayed to him, then he besieged and captured Potidaea, garrisoned by Athenian settlers, and handed it over to the Chalcidian League to gain its support. In the west, while Philip pressed the siege of Potidaea, his general Parmenio inflicted a crushing defeat on the Paeonians and Illyrians, whose rulers had concluded an alliance with Athens on 26 July.[1] As Philip was resting after his capture of Potidaea, the story goes, a messenger rode up bearing important dispatches. They announced Parmenio's victory, the success of the king's horse at Olympia, and, most important, the birth of a son at Pella to the queen Olympias. This happy coincidence, we are told, inspired the seers to prophesy that the boy, Alexander, whose birth was marked by three victories, would be invincible.[2] Unfortunately, like much else that it is told of Alexander, including the omens which supposedly preceded and attended his birth, this prophecy must be accounted an invention; for news of Alexander's birth, which occurred about 20 July, must surely have reached Philip before he heard of Parmenio's succeess or of his Olympic victory, probably late in August.

Alexander owed much both to his environment and to his heredity, and he was to reveal the qualities, good and bad, of both his parents. His mother Olympias, a princess of the Molossian royal house in Epirus, who numbered Achilles among her ancestors, was proud, passionate, and jealous, especially where Alexander's interests were concerned. She was a devotee of the wild, orgiastic cults of Dionysus, which were popular in Macedonia, and indulged to the terror of the men in the snake-handling which formed part of those cults.[3]

Indeed, she is credibly reported to have kept a pet snake, a fact which may have given rise to the rumour, at least after Alexander's visit to the temple of Ammon at Siwah, that he was the son of the god who visited the queen in the guise of a snake. Olympias was without question a masterful woman, intent on playing a part in affairs of state, a characteristic which did not endear her to the Macedonian nobles. Subject to ungovernable fits of rage, she twice displayed a savage cruelty that, even in a savage society, revolted her contemporaries. In 335, when Alexander was campaigning in the north, she murdered Europa, the infant daughter of Philip and Cleopatra, then forced Cleopatra to commit suicide, and in 317 she put to death Philip Arrhidaeus and his wife Eurydice together with a hundred of Cassander's adherents.[4]

Philip has sometimes been contrasted with Olympias as supplying the Apolline or rational element in Alexander's character. This is only partly true. Philip, too, was passionate, although unlike Olympias he almost always succeeded in mastering his passion and rarely allowed it to interfere with his policies. Towards their defeated enemies Philip and Alexander often displayed a generosity that may have accorded with their inclinations as much as with their interests, but where they judged severity to be necessary they did not hesitate to use it. We need only recall the very different treatment which both Philip after Chaeroneia and Alexander after the Theban revolt of 335 meted out to Thebes and to Athens. Although his policy of encouraging Hellenization in Macedonia was at least partly motivated by political and economic considerations, Philip was no uncultivated barbarian. As a hostage in Thebes he lived in the house of Epaminondas' father and, we are told, studied the teachings of Pythagoras. Certainly there is no reason to suppose that he learnt only military science. Perhaps, too, it may be significant that Philip and Olympias met during their initiation into the mysteries of the Cabiri on Samothrace.

Philip's drinking was notorious, and Alexander, despite the assertions of his apologists both ancient and modern, drank heavily, particularly towards the end of his life. But this need not be taken to be a hereditary trait; for heavy drinking was a feature of Macedonian life. Whether Alexander's attitude to women differed from his father's is uncertain. While Alexander married only twice, once from policy and once from policy and affection, Philip married several times; but doubtless, as the biographer Satyrus says,[5] most of his marriages were political alliances. However, it seems likely that Alexander was indifferent to women.[6] That this indifference was due to homosexual tendencies may be doubted—the Greeks after all combined homosexual with heterosexual love quite happily—but

Alexander's extravagant grief at Hephaestion's death suggests that their relations were not purely Platonic.

Of Alexander's childhood we know distressingly little, and some of the anecdotes told about him, chiefly by his biographer Plutarch, may be picturesque rather than true. We are told, for example, that once when Philip was absent from Pella Alexander entertained some Persian envoys and astonished them by asking not about the famous hanging gardens of Babylon or the royal attire but about the Persian army and the roads in the Persian empire. But it seems likely that an intelligent and inquiring child, as Alexander surely was, would have taken advantage of the presence of refugees at Philip's court—Artabazus, for example, who later became Alexander's satrap, and Memnon, who was to be his most formidable opponent in Asia Minor—to make such inquiries.

We need not doubt, however, that the dominant influence in Alexander's early years was his mother Olympias, who retained his affection throughout his life, although he never allowed her to meddle in affairs of state. As a child, he cannot have seen much of his father, who was often away fighting, sometimes even in winter. When Philip did appear he doubtless regaled his son with stories of his campaigns, and it would be strange indeed if Alexander had not admired his father, even if he complained, we are told, that Philip's successes would leave nothing for him to accomplish. Of Philip's relations with Olympias before the rupture brought about by his marriage to Cleopatra in 337 we know nothing. But it is likely that Olympias did not welcome the arrival of Philip's other wives and did not conceal her feelings. The atmosphere in the palace may well have been at times an unhappy one. However, even if Olympias did complain to her son of Philip's doings, we need not suppose that Alexander's relations with his father were other than cordial until Philip's marriage to Cleopatra.

Alexander was nursed by the well-born Lanike, a sister of 'Black' Cleitus, commander of the Royal Squadron of the Companion cavalry, whom he was later to murder in a drunken brawl. His early education was organized by Leonidas, a relative of Olympias, assisted by the Acarnanian Lysimachus and numerous teachers. Leonidas was a stern disciplinarian, whose lessons Alexander long remembered even if he did not perhaps much appreciate them at the time. For Alexander, it is said, could be led, but not driven. Lysimachus, who later accompanied Alexander on his expedition, was more indulgent. He encouraged the prince to think of himself as Achilles and called himself Phoenix, the hero's teacher. Homer, of course, had long been established as a text-book, and Alexander, as a descendant of Achilles, must have been particularly attracted to the *Iliad*. Although many writers elaborated the Achilles theme and Alexander himself was well aware of its propaganda value, it seems not unlikely that he regarded himself as a second Achilles. But it is never easy to be sure of this. Were his actions at Troy, for instance, at the beginning of the Persian expedition, which are certainly historical, simply propaganda for the Hellenic 'crusade', or did Alexander see himself as Achilles?

Besides learning to read, to write, and to play the lyre, Alexander must have been trained in the use of weapons—the sword, the bow, and the javelin. He was a fine runner, and, although he is said to have disliked athletes and athletics, he certainly maintained a group of professional ball-players at his court in Asia.[7] Like most Macedonian nobles, he doubtless learned to ride almost as soon as he could walk and he had many horses. His favourite was the great Thessalian stallion Bucephalas, who is reputed to have cost the quite un-exampled sum of thirteen talents. Plutarch tells the story of the 'breaking' of Bucephalas, probably on the authority of Chares who may have witnessed the event. The horse, he writes, would allow no one to mount him until Alexander, noticing that he was frightened by his own shadow, turned him to face the sun, vaulted on to his back, galloped him round the enclosure, and rode back proudly to his father. Philip's conflicting emotions—disbelief, anxiety, finally relief and joy—are vividly evoked by Plutarch's description and show his affection and concern for his son and heir at this time, when Alexander was probably eight or nine. In 343, when Alexander was thirteen, Philip decided that his son needed more advanced instruc-tion which would fit him for his position as heir to the Macedonian throne. To become the prince's tutor he invited to Pella the eminent philosopher Aristotle, whose father had been court physician to Amyntas II some fifty years earlier. But his choice may have been determined not so much by this distant connection or even by Aris-totle's abilities as by political considerations. For Aristotle was the son-in-law of the tyrant Hermeias of Atarneus in Asia Minor, at whose court he had established what we may call a branch of the Academy, and Hermeias was an ally of Philip. Indeed, it is likely that his kingdom was to serve as a bridgehead for the invasion of Asia which Philip already projected, an invasion which Hermeias did not live to see; for soon after he was betrayed to the Persians and impaled.[8]

For three years Aristotle taught Alexander and a few chosen com-panions at Mieza, a quiet spot remote from the distractions of the court and, we may suspect, from the influence of Olympias. About this important period of Alexander's life we are reduced for the most part to conjecture. A letter reproduced by Plutarch, in which Alexander complains to Aristotle that the publication of the *Meta-*

physics has made available to all and sundry the substance of his teaching, is almost certainly a forgery. However, another letter criticizing Aristotle's teaching, which purports to have been written by the aged Isocrates, may be genuine.[9] If it is, Aristotle will have instructed the prince in the philosophy which was taught in the Academy. Certainly, if we may judge by the number of philosophers who accompanied the expedition and by Alexander's offer of fifty talents to Xenocrates, the Academic philosopher who wrote for him a work on the duties of a king, Alexander retained an interest in the subject. Aristotle wrote a treatise *On Kingship*, perhaps for Alexander's accession, and must surely have talked to his pupil about political philosophy, but there is no indication that Alexander was in the least influenced by his views on politics. Quite the reverse, in fact; for, although Aristotle[10] had advised him to treat 'barbarians' like slaves and animals, Alexander did no such thing. Doubtless, when he met these 'barbarians' in the field and talked with Persian prisoners, he formed a very different opinion of their capabilities. Indeed, he may well have discounted Aristotle's teaching on this point much earlier after meeting Persian envoys and refugees who had fled to Philip's court.

But if Aristotle's teaching had little effect on his pupil's political thinking, the same cannot be said of other topics. Bertrand Russell is clearly very wide of the mark in supposing that the influence of 'the prosy old pedant' was nil! In fact, Aristotle was only just over forty in 343, and the 'Hymn to Virtue' which he wrote in memory of Hermeias shows him capable of sincere and passionate affection.[11] We may confidently assume that he won his pupil's respect and affection, and their relationship appears to have remained cordial until the arrest and execution of Callisthenes caused a certain coolness between them.

Aristotle consolidated and extended Alexander's appreciation of Greek literature. When, after the battle of Issus, the king captured a valuable casket among Darius' baggage, he chose to keep in it a copy of the *Iliad* which Aristotle is said to have annotated for him. He is often reported to have quoted Euripides, naturally a popular author in Macedonia, and his treasurer Harpalus, when asked by Alexander to obtain books from Greece, chose the works of the three great Attic tragedians, two volumes of fourth-century poetry, and Philistus' *History of Sicily*. Earlier, Alexander had shown his reverence for Pindar by sparing the poet's house and his descendants in the sack of Thebes.

Aristotle appears to have passed on his interest in medicine to his pupil, for Alexander did not hesitate to advise his doctors during his expedition. Again, the many scientists whom he took with him to

B

Asia sent back to Athens much valuable data on plants and animals which enabled Theophrastus and others in the Lyceum to make great advances in botany and zoology. Geography, too, much interested Alexander, although we may doubt whether Aristotle had much of value to tell him about the eastern part of the Persian empire. Certainly Aristotle knew that the Caspian was an inland sea and not, as many believed, a gulf running in from the northern ocean, and wrote in the *Meteorology* of *two* inland seas, which might suggest that he knew of the existence of the Aral.[12] But probably he was misled by the alternative names, Caspian and 'Hyrcanian', for the Caspian. Moreover, he shared the general misconception that the ocean lay not far beyond the eastern boundary of the Persian empire; in fact, he believed that it could be seen from the summit of the Hindu-Kush!

Some scholars have maintained that Aristotle inspired Alexander with a mission to carry Greek culture into the East.[13] It seems more likely that, while Greek culture followed in the wake of Alexander's conquests, Alexander himself had no such mission. The establishment of cities, as we shall see, can be explained otherwise, while the holding of Greek games surely does not prove Alexander's intention to Hellenize Asia.

4

CROWN PRINCE

Alexander's formal education came to an end in 340, when Philip
judged him old enough to assume the responsibilities of office.
Philip's subjugation of Thrace in 342 and 341 had brought him into
conflict with Athens, whose corn supply from the Black Sea was
now threatened at the Hellespont. It had also alarmed his allies,
Byzantium and Perinthus, who refused him assistance against the
Athenian settlements in the Thracian Chersonnese. Philip, therefore,
set out early in 340 to coerce them, leaving Alexander in Pella in
charge of the Royal Seal. This meant that he was in full charge of
Macedonia as Philip's deputy, although it is probable that the *Plutarch*
experienced Antipater was on hand to advise him.[1]
    We may suppose that the prince was not displeased to hear of the
revolt of the Maedi, a powerful Thracian tribe living on the Upper
Strymon, which gave him his first opportunity of action. He marched
out, defeated the Maedi, and took their capital, which he resettled as
a military colony. This he named Alexandropolis—surely with
Philip's approval—in imitation of Philippopolis which his father had
founded two years earlier. This may have been the occasion for
which Aristotle wrote at his request a treatise *On Colonies*.[2]
    Philip's siege of Byzantium and Perinthus, although pressed with
the greatest determination and skill, had failed, largely because of
the assistance given to the besieged by the Athenians and the neighbouring Persian satraps. In the spring of 339 he broke off the siege
and, in order to restore the morale of his troops and recover the cost
of the operations, turned north to subdue the Scythians at the mouth
of the Danube. The young Alexander was summoned from Mace- *Justin*
donia to gain further experience in war.[3] He had every opportunity
to do so; for, although Philip defeated the Scythians without
difficulty and secured a vast amount of booty, including captives,

cattle, and brood-mares, the Triballians refused him passage on his way back to Macedonia and he had to fight his way through their territory. Much of the booty was lost and Philip himself was severely wounded in the thigh.

In the following year Alexander had his first experience of a full-scale pitched battle, when on 2 August the Macedonian army, thirty thousand strong, met the army of the Greek allies of roughly the same strength at Chaeroneia in Boeotia.[4] The allies held a strong defensive position with their right wing resting on the River Cephisus and their left extending to the foothills east of the town. On the allied right were the Thebans, the most formidable infantry, with the famous 'Sacred Band' drawn up in depth on the flank; on the left stood the inexperienced Athenian troops, and in the centre the remaining allies and the mercenaries. On the Macedonian left Alexander, attended by the leading Macedonian generals, led two thousand Companion cavalry. His task was to spearhead the charge through the gap which Philip planned to open up in the allied line to the left of the 'Sacred Band', a task less difficult but more spectacular than that which he had set himself. He intended by an ordered withdrawal of the infantry on the Macedonian right, a manœuvre calling for discipline and skill of a very high order, to entice the Athenians to pursue him, thus separating them and the allied centre, which would inevitably follow, from the 'Sacred Band'; for the Thebans could not leave their position without exposing their flank to attack by Alexander's horsemen. The manœuvre was successful, and Alexander, charging through the gap, wheeled left to attack the 'Sacred Band'. The Thebans fell where they stood, on the spot now marked by the huge stone 'Lion of Chaeroneia'. Meanwhile Philip waited until the Athenians, pressing on in pursuit of an enemy they believed routed, were in disorder, then ordered the charge. A thousand Athenians fell, two thousand were taken prisoner. The victorious Macedonian wings turned inwards upon the allied centre and victory was complete. Philip did not press the pursuit; he had gained his objective.

The punishment of Thebes was severe, as befitted an ally of Macedon which had defected.[5] The leaders of the anti-Macedonian faction were executed or banished, and an oligarchy of 300 pro-Macedonian exiles was set up, supported by a Macedonian garrison in the Cadmeia, the citadel of Thebes. The Boeotian League was dissolved and orders were given for Plataea, Orchomenus, and Thespiae, destroyed by Thebes, to be restored. Theban prisoners, if not ransomed, were sold into slavery. Athens deserved punishment no less than Thebes, and expected it. Preparations were made to resist, but Philip expressed his willingness to negotiate and offered lenient terms. Athens was to disband her confederacy and give up her claim to the Chersonnese, but to retain her possessions in the Aegean and to recover Oropus from Thebes. She was to become an ally of Macedon, and Philip undertook not to send troops into Attica or warships into the Piraeus. Athenian prisoners were to be restored without ransom. Philip's offer was readily accepted, and Athenian relief and gratitude were expressed in the grant of citizenship to the king and his son and in the erection of a statue to Philip in the Agora.

Athens had fared much better than Thebes. No doubt the difficulty of besieging a city which could be supplied from the sea weighed with Philip, and admiration for the cultural achievements of Athens may perhaps have had some influence. But the most important consideration was undoubtedly the Athenian fleet, now numbering over 350 ships, which he required for his expedition against Persia, soon to be made public. We may guess that discussions were held about this between the leading Athenian statesmen and the envoys whom Philip sent to escort the ashes of the dead to Athens—Alexander, Antipater, and Alcimachus, who was later employed on diplomatic tasks in Asia. How high Alexander stood in his father's regard at this time we can see from his participation in the mission to Athens and from the part allotted to him at Chaeroneia. This was the only occasion on which Alexander saw Athens and we can only conjecture what impression the city and its fine buildings made upon him.

Philip now turned to deal with the other Greek states. Outside the Peloponnese he could rely on the support of the Phocians and the Thessalians, while Epirus, where in 342 he had installed Olympias' brother Alexander as king, was virtually a dependency of Macedon. To complete his domination Philip expelled the pro-Athenian leaders from Acarnania and established garrisons in Chalcis and Ambracia. Receiving the submission of Megara and Corinth, where another garrison was installed, he entered the Peloponnese. Sparta alone refused to submit, and in consequence was compelled to surrender much of her territory, including the valuable Cynuria, to her neighbours. As a further precaution against a Spartan recovery the Arcadian League was re-formed.

Philip now judged the time ripe to disclose his plan for a general settlement of Greece.[6] He issued an invitation to the states of mainland Greece and the islands to send representatives to a congress at Corinth, and all did so, with the exception of Sparta. Late in 338 Philip made public his manifesto. He proposed that the states should become members of a federal union (*The Greeks*) and should take an oath to observe a Common Peace (*Koine Eirene*). Each state was to be 'free and autonomous' under its existing constitution, which

could only be changed by constitutional process. Executions and
sentences of exile contrary to the existing laws, confiscations of
property, distributions of land, cancellation of debts, and the
liberation of slaves for revolutionary ends, were all expressly for-
bidden. Each state was to swear not to subvert the constitution of any
other state, including the kingdom of Philip and his descendants, and
common action was to be taken against any state which broke the
Peace.[7]

Demosthenes

?

Detailed machinery was proposed.[8] A Council (*Synhedrion*) was
to be set up to which states, cities, or ethnic groups should send
representatives in proportion to their military or naval strength.
Thessaly, we know, had ten votes. The decisions of this Council,
reached by a majority vote, were to be binding on all member states.
The competence of the Council was far-reaching, extending to
decisions on peace and war and to the appointment of arbitrators,
since one of the purposes of the League of Corinth, as we generally
call it, was to secure the peaceful settlement of disputes between
members. The Council also had judicial powers, to try offenders and
to impose sentences. To carry out the decisions of the Council a
federal leader (*Hegemon*) was to be appointed who, should armed
intervention be required, would command the League troops on
whom he was entitled to call. It must have been clear, whether
Philip's name was mentioned or not, that he would become *Hegemon*
in due course. Macedonia, however, did not become a member of
the League and sent no representatives to the Council.

These proposals were conveyed by the envoys to their respective
states and were eventually accepted by all, Sparta still excepted.
Representatives were chosen and assembled at Corinth in the early
summer of 337 for the first meeting of the Council. Philip was duly
elected *Hegemon* for life and an offensive and defensive alliance was
concluded between 'Philip and his descendants' on the one hand and
'the Greeks' on the other. At a subsequent meeting Philip revealed
his plans for an attack on Persia. He proposed that the allies should
declare war on the Persians to avenge the acts of sacrilege which
Xerxes had committed against the Greeks during his invasion in
480–479. This motion was carried, and Philip was unanimously
elected 'General with plenary powers' (*strategos autokrator*) to
command the allied expeditionary force.

The idea of a war against Persia was not new. Since the delivery
of his *Panegyricus* in 380 the Athenian rhetorician Isocrates had constantly urged the need for the Greeks to unite in a national crusade
against Persia, as Gorgias and Lysias had done before him. Unlike
them, however, Isocrates had suggested a leader for the expedition,
in the first instance Athens and Sparta, then, successively, the tyrants

Jason of Pherae and Dionysius of Syracuse; finally, on the conclusion of the Peace of Philocrates in 346, he had urged the Macedonian king in an open letter, entitled *Philip*, to undertake the task. Philip doubtless welcomed Isocrates' propaganda in favour of a proposal which agreed so well with his own intentions, but the settlement and the form which it took owed little, or nothing, to the Athenian. Isocrates had the welfare of Greece in mind; Philip, it can hardly be doubted, was influenced entirely by the interests of Macedon. Naturally he would have welcomed the wholehearted support of the Greek states, but this was obviously not forthcoming. The next best thing was to secure a peaceful Greece in his absence, and this Philip hoped to bring about through the machinery of the League. In 346 he had opposed the idea of a Common Peace, which would have had the effect of stabilizing the existing situation in Greece, for his plans were still incomplete. Eight years later he engineered such a Peace, since by his victory at Chaeroneia and his subsequent arrangements he had attained what he wanted. These arrangements were designed to place the supporters of Macedon in control in the various states, and a decade of bribery and propaganda had created in many, or most, of them groups of politicians who through conviction or self-interest favoured, or at least were prepared to accept, the dominance of Macedon. When we read the speeches of Demosthenes, it is only too easy to consider that all who took this course were traitors who had accepted Philip's money; on the contrary, many smaller states, particularly in the Peloponnese, genuinely welcomed a settlement which protected them from the ambitions of their stronger neighbours. The sincerity and devotion of Demosthenes should not blind us to the fact that his patriotism was Athenian, not Pan-Hellenic; if the liberty of the Greek city-state really perished on the field of Chaeroneia, its ambition lived on. Philip's settlement cannot be called a failure, but it was not, and perhaps never could have been, a complete success. It was not voluntary, and few Greeks can have been deceived about Philip's object, to *use* them against Persia. The Council passed resolutions, but Philip was master. As *Hegemon* he controlled the forces of the League, and behind him stood the powerful army of Macedon. If the Greeks were 'free and autonomous', Macedonian garrisons held four key positions in Greece, with the consent of the Greeks themselves. It is highly significant for the attitude of the Greeks and for Philip's understanding of it that he found it necessary to propose a motion outlawing any Greek who took service with the Persian king after the conclusion of the peace and alliance. Despite this many more Greeks fought for Darius than for Alexander.

Philip himself was never to set foot on Asian soil. The expedition got under way in the spring of 336 when an advance force under Parmenio and Attalus crossed the Hellespont, but before Philip could follow with the main body he was murdered. To the events leading up to his murder we must now turn.

Soon after Philip's return to Macedonia in 337 his good relations with his son were shattered, never to be completely restored.[9] Philip, we are told, had conceived 'an unseasonable passion' for a young Macedonian lady, Cleopatra, the niece of his general Attalus. Since his marriage to Olympias Philip had contracted several other alliances, but there was no possibility that Cleopatra could be just another wife; her birth forbade it. Olympias' position was threatened and, if Cleopatra should bear a son, there was no guarantee that Alexander would succeed. Still, this contingency lay far in the future, it seemed, and matters might not have come to a head but for an unfortunate incident at the wedding feast. Attalus, the worse for drink, called on the guests to pray for 'a legitimate heir', hinting no doubt at Olympias' 'barbarian' blood. Infuriated, Alexander sprang to his feet, shouting, 'Am I then a bastard, you villain,' and threw his cup at Attalus. Philip, as drunk as Attalus, drew his sword and made to attack his son. Fortunately for both, he tripped and fell headlong, and Alexander with a bitter jibe that 'the man who was preparing to cross from Europe into Asia could not cross from couch to couch' took his mother and fled the country. Leaving Olympias with her brother Alexander in Epirus, he sought refuge with the Illyrians.

It is remarkable that Philip, on the eve of his departure for Asia, should have contracted a marriage that could scarcely fail to alienate his heir. The ancient sources find the explanation in his infatuation for Cleopatra and it would be rash to dismiss this conjecture out of hand, for even as sensible a man as Philip may do strange things. But Attalus' words suggest another possibility, that there was an influential group of nobles who were reluctant to accept the son of the 'barbarian' Olympias as Philip's successor. Attalus was the son-in-law of Parmenio, and few of Alexander's close friends belonged to the great Macedonian families. Was Philip urged to marry and produce an heir of pure Macedonian stock, and did he consent, thinking that the question of a successor was unlikely to arise for many years? Our almost total ignorance of Macedonian court intrigues must leave us in the dark.

Presently, through the efforts of the Corinthian Demaratus, an old family friend, father and son were reconciled and Alexander returned to Pella. But the reconciliation was a hollow one, as the Pixodarus affair soon made plain.[10] Pixodarus was the ruler of Caria and owed allegiance to the Persian king. He hoped in the troubles that followed the death of Artaxerxes III in 338 to secure a more

Plutarch only

independent position and offered his daughter in marriage to Philip Arrhidaeus, a half-witted son of Philip and the Thessalian Philinna. Alexander, thinking that he was being slighted, sent envoys secretly to Pixodarus, offering to marry the princess. The Carian ruler was naturally delighted, but Philip learnt of Alexander's offer, perhaps from Philotas, Parmenio's son, and stopped the marriage. That Alexander proposed to marry the daughter of a Carian, a Persian vassal, shows beyond doubt how deeply he distrusted his father. Philip, for his part, will hardly have been pleased that an alliance which would have assisted his projected invasion of Asia had come to nought. Matters between father and son were not improved by Philip's banishment of Alexander's closest friends, including Ptolemy, Harpalus, and Nearchus, but not Philotas, for their part in the affair. They did not return to Macedon until Alexander's accession.

Olympias had remained in Epirus, where she attempted to persuade her brother Alexander to avenge the insult to her honour. But Philip, displaying his customary diplomatic skill, offered the king of Epirus the hand of Cleopatra, his daughter by Olympias, and Alexander, swallowing his family pride, accepted.

The wedding took place at Aegae in the early summer of 336. Elaborate games had been arranged for the following day, and as Philip entered the theatre, escorted by his son and son-in-law, and followed at a distance by his bodyguard, a young Macedonian nobleman named Pausanias detached himself from the waiting crowd, ran up to the king, and stabbed him in the chest. As the king fell, mortally wounded, his assailant made for the gates, where horses were waiting, but caught his foot in a vine. Struggling to his feet, he was overtaken by a group of bodyguards and run through by their javelins.

Such, at any rate, is Diodorus' version, which is not disproved by the other evidence. A very fragmentary papyrus epitome of uncertain date, whose contents do not, in general, inspire confidence, has been thought to refer to the execution of Pausanias, but may equally well refer to the crucifixion of his corpse.[11] In any case, the manner of Pausanias' death is of less importance than his motive for the crime. Diodorus, who is supported not only by Plutarch and Justin but also by Aristotle in his *Politics*, attributes to him a personal grudge against Philip;[12] for, according to Diodorus, Attalus had been responsible for a brutal assault on Pausanias, and Philip, despite the victim's repeated requests, had taken no action against his wife's uncle. But the death of the king occurred at so opportune a moment for Alexander and his mother that they were inevitably suspected of having instigated Pausanias to kill him. The difficulty of discovering

the truth of the matter is increased by the execution, perhaps at
Philip's funeral, of two Lyncestian nobles, the brothers Heromenes
and Arrhabaeus, for alleged complicity in the crime. A third brother,
Alexander, a son-in-law of Antipater, is said to have been implicated but to have survived because he had been the first to salute his
namesake as king.

The case against Alexander and Olympias is circumstantial, but
none the less strong. They were on bad terms with Philip, and they
were undoubtedly the chief beneficiaries by his death, while Alexander and his uncle, Alexander of Epirus, the brother of Olympias,
accompanied the king into the theatre. Moreover, if Diodorus'
version is correct, the bodyguards who killed Pausanias, Leonnatus,
Perdiccas, and Attalus (not the son-in-law of Parmenio), were all
friends of Alexander, and it has been plausibly maintained[13] that
they made no attempt to take him alive because he knew too much.
Tarn suggests that the attitude of Antipater clearly exculpates
Alexander; for it was Antipater who presented Alexander to the
assembled people for their acclamation. But, even if this is true, and
it rests only on the authority of the Alexander-Romance, we cannot
be sure that Antipater was not privy to the plot. He had advised
Alexander in 340, he had accompanied him to Athens after Chaeroneia, and he was a close friend of Aristotle, Alexander's tutor. It is
not impossible that a man who is later recorded to have disapproved
of Alexander's deification might have been alienated by Philip's
recent actions.[14] We know that after Chaeroneia Philip built at
Olympia the Philippeum, a circular building containing statues of
himself, his parents, his wife, and his son, while on the very day of
his death he had had a statue of himself carried in the procession
together with those of the twelve gods.[15] Nor can we argue that the
later enmity between Antipater and Olympias would have prevented
their cooperation in Philip's murder, since we know nothing of their
relationship at this time.

Many writers on Alexander (including myself) have rejected
Diodorus' attribution of a personal motive to Pausanias,[16] principally because he dates the events which led to the assault on Pausanias
to the time of a campaign against the Illyrian Pleurias and the last
known campaign by Philip against the Illyrians took place in 344.
Obviously, if the assault took place in 344, it is difficult to credit that
Pausanias waited eight years for his revenge. Difficult, but not quite
impossible; for Attalus' appointment as one of the generals of the
advance force sent to Asia preceded by the marriage of his niece to
Philip *might* have revived Pausanias' resentment and roused him to
murder. Moreover, the chronology of Diodorus' account is obscure,
perhaps even contradictory, since he assigns Pausanias' approaches

to Philip to a time when he was already married to Cleopatra and had appointed Attalus to his command.[17] If this is true, then the probability that Pausanias was acting on his own is clearly much strengthened.

If Alexander is to be put in the dock, the only prudent verdict would seem to be 'not proven'. Philip's marriage was clearly a great blow to Alexander, particularly as it affected the position of his beloved mother, he was suspicious and resentful of his father, and the murder was a piece of luck for him. But his career was by no means devoid of good luck.

5

KING ALEXANDER

In the event Alexander succeeded his father without difficulty. He was presented to the assembled army, perhaps by Antipater, and acclaimed king. Then, after executing the Lyncestians and carrying out the state funeral of Philip, he made a tactful speech in which he promised to follow the principles of his father's administration and announced that henceforth Macedonian citizens would be exempt from taxation. From the many envoys who had come to Aegae for the wedding he claimed the loyalty which they had given to his father, meaning the position of *Hegemon* of the League of Corinth; this he rightly considered to be hereditary.

But Alexander's position was by no means secure. His cousin, Amyntas, the son of Perdiccas III, for whom Philip had acted as regent and whom he had later succeeded, was still living at court and had recently married Cynane, Philip's daughter by an Illyrian woman.[1] Amyntas might become, and may well have become, the focus of a plot against Alexander;[2] at any rate, Alexander was taking no chances, and Amyntas was 'liquidated'. It was doubtless his execution that led his associate, Amyntas, the son of Antiochus, and other leading Macedonians to flee the country and make their way to the Persian court.[3] In Asia Minor Attalus was Parmenio's second-in-command. He is reported to have entered into treasonable correspondence with Demosthenes immediately after Philip's murder, then, when it became evident that there was to be no general rising against the new king, to have sent Demosthenes' letters to Alexander in the hope that this would prove his loyalty. If he did conspire with Demosthenes—flight to the Persian king would have been more sensible—it was in vain. He was too popular with the troops, and Alexander had not forgotten his insult at Cleopatra's wedding. Hecataeus, one of the Companions, was dispatched to Asia to bring

back Attalus, or, failing this, to kill him. Parmenio can hardly have
remained unaware of Hecataeus' mission and it is likely that he
agreed to sacrifice his son-in-law and support Alexander. Significantly, many of the key positions in the army at the start of the
expedition were occupied by his sons and relatives. In any case
Attalus was assassinated and the army in Asia made no move against
Alexander. For the murders of Philip's widow, Cleopatra, and her
infant daughter, probably in 335, Alexander bears no responsibility.
This was Olympias' doing and the king, who was absent at the time,
is credibly reported to have been distressed by her brutality. Nevertheless, his distress did not prevent him from putting to death
Cleopatra's male relatives, perhaps not unjustifiably according to
Macedonian standards. Throughout Macedonian history assassina-
tion had been a traditional method of gaining or safeguarding the
throne, and Alexander does not seem to have indulged in wanton
slaughter.

Outside Macedonia the news of Philip's death had caused a wave of
unrest. The northern peoples were reported to be on the verge of
revolt and the news from Greece was grave. At Athens Demosthenes
had once again come to the fore and, although his daughter had
died only a week earlier, he put a garland on his head, donned a
white robe, and offered thank-offerings for the death of Philip. He
may have entered into negotiations with Attalus; certainly he was
encouraging the other Greek states to revolt. The Aetolians had
voted to restore their exiles, the Thebans were bent on expelling the
Macedonian garrison from the Cadmeia, while the Ambraciots had
actually expelled their garrison and established a democracy. In
the Peloponnese, too, there was widespread unrest.

Faced with this critical situation, Alexander's advisers counselled
caution. Alexander, they said, should abandon his commitments in
Greece and gradually consolidate the position on Macedonia's
northern frontier. But the young king, characteristically, went his
own way; he would not abandon control of Greece: the barbarians
could wait.

Hurrying south, he outflanked the strong Thessalian position in
the Vale of Tempe—his engineers cut a path up the slopes of Mount
Ossa—and gained control of Thessaly without fighting. The Thessalians recognized him as *archon* of Thessaly in succession to his
father and placed their invaluable cavalry at his disposal. The
neighbouring tribes then submitted and the Amphictyonic League
acknowledged him as *Hegemon* of the Corinthian League. The speed
of Alexander's march had surprised the Greeks and they were in no
position to resist. The Ambraciots hastened to send envoys and,
when Alexander encamped in full battle order near the Cadmeia,

Theban resistance collapsed. The Athenians, too, lost no time in apologizing for failing to recognize him sooner. At Corinth Alexander summoned a meeting of the Council of the League and was duly elected *strategos autokrator* to conduct the war against Persia in place of Philip. On his return journey to Macedonia he visited Delphi, presumably to consult the oracle about his intended Persian campaign, and made a donation of 150 'Philips', the popular gold staters whose reverse type celebrated Philip's victory in the chariot race at Olympia.[4]

Alexander intended, when he set out for Asia, to leave Antipater behind in Macedonia to deal with any trouble that might arise in Greece. But in order that his deputy might not have to fight on two fronts it was necessary to bring the restless tribes of the north and west to realize the power of Macedon. Although Alexander had a personal score to settle with the Triballians for their 'insolence' in 339, he clearly aimed at more than a mere punitive expedition. In fact, it is probable that he had already determined to make the Danube the frontier in the north.

In the spring of 335 he set out from Amphipolis. He marched east past Philippi and Mount Orbelus, crossed the River Nestus (Mesta), and in ten days reached Mount Haemus (Balkan Mountains), probably by way of Philippopolis (Plovdiv). There, at the Shipka pass, he was confronted by a Thracian force whose waggons were drawn up at the head of the steep slope. There was no way round, and Alexander had no option but to make a frontal attack. His ability as a leader and the discipline of his troops was soon revealed. Divining that the intention of the Thracians was to launch the waggons down the slope and follow them up with a wild charge against the disorganized Macedonians, he instructed his men, where there was room, to leave gaps through which the waggons might pass harmlessly or, where the ground did not allow this, to kneel or lie down, linking their shields together like a Roman *testudo*, so that the waggons might bound over them and cause no damage. Alexander's plan worked perfectly. The waggons careered down the hill, passing between the Macedonian files or bouncing off their interlocked shields, and not a man was lost. Immensely heartened, the infantry rose and charged. The enemy fled, leaving 1500 dead and a great quantity of booty.

As Alexander crossed into Triballian territory and advanced towards the Danube, their king Syrmus fled with his suite and the women and children to an island called Peuke. The main body of the Triballians, who had doubled back, was surprised making camp but escaped to a wooded glen. To storm their position threatened to cost many Macedonian lives and, once again, Alexander used his wits to save his men. Advancing his archers and slingers, he kept his heavy infantry and cavalry out of sight in the rear, until the Triballians, harassed by the missiles and thinking to win an easy victory, rushed out of the glen, when he attacked them in front and on both flanks with his cavalry. Three thousand Triballians fell; Macedonian losses, we are told, totalled only eleven horsemen and forty infantrymen.

When he reached the Danube, Alexander was joined by the fleet which he had ordered to sail up the river from Byzantium, but the swift current and the steep banks prevented him from landing on Peuke. Meanwhile the Getae, a kindred Thracian tribe, had assembled in strength on the further bank and Alexander decided to attack them. Arrian attributes to him a 'longing' to land on the further side of the river, a word which he and other writers use elsewhere of 'a non-rational longing for the unknown, the uninvestigated and mysterious'.[5] It seems probable, however, that on this occasion at least his purpose was more pedestrian. Collecting all the native 'dugouts' he could find and filling tent-covers with hay, Alexander ferried across the Danube no fewer than five thousand men during the night. Despite their superiority in numbers, the Getae did not venture to oppose him, but fled first to their settlement nearby and, when the Macedonians approached, galloped off into the northern steppes. So impressed were the independent tribes along the river by Alexander's feat in crossing 'the greatest of rivers' that they made haste to submit. Syrmus followed suit, and even the Celts living along the eastern shore of the Adriatic sent envoys to conclude an alliance with Alexander. Not for over fifty years did Macedon have to cope with a serious threat to her northern borders.

As Alexander marched south-west towards the territory of the Agrianians and Paeonians, news reached him that Cleitus, an Illyrian chieftain, had seized Pellion, a border stronghold on the Apsus, and that the Taulantian king, Glaucias, who lived near Durazzo, was on his way to join Cleitus. The Autariatians, too, were said to be preparing to attack him. The situation was critical; all Illyria seemed likely to rise and engulf the western border of Macedonia.

Leaving Langarus, the Agrianian king, to deal with the Autariatians, Alexander hurried down the valleys of the Axius (Vardar) and the Erigon (Tzerna) and succeeded in reaching Pellion before Glaucias. He had driven Cleitus into the town and was preparing to invest it when Glaucias arrived and occupied the heights nearby. Alexander's impetuosity had landed him in serious trouble. He was caught between two fires, outnumbered and short of supplies, his only way out a narrow defile commanded by the enemy. But he did not panic; instead of trying to fight his way out, he had recourse to a stratagem. By a breathtaking display of arms-drill, precision marching and counter-marching, he drew the enemy down from their position on the heights, then ordered his men to raise their battle-cry and beat their spears on their shields. Astounded, the Taulantians fled to Pellion. But Alexander still had to cross the Apsus and, as an enemy force commanded the ford, his rearguard faced the prospect of heavy casualties. This problem, too, he solved. Taking the light-armed troops across first, he set up catapults on the far bank and by using these as field artillery (the first recorded instance) and by ordering his archers to fire from mid-stream he kept the enemy at a safe distance so that not a man was lost during the crossing. Three days later Alexander had his revenge. Learning that Cleitus and Glaucias were encamped without trenches or sentries—for they thought he had retreated in disorder—he recrossed the river and in a night attack killed or captured many of the enemy. The survivors, after setting fire to Pellion, fled to Glaucias' mountain stronghold in the west. Alexander's success had come none too soon, for the news from Greece forced him to abandon any thought of further operations. Yet this demonstration of Macedonian strength served its purpose and Illyria gave no trouble during his reign.

The situation in Greece was serious. Thebes had risen, Athens had promised support, and a Peloponnesian army had advanced to the Isthmus. The trouble, it seems, had begun soon after Alexander's departure for the north, when Persian agents arrived in Greece with a plentiful supply of gold. Darius III had succeeded to the Persian throne in 336, soon after the arrival in Asia Minor of the Macedonian advance party. He had perhaps thought at first that Philip's death would result in its withdrawal, but on learning that Alexander was firmly established in control of Greece he had realized that the invasion would go ahead as planned. Memnon was appointed to the command against Parmenio and Darius had recourse to the time-honoured method of dealing with the Greeks, the employment of Persian 'archers', as the Greeks called the gold darics which portrayed the Great King as a bowman.[6] Of the Greek states only Sparta is known to have taken his money, but Demosthenes, as documents later captured in Sardes revealed, accepted 300 talents.[7] Soon a rumour began to circulate throughout Greece that Alexander had fallen among the Triballians and Demosthenes, most opportunely, was able to produce a soldier who declared that he had been wounded in the same battle in which the king had been killed.[8] A party in Thebes now resolved to act. They invited the Theban exiles now living in Athens to return, surprised two of the garrison of the Cadmeia outside the fortress and put them to death. The Theban assembly voted to throw off the Macedonian yoke, and Demosthenes used some of the Persian money to supply arms. The Cadmeia was besieged, but held out.

Alexander feared a combination of the leading states. If he were quick, he might prevent it; but speed was vital. He called on his weary troops for a supreme effort, and in seven days reached Pelinna in Thessaly. A further six took him to Onchestus, seven miles north-west of Thebes, some 250 miles from his starting-point. The Theban leaders refused to believe that it was Alexander; it must, they said, be Antipater from Macedonia. When they were assured that the army was led by Alexander, they thought it must be Alexander the Lyncestian. But on the following day, when the king advanced to Thebes, the truth was plain.

Diodorus and Arrian, who follows Ptolemy, are agreed that for three days Alexander remained inactive near the Electra Gate, where the walls of the Cadmeia, now ringed by a double stockade, met the city walls and the road from Athens reached the city. He had no wish to leave behind him an embittered Greece and waited for an approach from the Thebans. Indeed, he issued a proclamation offering the Thebans an amnesty and demanding only the surrender of two of the leaders of the revolt. The Thebans replied by demanding the surrender of Antipater and Philotas, the commander of the garrison of the Cadmeia, and inviting anyone who wished to join them and the king of Persia in freeing Greece from the tyrant. Alexander, understandably, was infuriated and on the following day ordered the attack to begin. At first the Thebans held their own in fierce fighting outside the walls, but eventually the weight of the Macedonian phalanx and their superior numbers forced the Thebans to retire into the city. Some of the attackers entered with the fugitives and the remaining Macedonians scaled the walls, now held by their own men. As the Thebans tired, the Macedonians and their allies gained the upper hand and the battle became a slaughter. The Greek allies of Macedon, Phocians and Boeotians, whom Alexander had called out as members of the League of Corinth, indulged their lust for vengeance on armed and unarmed alike and when the massacre ended 6000 Thebans lay dead.

Alexander, quite properly, treated the revolt as an infringement of the Common Peace and handed over the decision about the fate of Thebes to the representatives of the allies. Her enemies recalled the Medism of Thebes in 480, the massacre of the Plataeans in 429, and the Theban proposal to enslave Athens at the end of the Pelo-ponnesian War, and the Council gave its verdict. The city of Thebes was to be razed to the ground, its territory divided among the Boeotian allies, and the survivors, men, women, and children, sold as slaves; Orchomenus and Plataea, destroyed by Thebes in 364 and 373 respectively, were to be rebuilt and fortified. As *Hegemon* of the League, Alexander carried out the decree. 30,000 Thebans were sold into slavery, realizing 440 talents. The Macedonian garrison remained in the Cadmeia.

The responsibility for the destruction of Thebes lies fairly and squarely on Alexander's shoulders, as even the kindly Plutarch implies. The delegates to whom he entrusted her fate were, as he well knew, her bitter enemies, whose behaviour in the battle and still more in the massacre which followed clearly indicated their feelings towards her. It was a calculated act of terrorism on Alexander's part. Had he wished to save Thebes, he could have done so; but he wanted to teach the other Greek states a lesson. His very different treatment of Athens, morally equally guilty, shows that political considerations were uppermost in his mind. Whether he was wise to destroy Thebes is debatable. It may be true to say that by doing so he destroyed the possibility of reaching an understanding with the Greeks, but the conduct of the Greek states in the past two years must have convinced him that the likelihood of their cooperating with him was remote.

One after another they hastened to make their excuses to Alexander and at Athens all thought of resistance vanished. The assembly voted to send an embassy to congratulate Alexander on his safe return from his northern campaign and on his punishment of Thebes! He replied by demanding the surrender of ten leading politicians and generals, including Demosthenes and Lycurgus. However, a second embassy, led by Phocion and Demades, persuaded him to be content with the exile of the irreconcilable Charidemus, a native of Euboea, granted Athenian citizenship for military services, who went off to the Persian court. Nevertheless, we know of a number of prominent Athenians who left the city at this time to take service with the Persian king.[9] Quite evidently Alexander's concessions did not secure the gratitude of the Athenians.

Returning to Macedonia, Alexander began his preparations for the invasion. He recalled Parmenio, now sixty-five but by far the most experienced Macedonian general, to act as his second-in-command. Then he summoned a meeting of his advisers to discuss the timing and strategy of the expedition. Antipater and Parmenio, characteristically, counselled delay, until Alexander should marry and produce an heir. Their advice was sound, as events after Alexander's death were to prove, but the king would not listen. He may simply have been impatient to conduct a major campaign—for his desire for glory is undoubted—but it is not impossible that he was thinking of the state of the Macedonian economy. Philip had died owing 500 talents, he himself had abolished direct taxation, and the maintenance of a great army required money that could only be got from conquest.[10] At any rate the king's will prevailed. It was agreed that the expedition should start in the early spring of the following year, and the member states of the League of Corinth were instructed to send their contingents to Pella before that time. Antipater was to remain in charge of Europe, acting in Macedonia as viceroy and in Greece as deputy for the *Hegemon* of the League, responsible in effect for the maintenance of peace throughout the country. This latter task, in particular, explains the large force of 12,000 Macedonian infantry and 1500 cavalry placed at his disposal, almost as large as the Macedonian contingent in Alexander's army; for the king had no illusions about the feelings of the Greeks towards him.

6

THE CONQUEST OF ASIA MINOR

Alexander set out from Pella early in the spring of 334 and covered the three hundred miles to the Hellespont in just under three weeks. Leaving Parmenio at Sestos to see to the transport of the army across the straits to Abydos, where the Macedonians still held a bridgehead, he took the opportunity to pay a visit to Troy. Such a visit, one might say, was inevitable. From boyhood the *Iliad* had been his favourite reading and the Homeric heroes, particularly his ancestor Achilles, were doubtless alive for him to an extent that we can hardly conceive. It would not be surprising if Alexander really thought of himself as a second Achilles.

His first action certainly recalled the Trojan war. With a small group he advanced to Elaeus at the tip of the Gallipoli peninsula, the point from which, according to tradition, Agamemnon's forces had crossed into Asia. There he offered sacrifice at the tomb of Protesilaus and prayed for better fortune; for, as Homer relates, Protesilaus had been the first Greek to set foot on the soil of Asia and had been killed immediately.[1] Then, setting up altars to Zeus of Safe Landings, Athena, and Heracles, an action he was to repeat on the Asiatic shore, he embarked on his flag-ship and took the helm. In mid-stream he sacrificed a bull to Poseidon and poured a libation to the Nereids. This has been supposed to show that Alexander had in mind Xerxes' actions at the Hellespont before his invasion of Greece in 480.[2] But, while it is true that his expedition professed to be a war of revenge for the acts of sacrilege committed by Xerxes, the only similarity between the actions of the two kings is that both poured a libation; for Xerxes offered no sacrifice and he made his libation from the shore before crossing the Hellespont, not to Elaeus but to Sestos. The war which Alexander had in mind was the Trojan war.

As Alexander reached the 'Achaean harbour', probably at or near Rhoeteum, Diodorus relates that he hurled his spear ashore, leaped after it, and declared Asia 'spear-won land'.[3] This means, if Diodorus is to be trusted, that at the start of the expedition Alexander was laying claim to the Persian empire, for this is the usual meaning of 'Asia' at this time. It is certainly not likely that Alexander doubted the ability of his large and well-trained army (with himself to command it) to achieve this aim. At Troy Alexander sacrificed to Athena of Ilium and dedicated his armour to the goddess, receiving in exchange a shield said to have been preserved from the Trojan war, which he had carried into battle before him. Next he laid a wreath on Achilles' tomb while his dearest friend, Hephaestion, laid one on the tomb of Patroclus; finally, we are told, he offered sacrifice to Priam to avert his anger from himself as a descendant of Achilles.

The ceremonies completed, Alexander marched north to rejoin his army now in camp at Arisbe, just east of Abydos. The crossing had taken place without incident, since the strong Persian fleet, most surprisingly, had made no effort to intervene. At Arisbe the king held a review of his forces, numbering probably 32,000 infantry and 5100 cavalry. Such, at any rate, are the totals given by Diodorus, who alone provides details of the various contingents, totals which agree with the figures given by Arrian.[4] It seems likely, however, that we must add to these the troops holding the bridgehead. How many these were is anyone's guess, but surely not the whole 10,000 that Parmenio is said to have had under his command in 335.[5]

The backbone of the infantry was the Macedonian phalanx, the Foot Companions, 6 battalions of about 1500 men each, organized on a tribal basis. The Macedonian infantryman was armed with the *sarissa* or pike, about 13 or 14 feet long, roughly half as long again as the Greek hoplite's spear, and, as the *sarissa* required two hands to wield it, he carried a smaller shield without the grip near the rim by which the hoplite held his shield; instead the Macedonian shield had an armband through which the left arm passed. Besides his pike the Macedonian carried a short sword and wore greaves and a helmet; whether, like his Greek counterpart, he wore a breastplate is disputed.[6] The phalanx, like the Greek hoplite line, was designed for pitched battles, but was more flexible. Each battalion had its own commander, although Craterus, in addition to commanding the battalion on the extreme left, had authority over the next two in line, and Coenus, who commanded the battalion on the extreme right, probably exercised a similar command over the two to his left. Nevertheless, there was a tendency for the phalanx to become separated on difficult ground. Its main function in Alexander's major battles was to hold the enemy infantry while the king at the head of his cavalry delivered the decisive blow.

The right or unshielded side of the phalanx was defended in battle by the Royal Hypaspists or Guards, three battalions of picked infantry each 1000 strong, one of which, the *agema*, was Alexander's personal guard.[7] They were constantly employed with the Agrianians, archers, and the Companion cavalry in independent operations, for skirmishing and mountain warfare, and in battle they acted as a link or hinge between the phalanx and the cavalry on their right. Although their mobility might suggest that they were more lightly armed than the men of the phalanx, Arrian sometimes writes of them as if they were part of the phalanx and they certainly shared the heavy infantry work. It is likely, therefore, that the difference between them and the infantry of the phalanx was roughly the same as that which distinguishes the modern Guards' regiment from the infantry of the line, a historical difference rather than one of armament.

Besides his Macedonian infantry Alexander had some 8000 Balkan troops and 12,000 Greeks. 5000 of the latter were mercenaries, perhaps as many as Alexander could afford; the remainder were provided by the member states of the Corinthian League, and their presence is due partly to Alexander's desire to preserve the pan-Hellenic character of the expedition, partly perhaps to a desire to have hostages for the good behaviour of the Greek states. The mercenaries were used largely as garrison troops, and their number steadily increased as the campaign progressed. The Balkan troops were light-armed javelin-men, mainly Thracians and Illyrians, but including the invaluable Agrianians, perhaps 1000 strong, who have been appropriately compared in quality and status with the Gurkhas. Finally, there was a regiment of 500 Cretan archers, the best archers in the Greek world, who were always in the forefront of the fighting.

Among the cavalry the Macedonian 'Companions' commanded by Philotas, the son of Parmenio, held pride of place. Seven of the squadrons consisted of just over 200 troopers each; the eighth, the Royal Squadron, numbered about 300 and served as Alexander's personal guard. Originally 1800 strong, they were reinforced in the winter of 334–333 and at Gaugamela numbered 2000. In pitched battles they were drawn up on the right of the Hypaspists and made the decisive charge, sometimes at least in wedge formation, spearheaded by the Royal Squadron. Their counterpart on the left of the phalanx was the Thessalian cavalry, of whom the 300 Pharsalians seem to have formed a personal guard for Parmenio, Alexander's second-in-command, who had charge of the entire left wing. The Thessalians, too, numbered 1800 at the start of the expedition and at the beginning of 333 received a reinforcement of 200 troopers. The

remainder of the cavalry was light horse, 600 from the Greek states
and 900 Thracians and Paeonians from the northern borders of
Macedonia. The Thracians probably included four squadrons of
'Scouts' (*Prodromoi*), although some consider these Macedonian.[8]
They were armed with the *sarissa*, presumably shorter than the infantry *sarissa* which required two hands to wield it; hence they are also
called 'Lancers' (*Sarissophoroi*). At the beginning of the campaign
Alexander does not seem to have had any mercenary cavalry, unless
there were some with the advance force at Abydos; at Gaugamela
he may have had about 1000.

Of Alexander's technical troops our sources tell us little.[9] Yet they
played an important part in the campaign, not merely in the sieges of
Tyre and Gaza, but also later in Bactria and India. We know the
names of four engineer officers, and there may have been others;
certainly Alexander had many engineers who worked under their
supervision. They built stone- and arrow-firing catapults, which the
king used on occasion as field artillery, as well as ladders, boarding
bridges, towers and rams. Most of the material used was wood, and
only the essential parts of the engines were transported from one
place to another, doubtless on pack mules like modern mountain
artillery. Alexander's engineers were also employed in constructing
boats (sometimes transported in sections and reassembled where
required), and in building bridges, as they did across the River Indus.
We hear, too, of architects, such as Deinocrates who laid out the
first and greatest Alexandria in Egypt, while a group of surveyors
(*bematists*) collected information about routes and camp sites and
kept a record of the distances covered, thereby contributing much
to Greek knowledge of the geography of Asia.

Alexander's personal staff consisted of a small group of 'Bodyguards' (*Somatophylakes*), never numbering as far as we know more
than eight at any one time. The basis for their selection was perhaps
personal rather than military. A much larger group, probably more
than one hundred—we know the names of sixty-two—was the
Companions (*Hetairoi*). They formed an unofficial Council and
from them Alexander drew his governors and administrators.[10] His
chief secretary was the Greek, Eumenes of Cardia, who had held this
post under Philip. Besides dealing with official correspondence, he
may have been responsible for keeping a journal or diary of important events. However, as has been said, the *Diary* from which Arrian
and Plutarch quote is probably not genuine.

From Arisbe Alexander marched east towards the River Granicus,
now the Koçabas, which flows northwards from Mt Ida into the
Sea of Marmora. Although Lampsacus and Colonae made no move
to welcome him, he was content to bypass them; the difficult decision

about their future could wait until he had dealt with the Persian forces in the area. Meanwhile the coastal satraps, Spithridates of Lydia and Arsites of Hellespontine Phrygia, had been joined at Zeleia (Sari-Keia), east of the Granicus, by the governors of Phrygia and Cappadocia, by Memnon who commanded the Greek mercenaries, and by many Persian barons. Arrian puts their combined forces at forty thousand, equally divided between infantry and cavalry. This is clearly an overestimate, for many of the mercenaries in Persian service were absent with the fleet and in the battle at the Granicus the Persians were evidently outnumbered. A Council was held and Memnon, stressing the superiority of the Macedonian phalanx, advised the Persian leaders to retire, destroying their towns and crops as they went, and to await Darius. Meanwhile, he advocated, they should take advantage of their naval superiority to carry the war into Greece. The plan was sound, but the Persian nobles, jealous and suspicious of Memnon and perhaps nettled by his reference to the inferiority of the Persian forces, would have none of it, and Arsites swore that he would not yield a foot of his territory. Instead they decided to fight and advanced to a position on the east bank of the Granicus. The position was a strong one, for the banks were steep and muddy and the river was swollen by spring rains, but the Persian commanders threw away their advantage by drawing up their cavalry along the top of the river bank and stationing the infantry in the rear. For this arrangement deprived the cavalry of the opportunity to charge and their light javelins were no match in hand-to-hand combat for the *sarissae* of the Companion cavalry. Tarn has suggested that their object was to kill Alexander; but, if it was, this was not the best way to do so. Major-General Fuller's explanation is altogether more likely. He does not deny that the Persians aimed to kill Alexander, but he conjectures that the Persian nobles declined to yield the place of honour in the forefront of the battle to Greek mercenaries, especially perhaps since their pride had been touched by Memnon's remarks. Possibly, too, they did not altogether trust Memnon and his men.[11]

When the Macedonian forces reached the Granicus, Parmenio advised the king not to attempt to cross immediately, but to wait for dawn. The Persians, he calculated, would retire from the river bank for the night, and at dawn Alexander would be able to cross without opposition. This advice the king rightly rejected. A dawn attack might increase his chances of victory, but it would deprive him of the thing he wanted most, the moral effect of a victory won on the enemy's ground.

Deciding to engage immediately, Alexander made his dispositions. In the centre he drew up the six battalions of the phalanx, and on their right the hypaspists commanded by Nicanor, one of Parmenio's sons. On the right of the hypaspists Amyntas commanded a cavalry group consisting of the Lancers, the Paeonian light horse, and one squadron of the Companions; then came the remaining squadrons of the Companions and on the flank the Cretan archers and the Agrianians. On the left of the phalanx were stationed the Thracian horse, the allied Greek cavalry, and the crack Thessalian cavalry. The left wing of the army, including three battalions of the phalanx, was under Parmenio's command.

The only exception to Alexander's normal battle line was that the cavalry group under Amyntas was interposed between the hypaspists and the Companions. The purpose of this change soon became evident. Seeing Alexander, a conspicuous figure in his shining armour and his helmet with its two enormous white plumes, on the Macedonian right, the Persians reinforced their left wing, thereby weakening their centre. Whereupon Alexander ordered Amyntas, with his cavalry force reinforced by a hypaspist battalion, to charge diagonally to his right against the massed Persian ranks. When Amyntas had pinned down the Persian left wing, Alexander gave the order for the charge and at the head of the Companions galloped diagonally to his left against the left centre of the enemy. Amyntas' group suffered heavy casualties, but Alexander was able to force his way up the steep banks and gradually the Companions, fighting with *sarissae* against javelins, gained the upper hand. The king himself was the target for the attacks of the Persian nobles, many of whom lost their lives in this phase of the battle. Arrian's narrative recalls the duels between Homeric heroes, but Fuller reminds the sceptics that 'war was still in its heroic phase' and remarks that 'the rather common assumption that when a classical historian depicts a duel between opposing protagonists, he does so to gain dramatic effect, or to champion a favourite general, should generally be discounted, for he is usually depicting the decisive incident in the battle'. Such a moment came just after Alexander had vanquished Mithridates, a son-in-law of Darius. Another Persian noble, Rhoesakes, dealt him a mighty blow with his sabre, severing part of his helmet together with one of its plumes, and, as the king ran him through with his lance, Rhoesakes' brother, Spithridates, rode up behind him. The Persian had already raised his sabre to cut down Alexander when Cleitus 'the Black' struck him a terrible blow and cut off his arm at the shoulder.

The battle now became what Arrian calls 'a cavalry battle but on infantry lines', in other words a hand-to-hand struggle, in which the superior weapons and superior strength of the Macedonians told. The Persian centre collapsed, the wings turned to flight, and the

Greek mercenaries were left to face the Macedonians. Surrounded,
they asked for terms, but Alexander refused and cut them down
except for two thousand who were taken prisoner. Alexander's
refusal was due to policy, not anger. He treated the Greeks as
traitors, in accordance with the resolution of the League of Corinth.
Later he was to change his policy. The prisoners were sent in chains
to Macedonia to work on the land, and to underline his position as
Hegemon of the League Alexander sent to Athens three hundred
suits of Persian armour as an offering to Athena from 'Alexander,
son of Philip, and the Greeks, except the Spartans'. The mention of
the Spartans is deliberate, to emphasize their refusal to join the
League; noteworthy, too, is the absence of any reference to the
Macedonians who had borne the brunt of the fighting. Clearly the
dedication was meant for Greek consumption. But at Dium in
Macedonia statues of the twenty-five Companions who had fallen
in the initial onslaught were set up.

The effect of the victory was immediate. Zeleia, a Greek town,
which had been the main Persian base, now surrendered; so, too, did
Lampsacus and Dascylium. Alexander accepted the plea of the
Zeleians that they had acted under duress but, when Calas was
appointed satrap of Hellespontine Phrygia, the town was apparently
treated no differently from the non-Greek towns which had to pay
to Alexander the tribute they had previously paid to Persia.[12]
Lampsacus and Dascylium presumably received similar treatment;
indeed, Alexander is said to have contemplated destroying Lampsacus and to have been dissuaded by its most eminent citizen, the
historian Anaximenes.

Many of the Persian leaders had fallen in the battle. Those who
survived, including Memnon, had retreated south to Miletus and
Alexander hastened in pursuit, making first for Sardes at the head
of the Royal Road to Susa. Near the city he was met by Mithrines,
the commander of the Persian garrison in the citadel, who surrendered the city and its valuable treasures. Alexander kept the
Persian with him, and treated him with the honour due to his rank;
such conduct as his was worth encouraging, and he might prove
useful in future negotiations. The inhabitants of Sardes were granted
their 'freedom', as were the other Lydians. What this amounted to
we can see in the appointment of a satrap, Asander, a financial
officer to assess and collect the tribute, and a garrison commander. In
fact, the position of the Lydians was unaltered. At Ephesus an
oligarchy had ruled in the Persian interest with the support of a
mercenary garrison. On the news of the Persian defeat the garrison
fled and the citizens welcomed Alexander, who established a democracy and restored the exiles but, commendably, intervened to prevent

a massacre of the oligarchs. Alexander offered to dedicate the new temple of Artemis—the old one is said to have been burnt down on the very day of his birth—but the Ephesians refused. Hence he did not remit the tribute, but ordered it to be paid to the temple.

Events now led Alexander to declare his policy towards the Greek cities. To Ephesus came envoys from Magnesia on the Maeander and from Tralles offering to hand over their cities, now presumably under democratic rule. Parmenio was dispatched with a squadron of cavalry and 5000 infantry to take them over and at the same time Alcimachus was sent with an equal force to the Aeolian and Ionian cities. These large forces suggest that resistance was expected, or provided for. Alcimachus' orders were to put down oligarchies and establish democracies, to restore to the cities their own laws and to remit the tribute paid to the Persian king. These orders do not indicate a preference on Alexander's part for democracy—he had, after all, little reason to be grateful to the Greek democracies, and in Greece tyrannies and oligarchies enjoyed Macedonian support—but, since Persia had maintained oligarchies in Asia Minor, Alexander was bound to take the opposite line. The cities probably became members of the League of Corinth, as the island states certainly did, and instead of supplying men or ships were required to make financial contributions (*syntaxeis*).[13] At Priene Alexander, remembering his rebuff at Ephesus, promised to donate a large sum of money towards the restoration of the temple of Athena in return for the right to dedicate it when completed; nevertheless, the city received a garrison and had to make a 'contribution' (later remitted).[14]

Although it is clear that Alexander interpreted 'liberation' in a very restricted sense, the only serious opposition he encountered in Asia Minor was at Miletus and Halicarnassus. At Miletus Hegesistratus, the garrison commander, who had written to Alexander offering to surrender the city, changed his mind when he learnt that the Persian fleet of 400 ships was nearby, and held out in the citadel. However, his hopes were soon dashed when the Greek fleet of 160 ships under Nicanor reached Miletus first and blocked the entrance to the harbour. Deprived of outside help, the city soon fell. A number of the defenders, including 300 mercenaries, escaped to a nearby islet. They were prepared to fight to the death, but Alexander, as Arrian puts it, 'was moved to pity by their courage and loyalty', and came to terms with them. The fact was that Alexander saw that his policy of treating such men as traitors was mistaken and, ready as always to learn by his mistakes, decided to enrol in his army 300 valuable recruits whom by now he could well afford to pay.

It was at this point that Alexander took the hazardous step of disbanding his fleet, except for twenty Athenian ships and a few others which he retained for the transport of his siege equipment. His reasons, we are told, were lack of money, the inability of his fleet to face the larger Persian navy, and his intention to break up the enemy fleet by capturing its bases. Despite the high cost of maintaining a fleet, we may doubt whether money was the deciding factor. By this time Alexander was in possession of the treasure in Sardes and the 'contributions' of a number of Greek cities, perhaps a substantial sum if the fifty talents later 'asked' from Aspendus is any guide. At any rate he was able in the spring of the following year to give Hegelochus 500 talents to raise another fleet, to send 600 talents to Antipater, and to send Cleander to the Peloponnese to hire mercenaries. His conquest of the coast of Asia Minor, too, was by no means complete as yet, and at least half of the Persian fleet came from Cyprus and Phoenicia. Arrian gives us a clue to Alexander's main reason when he remarks that the king 'had no wish to subject any part of his strength, in ships or men, to the risk of disaster'. At Miletus Alexander had rejected Parmenio's advice to fight a naval battle on the ground that news of a Persian success would encourage the Greeks to revolt, and it seems clear that Alexander's real worry was the loyalty of the Greek sailors. The crews of the twenty Athenian ships which he retained are perhaps best regarded as hostages. Alexander took a calculated risk, which very nearly cost him dear, that during the winter the enemy fleet would be restricted in its operations and that in 333 he could, as he did, raise another fleet which would suffice at least to defend the shores of Greece.

In the autumn of 334 Alexander marched, probably by way of Alabanda and the Marsyas valley, into Caria.[15] Pixodarus, whose daughter he had once proposed to marry, was now dead and his brother-in-law Orontopates, a Persian, ruled the country. However, Ada, the former queen, still held the fortress of Alinda to which she had withdrawn on being deposed by her brother, Pixodarus, and advancing to meet Alexander she offered to surrender the town. Seeing in her a valuable ally, he confirmed her in possession of Alinda and recognized her as queen of all Caria. He agreed, too, to her proposal that she adopt him as her son; for this meant that on her death he would possess a valid title to the country.

At Halicarnassus (Bodrum), the Carian capital, Orontopates and Memnon with at least two thousand mercenaries and a large body of Asiatic troops had made extensive preparations to withstand a siege.[16] The town with its three fortresses and high brick wall was immensely strong, and the defenders had surrounded it with a moat 45 feet wide and 22 feet deep. Moreover, as the Persians were now unchallenged at sea, the city could not be starved into submission.

But, if Alexander was to deny the Persian fleet bases in the eastern
Mediterranean, it was essential to take Halicarnassus. Accordingly
the siege was pressed with vigour, the moat was filled in and siege
engines brought up. The defenders replied with courage and resource.
Attempts to set fire to the engines failed, but heavy casualties were
inflicted on the Macedonians. When two towers and the intervening
curtain wall had been demolished, a crescent-shaped brick wall was
hastily built to cover the breach and held up the attackers for several
days; for they were exposed to cross-fire from the towers at each end
of the breach. Gradually, however, the Macedonians gained the
upper hand, the city almost fell, and Memnon and Orontopates
decided to stake all on an offensive. When this failed, they abandoned the city, perhaps fearing a popular rising, and Memnon
escaped to Cos while Orontopates led the defence of the citadels,
Salmakis and Arconnesus, at the entrance to the harbour. Seeing
their strength, Alexander decided against attempting to take them
by storm—wisely, as they held out for another twelve months.
Instead, he left a force of 3000 mercenaries and 200 cavalry to invest
them, and to garrison the country.

As it was now late in the year Alexander, with his usual care for
the welfare of his troops, ordered home for the winter those Macedonians who had married just before the start of the campaign.
'No act of Alexander's', says Arrian, 'ever made him better loved by
his Macedonians.' The officers in charge were directed to comb Macedonia for reinforcements, and Cleander went with them to hire
troops in the Peloponnese. They were ordered to rendezvous with
Alexander at Gordium in Phrygia in the spring.

Parmenio was now detached. With a strong force of cavalry,
consisting of the Thessalians and a 'hipparchy' (presumably two or
more squadrons) of the Companions, the siege engines, and the
heavy baggage, he was ordered to return to Sardes and from there
to make for Gordium where Alexander would join him. The composition of his force shows clearly how well Alexander was informed
about the nature of the terrain that lay ahead, which would afford
little scope for the employment of large masses of cavalry. He himself
proposed to secure the coasts of Lycia and Pamphylia in accordance
with his plan to neutralize the Persian navy. He entered Lycia by the
line of the modern road and received the surrender of Telmissus,
where his seer Aristander doubtless had relatives or friends, Xanthus,
and other smaller towns, and after campaigning against the hill
tribes of the interior marched on to Phaselis. It was at Phaselis,
while he waited for the Thracians to build a road through the
mountain passes to Perge, that he received word from Parmenio that
Darius had attempted to bribe his namesake, Alexander of Lyncestis,

to assassinate him. This was a serious matter. A meeting of the Council was called to discuss the Lyncestian's fate and the king was advised 'to get rid of him as soon as possible', before he headed a revolt. Nevertheless, although Alexander was arrested and kept under guard, he was not put to death for another three years, at the time of the 'plot' of Philotas. The Lyncestian Alexander's relationship to Antipater may have had some influence on the king's decision, but he was evidently less fearful of plots than he later became.

Leaving a garrison in Phaselis and appointing his friend Nearchus to govern Lycia and Pamphylia, Alexander sent the bulk of his forces through the mountains by way of the new road, the 'Climax' or 'Ladder', while with his staff he took the direct route along the coast. Strong southerlies, which make the passage all but impossible, had been blowing for some time, but, as Alexander and his party struggled on, the wind suddenly swung round to the north and they were able to complete their journey without difficulty. The official historian, Callisthenes, recalled, surely with Alexander's approval, the passage in Homer (*Iliad* 13.26ff.) where the waves did obeisance to Poseidon.[17] While it is likely enough that Alexander and his staff saw in this incident the hand of the gods, another expression of their goodwill, Callisthenes was not suggesting, as some scholars have argued, that Alexander was a god. The reference to the *Iliad* is merely 'courtly reminiscence' of Homer; for at this time the king was not seeking recognition as a god. That was to come later.

From Perge Alexander marched to Side (Selimiye) at the eastern end of the fertile Pamphylian plain, where he left a garrison before turning west again. The country beyond Side was wild and desolate, lacking harbours and good roads, as far as the Cilician border; it could safely be left unconquered. Near Sillyum news came that the Aspendians had repudiated the agreement that Alexander had made with their envoys. Not surprisingly, for the king, in return for a promise not to garrison their city, had demanded, in addition to the tribute of horses which they had paid to the king of Persia, a 'contribution' of 50 talents towards his soldiers' pay. Doubtless the Aspendians expected that Alexander would be too busy to trouble with them. But they had misjudged him. He turned east again and, when the Aspendians submitted, imposed harsher terms. In addition to the tribute of horses, Aspendus had to pay an annual tribute in cash, as if it was a 'barbarian' city, while the 'contribution' was increased to 100 talents, and the leading men were taken as hostages. These terms may be justified or excused; for the Aspendians had broken an agreement and put Alexander to some inconvenience; but the original 'contribution' of 50 talents—a truly enormous sum— shows what 'liberation' meant.

Alexander now resumed his march towards Phrygia. The only serious resistance came from the Pisidians of Sagalassus, where some twenty Macedonians were killed, and their defeat was followed by the submission or subjugation of the remaining strongholds. At Celaenae, an important centre of communications from which roads ran west to the Hermus and Maeander valleys and north to Gordium, the satrap of Phrygia held the acropolis with 1000 native troops and 100 mercenaries. However, he agreed to surrender if not relieved by a certain date, an offer that Alexander was happy to accept. The region was vital to his communications with the north and west and Alexander chose as governor a fine soldier, Antigonus 'the One-Eyed', perhaps the greatest of his Successors, assigning him a garrison of 1500 men.

In the spring of 333 Alexander reached Gordium on the River Sangarius, south-west of Ankara, to be joined there by Parmenio with the remainder of the army. The troops who had been on furlough in Macedonia also rejoined, and with them came strong reinforcements—3000 Macedonian foot and 300 horse, 200 cavalry from Thessaly and 150 from Elis. Lastly, from Athens came envoys requesting the release of the Athenian mercenaries captured at the Granicus and now undergoing hard labour in Macedonia. Their request was refused; they might approach him again, said Alexander, when circumstances were favourable.

Certainly this was no time to indulge the Athenians. During the past year the war on land had gone his way—the western satraps had been defeated and, if much of the interior still remained to be conquered, all coastal Asia Minor was in his hands—but since the disbanding of the allied fleet the Persians controlled the entire Aegean, and after Halicarnassus Darius had instructed Memnon to put into operation the plan he had advocated at Zeleia and carry the war into Greece.[18] With 300 ships and a large force of mercenaries Memnon quickly won back Chios and all Lesbos with the exception of Mytilene which he proceeded to besiege by land and sea. Quick to see the danger and quick to act, Alexander gave Hegelochus 500 talents and ordered him to raise a fleet from the Greek allies, while he sent Antipater 600 talents in case he should need to take action in Greece, where Memnon's agents were active. Then Alexander had a great stroke of luck, when Memnon, his most formidable opponent, died during the siege of Mytilene—'the most serious setback which Persia received during this period of the war'. Nevertheless, under Pharnabazus, Memnon's nephew, who now assumed command, and Autophradates, the Persian fleet won success after success throughout 333. Mytilene was forced to capitulate and to receive a garrison and a tyrant and, although the Persian

force was soon depleted by the withdrawal of the mercenaries whom
Darius recalled to join his army, Tenedos was retaken, while Miletus
and Halicarnassus, at least in part, came under Persian control.
Doubtless there were other Persian gains which our sources, interested primarily in Alexander, do not permit us to recover. According
to Plutarch,[19] it was on Samothrace that Autophradates captured
Antigone, who later fell into Macedonian hands and became the
mistress of Philotas. Nor is there any reason to doubt Diodorus'
statement that 'most of the Cyclades' sent envoys to the Persian
commander.[20] In the summer of 333 a Persian reconnaissance
squadron was defeated off Siphnos, but by the end of the year the
main Persian fleet under Pharnabazus was using the island as a
base. It was only the news of the Persian defeat at Issus that wrecked
the naval offensive. But this lay several months ahead. Meanwhile
we must return to Alexander.

Just before leaving Gordium he 'conceived a longing' to visit the
acropolis to see the ancient waggon dedicated to Zeus the King by
Midas, the founder of the Phrygian dynasty.[21] According to local
tradition the waggon had carried Midas and his parents from Telmissus at the very time that an oracle had declared that a waggon
would bring the Phrygians a king, but another legend, current in
Macedonia and probably known to Alexander, related that Midas
had driven this waggon from Mt Bermium, near Mieza where Aristotle had taught the prince. But it was not mere curiosity that led
Alexander to visit the acropolis; for the yoke of the waggon was
fastened to the pole by a knot so intricately tied that 'no one could
see where it began or where it ended', and tradition had it that the
man who untied it would rule 'Asia', which in Alexander's day meant
the Persian empire. Failing to find the ends of the knot, Alexander
drew his sword and cut the knot or (according to Aristobulus) drew
out the pin that passed through the pole and held the knot together.
Which version is true, we cannot know and, in any case, does not
matter. What does matter is whether Alexander really believed that
he had performed the task and was therefore destined to rule the
Persian empire, whether it was perhaps this episode that decided
him to take Darius' place. We cannot be sure. Naturally, when there
was thunder and lightning during the following night, Alexander
affirmed that the gods certified his performance. But can he really
have believed that he had 'untied' the knot? Whichever method he
adopted, he cheated, only a little less blatantly in Aristobulus'
account. It is easier to suppose that Alexander was well aware of
the propaganda value of 'solving' the problem, and that he had no
intention of failing.

7

ISSUS AND ITS AFTERMATH

From Gordium Alexander advanced to Ancyra, the modern Ankara, where Paphlagonian envoys met him, offering submission. The king readily accepted; he was eager to get through the Taurus passes and into Cilicia and had no time to spare for the conquest of Paphlagonia. Similarly in southern Cappadocia he appointed Sabictas, probably a native chieftain, as satrap, but took no steps to subdue the country. Ahead lay the Cilician Gates, a steep, narrow pass, 'impassable for an army if there was any opposition', as Xenophon described it without exaggeration; for in ancient times a loaded camel could not pass through.[1] A resolute defence might have held up Alexander indefinitely, but although he failed to surprise the defenders they fled at his approach and the Macedonians passed through at their leisure. The rich Cilician plain could not be defended but Arsames, the Persian satrap, planned to plunder the prosperous city of Tarsus before he withdrew. However, he was too late. Learning of his intention, Alexander galloped on ahead with his cavalry and a picked body of light-armed infantry and saved the city.

Hot and weary from his exertions and perhaps already ill, the king plunged into the icy waters of the Cydnus and was soon in the grip of a raging fever. His other doctors despaired of saving his life, but Philip the Acarnanian, an old friend, resolved to administer a strong purge. The story goes that as Alexander was on the point of drinking the draught a message arrived from Parmenio warning him that Philip had been bribed by Darius to poison him, and the king, as he drank, handed the letter to Philip who simply remarked that if he obeyed his instructions he would recover. Such was his confidence in his friends, and their confidence in him. Later it was to be different.

C

When he had recovered, the king dispatched Parmenio with the Thessalians and a strong body of infantry to occupy the Syrian Gates, now known as the Beilan pass, leading through the Amanus mountains into the plains of northern Syria, and no doubt to find out where the Persians were; for Alexander seems to have been poorly informed about Darius' movements. He himself set out westwards to secure his rear by a campaign against the mountain tribes in the west of the province. At Soli he fined the inhabitants the truly remarkable sum of 200 talents for their pro-Persian sympathies, imposed a garrison and exacted hostages. He was evidently still short of money and determined to have it; for although after Issus he remitted the sum outstanding this amounted to only 50 talents. It was in Soli, after his return from his successful week-long campaign, that he held the first of his many ceremonial parades and competitions in athletics, music, and acting. During these games the welcome news came from Halicarnassus that Orontopates had been defeated and much of the surrounding countryside subdued. At Mallus the democrats had risen and were massacring the oligarchs. Alexander put a stop to this, as he had done at Ephesus, and remitted the tribute paid to Persia, ostensibly because Mallus was an Argive foundation; more probably, the favourable treatment of the Mallians was the result of their efforts to free themselves from Persian domination.

At Mallus a dispatch from Parmenio reached him; the Persian army under Darius was encamped at Sochi, two days' march east of the Syrian Gates. This was the news that Alexander had been waiting for; he saw the prospect of a decisive battle, and in two days he covered the seventy miles to Myriandrus near Alexandretta (Iskanderun). Then, to his utter amazement, he heard that Darius was in his rear, astride his communications. A naval reconnaissance confirmed the presence of the Persian army at Issus.[2] To see how this extraordinary situation had arisen, we must turn to the Persians and Darius.

The Persian empire was a slow-moving giant, its size at once its strength and its weakness, and it was not until the early summer of 333 that Darius assembled an army from the central satrapies at Babylon. Its size is variously reported at between 300,000 and 600,000 men and although the correct figure cannot be recovered it is clear that the Persian army considerably outnumbered Alexander's forces; perhaps 75,000 would not be wildly wrong. With his fighting men, his family and harem, and the wives of his officers, Darius crossed the Euphrates in early autumn and encamped at Sochi, where the extensive plains of Syria afforded his cavalry and his numerous infantry scope for manœuvre. He was doubtless informed of Alexander's arrival at Tarsus by Arsames, the satrap of Cilicia, who had fled to him, and when Alexander, delayed by his illness and his Cilician campaign, did not appear Darius began to think that he had decided to remain in Cilicia. Eventually, we are told, Darius was gradually convinced by his staff who, from conviction or a desire to flatter, maintained that Alexander was afraid to meet the Persian army. But the difficulty of supplying a large force now that winter was approaching may have been a more persuasive argument for Darius' decision to seek out Alexander. When Parmenio sent his message to Alexander, Darius must have been on the point of marching north and, as Alexander was hurrying down the coastal road west of the Amanus mountains, he was completing his march up the eastern side of the range. By the time that Alexander reached Myriandrus, Darius had entered eastern Cilicia through the Amanic Gates (the Bogtche Pass) north of Issus. Alexander had blundered badly; either he had failed to discover the existence of the Gates, or, less probably, he had taken no precautions to guard them. But it is likely that Darius received just as great a shock as Alexander had done when, on reaching Issus, he came upon the Macedonian sick and wounded who had been left there and discovered that Alexander had already moved south. After mutilating and killing the captives, Darius set off in pursuit, probably hoping to engage the Macedonians on the plains as he had originally intended, but he had advanced no further than the River Pinarus (Deli) when his scouts reported that the enemy was marching north.

Alexander's blunder had turned out to his advantage. For the speed with which he had been informed of the Persian presence at Issus enabled him to surprise Darius on the narrow coastal plain. Although it must have been a severe psychological blow for the Macedonians to find the Persians astride their communications, Alexander was quick to see that his troops would have the opportunity of meeting the enemy on ground that would nullify their numerical superiority, particularly in cavalry. Accordingly, he hurried north and by midnight he had occupied the Pillars of Jonah, a pass some 12 miles south of the Pinarus, where he posted sentries and allowed his men to rest. At dawn he descended into the plain, deploying his infantry into line as the ground permitted and bringing up his cavalry. The allied horse he sent to the left, the remainder to the right; his final preparations he left until he should see the Persian dispositions.

Darius meanwhile was deploying his infantry behind a screen of cavalry and light infantry. In the centre of his line he placed his best infantry, the Greek mercenaries, perhaps 20,000 in number since 14,000 of them escaped from the battle.[3] On either side of them were stationed the Cardaces, supposedly heavy infantry but, as they were screened by archers, probably light-armed troops. Darius intended his infantry to hold the line of the Pinarus and, where the banks of the river afforded insufficient protection, he had erected some kind of stockade. In the rear stood the mass of the Asiatic levies, for lack of space prevented their deployment in the battle-line, and on the extreme left, along the foothills, was posted a strong force of light-armed troops to take the Macedonians in flank and rear as they advanced. When these preparations were complete, Darius withdrew his advanced troops behind the Pinarus and took up his position in the centre of the Persian line. Almost all the cavalry were sent to the right wing under Nabarzanes' command; for the Persian plan seems to have been to contain the Macedonian infantry while the cavalry broke through the Macedonian left, took the phalanx in flank and rear and drove it towards the mountains.

Seeing the masses of cavalry on the Persian right, Alexander ordered the Thessalians to ride behind the lines to join the allied cavalry on the Macedonian left, where Parmenio was in command. He was given strict instructions to leave no gap between the Macedonian left and the sea. Behind Parmenio's cavalry were posted the archers and javelin-men, then in their usual order came the six battalions of the phalanx, the hypaspists, and the Companions, supported on their right by the Lancers and the Paeonians. In the rear were stationed the mercenary infantry. To counter the threat posed by the Persian troops in the foothills Alexander had detailed a force of light-armed, but as the Persians withdrew up the hillside on the approach of the Macedonians he was able to use this force to strengthen his right wing, leaving only 300 light cavalry to keep watch on them.

Alexander now moved steadily forward, resting his troops at intervals to preserve the line of the phalanx. Then, as he came within range of the Persian bowmen, he ordered the charge and led his Companions at a gallop into the river, up the bank, over the archers, and into the ranks of the Cardaces. On the right the Agrianians and the light cavalry followed; so, too, on his left did the first two battalions of the phalanx. But the remaining battalions, unable to force their way up the bank, failed to maintain contact and a gap opened up in the Macedonian line. Into this gap poured Darius' mercenaries, striving to push the Macedonians back into the river, and a fierce struggle developed. Ptolemy, son of Seleucus, and 120 Macedonians fell, and the issue was not decided until the two battalions on the right, having disposed of their immediate opponents, were able to take the mercenaries in the flank.

Meanwhile on the Macedonian left the heavy Persian cavalry, both horses and riders clad in chain mail, had crossed the Pinarus and forced back the Thessalians. But, outnumbered and outweighted though they were, they held on tenaciously and prevented the Persians from outflanking their line. Nevertheless it was touch and go until their opponents, seeing that the mercenaries were being cut down and Darius had fled before the onslaught of Alexander and his Companions, turned and rode for their lives. Then the Macedonians had their revenge; for the heavily-armed Persians were easily over-taken on the narrow, crowded roads.

Not until he saw that his army was victorious did Alexander set off after Darius. He kept up the pursuit as long as the light lasted but, although he captured the chariot and weapons which the king had abandoned in his flight, he failed to overtake Darius. The Persian king, joined by 4000 survivors, half of them Greek mer-cenaries, crossed the Euphrates at Thapsacus (perhaps near Sura) and made his escape to Babylon.

Returning to the Pinarus, Alexander found that the Persian royal family had been captured in the Persian camp. He treated them with every mark of honour, probably as much from inclination as policy, although they were certainly valuable as hostages. We need not doubt that when Darius' wife died in childbirth early in 332 he was much distressed or that he was particularly attached to the queen-mother, Sisygambis, at whose request he later spared the Uxians. It was here that Alexander had his first sight of Oriental luxury. Although Darius had deposited the bulk of his baggage at Damascus, where Parmenio and the Thessalians later took possession of it, what remained was impressive enough—'basins, pitchers, bathing-tubs and vases for perfumes, all of gold', and three thousand talents in money, not to mention the army of attendants.

The victory had been costly; for Diodorus and Curtius, credibly enough, put Macedonian casualties at 450 killed and ten times as many wounded. Persian losses are unknown, for the 10,000 horse and 100,000 foot are mere propaganda figures. But five commanders fell and, the most serious blow of all, only 2000 mercenaries remained with Darius. The majority, indeed, escaped, but they were lost to Persia. One body of 8000 withdrew in good order under their com-manders and reached Tripolis in Phoenicia over the mountains. There they split up, half of them led by Amyntas sailing by way of Cyprus to Egypt, only to perish at the hands of the Persian garrisons. The remainder, together with another body of 4000 (probably part of the force against which Antigonus is recorded to have fought three battles in central Asia Minor), found their way into the service of King Agis of Sparta.

The battle of Issus brought the Persian naval offensive to an abrupt halt, for as soon as the news reached the Persian admirals they

hastened to retire from Siphnos, Pharnabazus to Chios and Autophradates to Halicarnassus. At Siphnos King Agis, intent on raising
Greece against Macedon, had been negotiating for ships and money
with which to hire mercenaries in Crete. Obtaining ten ships and
30 talents, with Autophradates' help he enlisted 8000 of Darius' old
mercenaries, joined his brother Agesilaus in Crete and 'captured
most of the cities and forced them to take the Persian side'.[4] Then,
doubtless with more mercenaries, he sailed back to Greece. There
the news of Issus had confounded Alexander's enemies, particularly
Demosthenes, who had been predicting that the Persian cavalry
would trample the Macedonian army into the ground,[5] and had
greatly strengthened the hand of the Macedonian sympathizers. The
Council of the Corinthian League, meeting at the Isthmian games in
332, thought it prudent to send envoys to Alexander with a golden
wreath to congratulate him on his victory.

Alexander resisted the temptation to march east in pursuit of
Darius; instead he moved south along the coast to Phoenicia. His
motives are well set out in the speech delivered (according to
Arrian) to his officers before the siege of Tyre.[6] If Cyprus and Egypt
remained in Persian hands, he said, there was danger of an attack on
Greece, where Sparta was openly hostile and Athens restrained only
by fear. But the capture of Phoenicia would cause the defection of
the Phoenician contingents serving with the Persian navy, and those
from the cities of Cyprus would either follow suit or the island could
be overcome by a naval expedition. An attack on Egypt would then
be easy and, once Egypt was in their power, they would have nothing
to fear from Greece and could march against Darius with enhanced
prestige. Indeed, Alexander might look for a welcome from the
Phoenician cities, particularly from Sidon which had led a revolt
against Persia some thirteen years earlier and had suffered destruction, while Egypt had been brought back into the Persian empire
only in 343–342 after more than sixty years of independence.

Alexander was met on his march by Strato, the son of the ruler of
Aradus, who was serving with the Persian fleet. Strato surrendered
the island city and its mainland possessions, including Marathus.
There, the first embassy from Darius reached him. In his letter, as
Arrian reports it, Darius offered friendship and alliance in return
for the restoration of his family, but made no mention of a ransom
or of the cession of territory; in addition, he blamed Philip for
starting the war without provocation. The blatant untruth of the last
statement—the Persians had aided Perinthus in 340—and the arrogant tone of the letter, remarkable in one who had been so decisively
defeated only a few weeks before, lend some support to Diodorus'
statement that Alexander suppressed the original letter and substi-

tuted one 'more in accordance with his interests'.[7] According to Diodorus, Darius offered, in addition to the payment of a ransom, to cede all territory west of the River Halys, which sounds reasonable in view of his later offer of all territory west of the Euphrates. If Alexander did substitute a forged letter, his motive was obviously to secure support for the decision he had already made; for he flatly rejected the king's proposals. After laying the blame for hostilities squarely on Persian shoulders, he accused Darius of procuring the murder of Philip and of trying to stir up trouble in Greece. Finally, Alexander instructed Darius to address him as 'King of Asia', that is, 'King of the Persian Empire': if he wished to dispute this title, he must fight. The reference to 'King of Asia' was clearly made to induce Darius to fight a third and, as Alexander hoped, decisive battle, and he did not officially adopt this title until after Gaugamela; nevertheless, it is clear that Alexander was resolved to conquer the Persian empire, and that, despite the reference in his letter to his position as *Hegemon*, his ambitions were not confined to the liberation of the Greeks of Asia.

As Alexander advanced, Byblos opened its gates and he received a warm welcome at Sidon, where another Strato, presumably a Persian nominee, was deprived of his throne, and perhaps put to death, on Alexander's orders. The Tyrians, whose king, Azemilcus, was commanding the Tyrian squadron in the Persian fleet, sent envoys and expressed their willingness to do whatever Alexander wished. To test their loyalty—for it seems unlikely that, with the Sidonians to advise him, he acted in ignorance—Alexander announced his intention of sacrificing in the city to Heracles (Melcarth), a thing which according to Tyrian custom only the king might do.[8] When the Tyrians declared that they would admit neither Persian nor Macedonian and indicated a temple of Melcarth at Old Tyre where Alexander might offer sacrifice, he angrily dismissed the envoys and prepared for a siege.[9]

TYRE.

To besiege Tyre was a formidable undertaking. It stood on an island, half a mile off-shore, with walls in places 150 feet high and thick in proportion. Alexander had few ships, but Old Tyre nearby could provide an abundance of stone and there was timber in plenty in the forests of Mount Libanon. Accordingly, he decided to construct a mole from the mainland to the island.

In January 332 the work began under the direction of the Thessalian engineer Diades. The inhabitants of the neighbouring villages were pressed into service in their thousands, and at first in the shallow water near the shore the mole, 200 feet wide, advanced steadily. But as the depth of water increased—round the island it was nearly 20 feet deep—the Tyrians were able to harass the workers from the walls and from galleys which they rowed right up to the mole. To protect the workmen and to command the walls Alexander had two 150-foot towers built, reputedly the highest in antiquity, protected against fire arrows by raw hides, on which catapults were mounted. The Tyrians replied by filling a transport with combustible material, towing it against the mole and setting fire to the towers. But Alexander did not give up, for the capture of Tyre was vital to his strategy and his prestige. He ordered the construction of a wider mole to accommodate more towers and built more siege engines.

The siege continued with thrust and counter-thrust. Then came the news which Alexander had been waiting for. On hearing that their cities were in his hands, the Phoenician contingents had left the Persian fleet and returned home. At Sidon Alexander found not only the 80 Phoenician vessels but 25 others from Soli, Mallus, Rhodes, and Lycia, and soon after the Cypriot kings, deciding that Alexander was winning, joined him with another 120 ships. Although Azemilcus returned to Tyre at the same time with the Tyrian ships, Alexander now had an overwhelming superiority at sea.

As Alexander sailed back to Tyre, the Tyrians came out to meet him but, observing the size of the enemy fleet, prudently withdrew into the harbours and blocked the entrances. Henceforth the defeat of the Tyrians was certain. However, they continued to fight with great courage and resource. When Alexander, not content with bombarding the wall from the mole, mounted engines on transports and attacked at many points, the defenders returned the fire from towers erected on the walls and directed fire arrows against the ships. Then they dropped masses of stone into the water, so that the attackers had difficulty in getting in close. When Alexander brought up transports to clear the obstruction they cut their cables with armoured ships, and when Alexander countered by mooring ships, similarly armoured, in front of the anchors, they sent down divers to cut the cables. But when Alexander substituted chains for cables, the Tyrians had no answer; the stones were removed, and the ships could lie alongside the wall.

Failing to make any impression on the wall opposite the mole, Alexander began to probe the other parts of the wall with rams mounted on ships. He had no success in the north, but just south of the Egyptian harbour he broke down a portion of the wall. On this occasion the Tyrians were able to repulse his attempt to enter the city by means of boarding-bridges, but three days later a much more serious attempt was made. Alexander fitted two ships with gangways and manned one with the hypaspists under Admetus, the other with Coenus' infantry battalion. When the engines had battered down a large stretch of the wall, he ordered the ships to lie alongside; gangways were thrown on to the rubble and, led by Admetus, the hypaspists mounted the wall. Admetus was killed by a spear-thrust, but Alexander led the second wave of attackers, gained the wall and advanced towards the palace. Meanwhile the Cypriot and Phoenician fleets had forced their way into the harbours and Coenus' battalion had entered the city. In the face of this three-pronged attack the Tyrians abandoned the walls and massed at the shrine of Agenor, but were forced by Alexander and the Guards to flee. A bloody massacre followed, as the Macedonians gave vent to their exasperation at the length of the siege, which had lasted for seven months, and their anger at the murder, in full view of their comrades, of some Macedonians recently captured at sea. Eight thousand Tyrians are reported to have perished compared with Macedonian losses of 400 in the entire siege. Alexander pardoned the Carthaginian envoys and a number of Tyrian notables who had taken refuge in the temple of Melcarth, but the remaining inhabitants, some 30,000, he sold into slavery. This was an accepted practice of ancient warfare, carried out with some justification here and at Cyropolis, where his troops were again murdered, at Thebes and Gaza. Alexander then sacrificed to Melcarth, as he had promised, and dedicated to the god a siege-engine and the sacred ship of Tyre.

Before the city fell a second embassy came from Darius.[10] The Persian king offered Alexander a ransom of 10,000 talents for his family, and all territory west of the Euphrates, and proposed that Alexander should become his ally and marry his daughter. We are not told when this offer was made, whether before or after the break-up of the Persian fleet, but once again Alexander completely rejected Darius' offer. The country and its treasures, he asserted, were already his; if he wished, he would marry Darius' daughter with or without his permission. Parmenio, we are told, remarked that if he were Alexander he would accept the offer, to which Alexander made the celebrated reply, 'So would I, if I were Parmenio.' This exchange may simply be part of the denigration of Parmenio, but even if it actually took place, we are not entitled to assume, as many do,[11] that Philip would have agreed with his marshal. We just do not know.

From Tyre Alexander marched for Egypt. All the coastal cities submitted except Gaza, a strongly-walled town on a mound about two miles from the sea, whose ruler Batis had collected a band of Arabian mercenaries and laid in provisions for a siege. Motivated perhaps more by the effect its capture would produce than by its strategic importance, Alexander decided on an assault. Initially the Macedonians made little progress and Alexander himself was wounded. Not until the counter-mound was raised to a height of 55 feet and extended all round the town and the engines he had used at Tyre arrived by sea did the Macedonians succeed in demolishing part of the wall and forcing their way into the town. Fighting was bitter and the entire male population died at their posts. The women and children were sold as slaves and the town, resettled with neighbouring tribesmen, became a Macedonian fortress.

The Egyptians had asserted their independence of Persia in 404 and thanks to the help of Greek mercenaries and dissensions within the Persian empire they had preserved it until 343–342, when the generals of Artaxerxes III (Ochus) had defeated the last native ruler, Nectanebo II. Ochus had outdone the frightfulness of Cambyses, desecrating the temples and roasting the sacred Apis calf, and the Egyptians, a very religious people, were ready to welcome any challenge to Persian rule. Only a few months before the arrival of Alexander they had flocked to support Amyntas.

Mazaces, appointed satrap only after Issus, with few troops and no prospect of outside help, had no option but to submit to Alexander and handed over to him '800 talents and all the royal furniture'. Leaving a garrison in the frontier town of Pelusium, Alexander marched up country by way of Heliopolis to Memphis while his fleet sailed up the Nile. At Memphis he was officially enthroned as Pharaoh and became, in Egypt, a god and son of the sun-god, Amon-Ra.[12] In contrast to Ochus, he treated the native religion with tolerance and understanding, as he had treated the gods of Lydia and Caria, and sacrificed to Apis and the other Egyptian gods; for policy and inclination harmonized once again. At Memphis too he held athletic and literary contests, as he had done at Tarsus and was to do many times later, in which famous artists from Greece took part. Wilcken regards this as an attempt to promote Greek culture in Egypt, but it seems altogether more likely that the obvious reason, relaxation for the troops, is correct.

At the end of the festivities, perhaps about the beginning of 331, Alexander set sail down the western arm of the Nile with a small body of troops including the Guards and the Royal squadron of the Companions. With him also went Callisthenes and other members of his staff. On reaching the coast, he sailed westwards and passing Canobus (Abukir) came to the ancient fishing village of Rhacotis. There, between Lake Mareotis and the island of Pharos, he marked out the ground plan of the city which he called Alexandria, destined to become the most famous of all his many foundations.[13] Evidently designed not as a fortress but as the great trading centre of the eastern Mediterranean to replace Tyre, the city was laid out by the Rhodian architect Deinocrates on the principles formulated by Hippodamus of Miletus with wide, straight streets and rectangular blocks of houses. Alexander (or his advisers) chose well. The harbour was sheltered by Pharos and, being situated west of the Nile delta, was not plagued by the silt brought down by the river, while in summer the westerly breezes kept the city cool.

While Alexander was still busy with the planning of his new city, his admiral Hegelochus and his deputy Amphoterus arrived with welcome news. The allied fleet was now in command of the eastern Mediterranean; Tenedos, Chios, Lesbos, and Cos had all been captured and no fewer than 5000 Greek mercenaries had transferred their allegiance to Alexander. They brought with them the oligarchs whom Pharnabazus had established in power at Chios and various tyrants, including Aristonicus of Methymna and Agonippus and Eurysilaus of Eresus.[14] Pharnabazus himself had been taken at Chios, but had escaped in Cos. The tyrants were returned to their cities for punishment, and the Chians were dispatched under guard to Elephantine, the most southerly city in Egypt, although about a year earlier Alexander had declared his intention of having them tried, when captured, by the *Synhedrion*, the judicial organ of the Corinthian League.[15] The king's action clearly reveals his increasing independence of the League.

Far to the south-west of Alexandria across a vast stretch of desert lay the tiny oasis of Siwah, the site of the ancient oracle of Ammon, an offshoot of the oracle of Amon-Ra at Thebes.[16] By the beginning of the fifth century the cult of Ammon had established itself in the Greek colony of Cyrene, where Ammon was identified with Zeus so that Pindar in his *Hymn to Ammon* addresses the god as 'Ammon, lord of Olympus'.[17] From Cyrene knowledge of Zeus Ammon spread to the Peloponnese and to Athens, and eminent Greeks, such as Lysander and Cimon, consulted the oracle at Siwah. At Sparta the god had a temple, while the Athenians paid cult to him in the fourth century and renamed the sacred trireme, Salaminia, 'Ammonias', ship of Ammon.

While he was on the coast, Alexander, we are told, 'conceived a longing' (*pothos*) to consult the oracle,[18] but it is more likely that he had in mind to visit Siwah from the time that he left Memphis. At any rate he now set out westwards following the coastline. At Mersa Matruh envoys from Cyrene met him, perhaps not unexpectedly, and he concluded with them a pact of friendship and alliance. Then Alexander struck inland, following the old caravan route across the desert to Siwah, 200 miles to the south-west. Their water ran out and when the south wind obliterated the landmarks the guides lost their way. But heavy rain fell and the party reached their destination without mishap, following birds returning to the oasis. The hardships of the march were real enough, but Callisthenes evidently treated it, as he had treated the march along the Pamphylian coast, in heroic

vein, attributing the rain and the guidance of the birds to divine
favour. We may note also that according to Ptolemy, who is usually
considered a 'prosaic' writer, Alexander and his party were guided
to the oasis (and back again) by two talking snakes!

When Alexander arrived at the oasis, the first Pharaoh to make
the journey, the chief priest greeted him, as he would have done any
other Pharaoh, as 'son of Ammon'; or possibly, as Professor Parke
has argued, he used in deference to Alexander the Greek equivalent
'son of Zeus', as Callisthenes relates. Then, while the other members
of his party remained outside, the priest escorted Alexander into the
inner shrine where the king put certain questions to the god and, as
Arrian has it, 'received the answer he desired'. Plutarch and the
'vulgate' writers claim to tell us the substance of his questions. He
asked first, they say, whether he would rule the world and then
whether all his father's murderers had been punished. To the first
question the god replied in the affirmative, but in answer to his second
bade him be silent; all Philip's murderers had indeed been punished,
but Alexander's divine origin would be shown by his invincibility.
However, as only the king and the priest knew what had occurred
in the shrine, we must, unless we envisage the possibility of a dis-
closure by the priest or an 'inspired leak' by Alexander himself,
regard these questions as pure speculation. Men were naturally eager
to know what questions Alexander put to the oracle, and the source
of the 'vulgate' and of Plutarch, probably Cleitarchus, may well have
endeavoured to satisfy their curiosity. The only hint we have of what
occurred in the shrine is contained in a letter cited by Plutarch which
Alexander later wrote to Olympias. He had received, he said, 'certain
secret responses', which he would reveal to her alone; but, of course,
as he never saw his mother again, the secret was never revealed. If the
letter is genuine, as seems likely, there is much to be said for Tarn's
suggestion[19] that the priest explained the sense in which Alexander
as Pharaoh was the son of the god.

But why did Alexander make this long and arduous journey to
Siwah? Our sources write of his 'longing', his desire to emulate his
ancestors Perseus and Heracles, his wish to consult an oracle
reputedly infallible, and his eagerness to learn about his relationship
to Ammon. This last reason is supported by his letter to his mother,
if it is authentic. The others do not take us very far, although his
rivalry with Perseus and Heracles, since it is reported by Callisthenes,
must at least be what Alexander wished to be believed and it does, in
fact, correspond with one of the motives advanced by Nearchus for
Alexander's march through Gedrosia late in 325, namely the desire
to emulate Cyrus and Semiramis. Tarn points to Alexander's statement (Arrian, *Anabasis* 6.19.4) that Ammon had told him to what

gods he should sacrifice, as Apollo had told Xenophon (*Anabasis* 3.1.6), and it is entirely credible that he should have asked about his forthcoming expedition. If Alexandria had not yet been officially founded, as is possible since its official birthday was 7 April, then Welles' argument, that a man so punctilious as Alexander in his observance of ritual must have obtained divine sanction for its foundation, deserves consideration.

Although Callisthenes, doubtless in accordance with Alexander's wishes, was very reticent about what went on in the inner shrine, he stated quite explicitly that the priest greeted the king as 'son of Zeus', and later, in his account of Gaugamela, he related that Alexander in a prayer referred to himself as 'son of Zeus'. He is beyond doubt striving to create a picture of a 'hero', beloved of the gods. Now, Alexander could have obtained from the priests at Memphis the information that the priest at Siwah would greet him as 'son of Ammon' and, if we make the assumption not unreasonable in the case of one so curious as Alexander, that he did inquire about this, he may fairly be said to have gone to Siwah to proclaim his divine descent. Certainly he used the greeting for purposes of propaganda. This does not mean, of course, that he did not think of himself as son of Zeus Ammon; indeed, consciousness of this may have been one factor in leading him in 324, as I believe he did, to request recognition from the Greeks as a god. But there is a world of difference between being the son of a god and being a god, and it is quite inadmissible to talk of the priest recognizing Alexander as a god. Nor did Alexander seek through Callisthenes to have himself recognized as such. His consciousness of his divine powers came later.

From Siwah Alexander returned to Memphis by a direct route across the desert and proceeded to make arrangements for the government of Egypt. These reveal his appreciation of the strength and prosperity of the country. Instead of entrusting the government of the whole country to a single satrap, he appointed two Egyptians as rulers of Upper and Lower Egypt respectively, while a Greek, Apollonius, was made governor of 'Libya', the western frontier districts of Egypt, and another Greek, Cleomenes, born at Naucratis in Egypt, was to govern 'Arabia', the area around Heroopolis to the east of the delta. To Cleomenes the native tax-collectors were instructed to pay all the taxes. Two Macedonians commanded garrisons at Pelusium and Memphis and, in addition, military commanders were appointed for Upper and Lower Egypt. The mercenaries left in Egypt, 4000 in number, had their own commander, clerk, and overseers. This highly complicated structure was clearly designed to prevent any one man from becoming too powerful and perhaps also to protect the natives from oppression. However, Alexander's arrangements did not last. When one of the native governors declined his post the other governed both Upper and Lower Egypt, and before Alexander's death Cleomenes had established himself as satrap of the whole country, including the eastern and western frontier districts.

In the spring of 331 Alexander returned to Tyre where embassies from Athens, Chios, and Rhodes awaited him. He agreed to remove his garrisons from the two islands and granted the Athenian request, which he had earlier refused, for the liberation of the prisoners taken at the Granicus. Alexander no doubt judged it politic to be generous to Athens in view of the dangerous situation in Greece of which news had just reached him. Memnon, the governor of Thrace, acting, it seems likely, in concert with the Spartan king, Agis,[20] had risen in revolt with the support of the natives, while in the Peloponnese Agis had called out the Spartan levy, collected 10,000 mercenaries, most of them survivors of Issus, and gained the support of Tegea, Elis, Achaea (except Pellene, where Antipater was supporting a tyrant), and Arcadia (except Megalopolis). With 'some of the northern Greeks' his army totalled over 30,000 men. Fortunately, Athens had not joined; indeed, she had refused to contribute any of her 400 ships. Confident in Antipater's ability to handle the situation, or underestimating the danger, Alexander was content to divert the fleet under Amphoterus, who was engaged in subduing Crete and the pirates, to protect the loyal Peloponnesians, and to order the Phoenicians and Cypriots to send 100 vessels to join him.

Alexander was now bent on meeting Darius, but before leaving Tyre he completed his arrangements for the territories conquered so far. Shortly before Issus Harpalus, who had been in charge of Alexander's war-chest, had fled to Megara. He now returned and was reinstated in his old post. Coeranus and Philoxenus, who had divided his responsibilities, were given new posts.[21] According to Arrian, 'Alexander entrusted Coeranus with the collection of tribute in Phoenicia, and Philoxenus in Asia west of Taurus'. As Phoenicia was not made subject to a satrap, Coeranus' task was evidently to collect the tribute from the various city states and remit it to Alexander. Philoxenus' task was probably similar. His area comprised the coastal satrapies from Hellespontine Phrygia to Pamphylia, and he would have been responsible for the collection and forwarding of the 'contributions' of the Greek cities. He may also have forwarded to the king the tribute of the satrapies, although the actual collection of the tribute must have been in the hands of the satraps or of the financial officials in the satrapies, if they existed. The only such appointment recorded by Arrian, apart from the special case of

Egypt, is that of Nicias in Lydia, but this may merely mean that Arrian (or Ptolemy) did not think it worth while to mention the others. Such officials would certainly serve to keep a check on the satraps, as procurators kept a check on governors of imperial provinces in the Roman empire.

Philoxenus evidently remained in Asia Minor during Alexander's absence in the east, and after the 'contributions' of the Greek cities were discontinued at the end of the 'crusade', as seems certain, he probably held a position as their 'protector' analogous to that of Antipater in Europe. At any rate, he intervened in the affairs of the cities, and presumably he was competent to do so. Of Coeranus we hear no more. This may be due to the preoccupation of the sources with Alexander's activities and their neglect of events in the west; alternatively, he may have been replaced by Menes, who in 330 was appointed '*hyparchos* of Syria, Phoenicia, and Cilicia'. Menes was responsible for sea communications, for securing the safe passage of reinforcements to Alexander and later for the repatriation of Greek troops; but he conceivably had financial duties as well, for *hyparchos* in the Alexander-historians is 'a vague term for one exercising any sort of command or control'.[22]

Both Philoxenus and Coeranus were doubtless responsible for supervising the working of the royal mints in their respective areas. Sardes, Tarsus, Aradus, Sidon, and other mints all begin to issue large quantities of gold and silver coinage at this time, for Alexander had resolved to replace the various coinages of the western and central satrapies by a Macedonian imperial coinage bearing his own name and types.[23]

8

THE YEAR OF DECISION

Nearly a year had passed since Alexander's rejection of the second Persian embassy.[1] In the interval Darius had made strenuous efforts to tap the resources of the eastern satrapies and had assembled a formidable army at Babylon. How many infantry he had we do not know, for the figures given by our sources, ranging from Curtius' 200,000 to Arrian's 1,000,000, are clearly incredible. In any case, now that Greek mercenaries were no longer to be had, the infantry was a negligible factor. The strength of the Persian army lay in its cavalry, which now numbered almost 35,000, much of it of high quality.

On learning of the presence of Darius at Babylon, Alexander advanced north-eastwards from Tyre and reached Thapsacus on the Euphrates late in July. There Mazaeus, satrap of Babylonia, was encamped on the far bank with 3000 cavalry. His orders were not to dispute the crossing, but to observe the movements of the Macedonians and to lay waste the territory along the river should they advance southwards on Babylon, as the Ten Thousand had done and as Darius doubtless expected Alexander to do. But once over the Euphrates, Alexander did not march on Babylon; instead he turned north towards Nisibis and the Tigris. His reasons, we are told, were that there was more fodder for the horses and that the heat was less intense. However, it is probable that he also planned to draw Darius northwards to fight on ground less favourable to cavalry than the extensive plains that surrounded Babylon. This, at any rate, is what happened. Informed by Mazaeus of Alexander's movements, Darius ordered his army to march north, intending to intercept the Macedonians at one of several fords across the Tigris. But Alexander was too quick for the cumbersome Persian army and crossed the river without opposition north of Mosul before turning south in the direction of Arbela. Out-generalled by Alexander, the Persian king now had to search for a suitable battlefield, which he was lucky enough to find not far from the village of Gaugamela, about 75 miles north-west of Arbela.

Meanwhile Alexander, learning from captives taken in a cavalry skirmish that Darius was nearby at the head of a large army, had halted about seven or eight miles from Gaugamela to rest his troops and to fortify a camp where he might leave his baggage and non-combatants. Four days later, just before dawn on 30 September,[2] he broke camp and advanced to a ridge from which he could observe the Persian dispositions and see the overwhelming superiority—about five to one—which they possessed in cavalry. When Parmenio advised against an immediate attack, the king readily agreed. The reason he gave to his commanders was the possibility that the ground, which Darius had levelled, might have been 'mined', but it is perhaps more likely that Alexander wished to have time to solve the problem posed by the presence of masses of fine Persian horse. After carrying out a thorough reconnaissance of the ground without interference from Darius, Alexander gave orders for his men to have a meal and rest, then retired to his tent to put the finishing touches to his plan of attack. Darius, on the other hand, kept his troops on stand-to all night, a serious error of judgement which Arrian regards as the chief reason for his defeat.

The Persian dispositions are known to us from a captured battle-order preserved by Aristobulus. Darius took up the traditional position of the Persian king in the centre of the line, flanked by his 2000 surviving Greek mercenaries, his bodyguard of spearmen, the royal horseguards, and 1000 Indian cavalry. The wings were commanded respectively by Mazaeus and Bessus, the satrap of Bactria and Sogdiana. On the right Mazaeus had at his disposal 14,000 cavalry, drawn mainly from the central satrapies, of whom 3000 were stationed in advance of the main line. On the left the arrangement was similar, except that Bessus had some 3000 Persian infantry under his command in addition to his 18,000 cavalry and the cavalry in the main line were probably drawn up in a double line in order to cope with Alexander's main thrust. In front of the line Darius had placed 200 scythe-chariots, half of them opposite the Companions, and fifteen elephants. The chariots had proved remarkably unsuccessful in the past and the reason for their resurrection was presumably the weakness of the Persian infantry. The remaining foot soldiers were drawn up behind the line and played no part in the battle.

For this decisive battle Alexander had reinforced his army to a strength of 40,000 infantry and 7000 cavalry, mainly by recruiting mercenaries. The Macedonian dispositions were basically the same

GAUGAMELA

as at Issus. On the right the Companions were led by Philotas, with Cleitus in command of the Royal Squadron; then came the hypaspists, the six battalions of the phalanx, the Greek cavalry, and on the extreme left the Thessalian squadrons. However, at Gaugamela, in view of the enemy strength in cavalry, Alexander had devised strong flank guards for both wings. On the right, facing the Persian line, Menidas led some 600 mercenary cavalry; behind him rode the Paeonians and the Lancers, 900 in all, and in support were drawn up the veteran mercenaries, 6700 strong, led by Cleander. The Macedonian archers and half of the Agrianians formed a flexible link with the Companions, who were screened by the remainder of the Agrianians, the Cretan archers, and Balacrus' javelin-men. The arrangement on the left was similar. Facing the Persians were the remaining 400 mercenary cavalry led by Andromachus; behind them came the Greek and Odrysian (Thracian) horse led by Coeranus and Agathon respectively, a total of just over 1000. They were supported by 5500 Thracian infantry under Sitalces. Behind the phalanx Alexander stationed a second line of infantry, 12,000 strong, who had orders to face about should the enemy penetrate to their rear. At some distance behind the battle line were posted the Thracians to guard the baggage and the prisoners.

The tactics of the two commanders did not differ materially from those at Issus. On the Persian left Bessus was to absorb Alexander's charge and, if possible, destroy the Companions, while on the right Mazaeus was again to try conclusions with the Thessalians, but with a much superior force; once the Macedonian cavalry had been disposed of, the phalanx could be dealt with at leisure. Alexander's plan was to reduce the odds against the Companions, who once again were intended to strike the decisive blow, to such dimensions that their charge might have a reasonable prospect of success. This involved inducing the Persians to attack his right flank and relying on his right flank guard to cope with the bulk of the cavalry on the Persian left—a tall order. On the left Parmenio was set the equally difficult task of holding Mazaeus' attack until the Companions could deliver their charge.

On 1 October Alexander slept late and awakened, according to Callisthenes, full of confidence; if he had any doubts about the outcome, he kept them to himself. After riding along the lines and briefly exhorting his troops—Parmenio had ordered them to have breakfast and to prepare for action—Alexander gave the order to advance. He allowed the Persians a considerable overlap on their left in the hope that they would be induced to attack his right flank, and continued his advance towards the right until his troops on that wing had almost reached the edge of the prepared ground. Meanwhile, the Persians had moved to their left to conform with Alexander's line of advance and Darius, perhaps fearing that his chariots would soon be rendered useless, ordered the Scythians and the thousand Bactrians posted in front of his left wing to ride round the Macedonian right and check their move to the right. They were promptly charged by Menidas' mercenaries and, although they drove them back by weight of numbers, they were held up by the Paeonians operating in front of the infantry screen. Thereupon Bessus decided to commit his 8000 Bactrians but, despite having the better of matters, he was unable to break through the stubborn Macedonian defence.

Darius now launched 100 scythe-chariots against the phalanx; but the attack failed utterly. Most of the chariots were stopped by the javelins of Balacrus' men and the Agrianians, who had been thrown well forward to meet this threat; the few that did get through this screen were allowed to pass between the columns of the phalanx—the Macedonian discipline must have been first-rate—and were mopped up in the rear. Immediately after this Darius ordered a general offensive. Mazaeus was launched against Parmenio's wing, and the remainder of the cavalry on the Persian left moved round in support of Bessus, only to be charged by the Lancers under Aretes. At this point a gap opened up in the Persian line to the left of the centre. This was the moment Alexander had been waiting for. He wheeled the great wedge of cavalry to the left and made for the gap. On their left the Companions were supported by the hypaspists and the battalions of the phalanx—or, to be more precise, the four battalions on the right. For Simmias, commanding the battalion second from the left in the absence of his brother Amyntas, saw that as the Macedonian left wing was securely held by Mazaeus' attack a break in the line was inevitable and wisely decided to stand fast. Fortunately for Alexander there was no enemy force at this point capable of exploiting the opportunity. 'Some of the Indian and Persian cavalry' did burst through the gap, break through the second line of infantry, reach the baggage lines, and free the prisoners; but the allied infantry turned about, killed most of the raiders and put the remainder to flight.

Meanwhile, the Companions had smashed through the attenuated Persian line and had begun to fight their way towards the Persian centre, where Darius could be seen standing in his chariot. However, their advance was held up, even if only briefly, by the Persian horse-guards and the Greek mercenaries and this delay enabled Darius, who had now concluded that the battle was lost, to make good his escape. On the Persian left Bessus and his Bactrians broke off the engagement and retired in good order, although they lost many men

in the process. Meanwhile, on the Macedonian left Parmenio was
still being hard pressed by Mazaeus.

Alexander's movements after his breakthrough and Darius' flight
are far from clear. One thing is certain: he did not set off in pursuit
of Darius, as our sources assert. At Issus he had not pursued Darius
until he was sure the battle had been won, and it is unlikely that he
did so now. Moreover, the sources are unanimous that a messenger
sent by Parmenio to request assistance was able to reach him, surely
impossible had Alexander been galloping in hot pursuit of Darius.
Was it the approach of Alexander, wheeling right to support his
hard-pressed right wing, that forced Bessus to retire? Or was he
already on his way left to encircle the Persian centre and right wing
when the message reached him?[3] We cannot be certain, but the latter
is perhaps more likely. Bessus' withdrawal is sufficiently explained
by the continued resistance of the Macedonian flank guard and the
threat of Alexander's attack on his exposed right flank. Moreover,
when Alexander rode left in response to Parmenio's summons, the
cavalry he encountered were 'Parthians, some of the Indians, and
the main body of the Persian royal guard', evidently bent on escape.
It seems unlikely, although perhaps not impossible, that had Alexander gone first to the assistance of his right wing these troops would
still have been in a position to meet him when he galloped towards
Parmenio's wing. It was at this point that Alexander met the fiercest
resistance and no fewer than 60 Companions fell before the desperate
enemy striving to break through to safety. By the time that Alexander
had succeeded in disengaging himself the situation on his left no
longer required his attention. Mazaeus, learning of Darius' flight, had
broken off the engagement and his troops were in flight, hotly pursued by the gallant Thessalians.

Once again Alexander had been victorious, and once again he had
failed in his ultimate objective, to kill or capture Darius. Although
he set off at once and rode through the night with only a brief rest,
he failed to overtake the Persian king. When he reached Arbela, he
learned that Darius, accompanied by Bessus and his Bactrians,
some household troops and 2000 mercenaries, had abandoned the
main road and was making for Media over the mountains. Alexander
decided not to follow him. It was not the difficulty of the terrain,
which Darius had thought would deter him, that determined Alexander; rather, he judged it more important to occupy the nerve-
centres of the Persian empire, and their treasures, than to pursue the
beaten remnants of the Persian army. Considering Gaugamela to
be decisive, he planned to take Darius' place as the rightful ruler of
the Persian empire and lost no time in proclaiming himself 'King of
Asia'. This was probably done by the assembly of the Macedonian

army, as Plutarch states;[4] even if it was not competent to proclaim Alexander Darius' successor, he was not troubled by constitutional niceties but was concerned only with the propaganda value of the proclamation.

As Alexander approached Babylon in battle order, Mazaeus, who had escaped from Gaugamela, came out to surrender the city. The inhabitants were probably not inclined to resist; for following a revolt Xerxes had (? partially) destroyed E-Sagila, the great temple of Marduk, and removed from it the statue of the god.[5] As he had done in Egypt, Alexander exploited the anti-Persian feeling. He ordered the rebuilding of the temple and showed great favour to the priests, gaining thereby much popularity.

When Alexander came to organize the province, he took the bold step of reinstating Mazaeus as satrap and even of granting him the satrap's traditional right to issue silver coins bearing his own name. Why Alexander gave him this privilege, which was never repeated, we do not know. As to the appointment itself, there is no need to suppose that it was due to Alexander's appreciation of Mazaeus' gallant fight at Gaugamela or to an agreement to surrender Babylon without a fight.[6] Alexander was announcing his future policy as king of Persia and calling for the cooperation of the Persian nobility. The *homonoia* between Macedonians and Persians for which he was to pray at Opis in 324 may not yet have been in his mind, but he doubtless hoped that those satraps who remained loyal to Darius would be encouraged to make their submission to the new ruler.

This policy of appointing or, where possible, reappointing Persians as governors Alexander adhered to consistently in the satrapies west of India. Even satraps who remained loyal to Darius until his death were given back their satrapies, although other governors had been appointed in the meantime. Phrataphernes, for example, was made governor of his old satrapy, Parthia, soon after his surrender, although the existing governor, Amminapes, had done no wrong so far as we know and had formerly been a refugee at Philip's court. Atropates, the governor of Media, also got back his satrapy, although he had to wait until 328–327, but the satrap of Persis, Ariobarzanes, a son of Artabazus, who surrendered with his father after Darius' death, was not reinstated in his former office. Perhaps Alexander had not forgotten the humiliation that Ariobarzanes had inflicted on him at the Persian Gates (below). The only satrapy in this region which did not receive a Persian governor initially was Arachosia, where in the winter of 330 Menon, a Macedonian or perhaps a Greek, was made governor. Possibly the supply of reliable Persians had run out or possibly, since Arachosia had been governed by Barsaentes, one of the murderers of Darius, the situation there was especially delicate.

As satrap Mazaeus was very probably commander-in-chief of his province but Apollodorus, a Greek from Amphipolis, was appointed to command the troops left with Mazaeus. He may have been technically subordinate to the satrap but he would act as a useful watchdog, to ensure that Mazaeus remained loyal to Alexander. Not all Persian satraps are recorded to have had *strategi* in their provinces, but this may mean no more than that Arrian (or Ptolemy) has failed to register them. In Babylonia Alexander also appointed a collector of revenues, as he had done in Lydia and Egypt, but no further appointments are mentioned and it is likely that no more were made. The satraps probably bore the odium of collecting taxes themselves, on the principle that to pay taxes to a fellow-countryman was less painful than to pay them to a Macedonian or a Greek.[7]

Before setting out for Susa Alexander spent more than a month in Babylon. Even if we need not take too seriously the lurid scenes of debauchery which Curtius describes, discipline was doubtless relaxed and the money captured in the city enabled Alexander to distribute more than six months' pay to his Macedonian troops and two months' pay to the mercenaries. Money, in fact, had ceased to be a problem and on his way east he received the welcome news that Susa and its treasure of 50,000 talents was in safe keeping. In Susa he confirmed Abulites in his satrapy, installed a garrison-commander in the city, and left a *strategus* with 3000 troops. Amyntas, who had been sent to Macedonia at the beginning of the year, had overtaken the army with large reinforcements from Antipater,[8] including 6000 Macedonian infantry and 500 Macedonian horse, which enabled Alexander to reorganize his forces in the light of the very different type of warfare to be expected in the future. The squadrons of the Companions, surely now considerably over strength, were divided into two companies to provide greater mobility, and it is likely that it was at this time that Alexander formed a seventh battalion of the phalanx; certainly a little later in the year he had more than six.[9] A somewhat garbled account in Diodorus and Curtius suggests that he also carried out certain changes in the organization of the infantry, perhaps involving an increase in the strength of a hypaspist battalion from 500 to 1000.[10]

Amyntas also brought disquieting news of the progress of hostilities in Greece which led Alexander to send Menes to the coast with the immense sum of 3000 talents to be put at Antipater's disposal. He also entrusted him with the task of returning to Athens the statues of the tyrannicides, Harmodius and Aristogeiton, which Xerxes had removed from the city in 480.[11] Their restoration at this time was an evident attempt by Alexander to maintain the support, or at least the neutrality, of the Athenians.

In Greece Antipater, faced with the prospect of war on two fronts, had kept his head like the experienced campaigner he was. He had turned first to deal with Memnon in Thrace and had arranged a settlement 'on the best terms he could'. As a result Memnon kept his post until 327–326, when he was sent east with reinforcements for Alexander. Meanwhile, in the Peloponnese, a Macedonian commander, Corrhagus, had been defeated and Megalopolis was being besieged by the Eleans and the Achaeans. It must have been at this juncture, perhaps in July, that Amyntas left Macedonia; despite the critical situation, reinforcements for Alexander had first priority. Antipater now proceeded methodically to gather a force of some 40,000 men and marched to relieve Megalopolis which by this time was in dire straits. Near the city, about the time when Gaugamela was fought,[12] he met the allied army and won a fiercely-contested battle which cost the Macedonians 3500 lives. Among the 5300 Greek casualties was King Agis, who fell fighting bravely. Antipater took fifty noble Spartans as hostages and, perhaps seeking to avoid responsibility, referred the decision about the punishment of Sparta to the Council of the League of Corinth. However, the *Synhedrion*, acting quite correctly since Sparta was not a member of the League, simply handed over the matter to the king. His decision was that Sparta should enter the League—which meant that she no longer enjoyed an independent foreign policy—and that the Eleans and the Achaeans should pay the people of Megalopolis 120 talents as compensation.

At the turn of the year Alexander left Susa for Persepolis, about 400 miles to the south-east. He has been criticized for not pursuing Darius, who was now at Ecbatana in Media, and from the point of view of the war in Asia this is perhaps just.[13] But we may suspect that Alexander was more concerned at this time about the outcome of the war in Greece, which was still, so far as he knew, very much in the balance. Although the uninviting prospect of a winter march over the mountains would not have deterred him, the possibility of a long pursuit cannot have appealed to him and he may have hoped that Darius, given time, would once again offer battle. Besides, he must have been eager to secure the main Persian treasury at Persepolis and to deny Darius the manpower of the Persian homeland.

The march was not without incident. East of the Pasitigris he encountered the Uxian hillmen, who refused to let him pass through their territory unless he paid the tribute which the Persians had been accustomed to pay. Alexander had no intention of paying, but he promised to do so when he reached the pass which barred the entrance to Persis. Then, making use of native guides, as he always did, he led a picked force to their mountain stronghold, destroyed their villages, and came down in the rear of the pass. The Uxians fled, 'amazed at his speed', but ran into Craterus' men who had been posted there to intercept them. Sisygambis, the Persian queen-mother, whose niece was the chief's wife, interceded for the Uxians and they were allowed to remain in their territory but were required to pay annually 30,000 sheep, mules and horses; for they had no money.

Parmenio was now dispatched with the baggage-trains by the main road through the plains by way of Kazarun and Shiraz, while Alexander with a picked force of infantry and cavalry marched at full speed for the Persian Gates, hoping to surprise the defenders. But Ariobarzanes, the satrap of Persis, had built a wall at the head of the pass and was encamped there with 25,000 men.[14] Over-confident, Alexander resolved to make a frontal attack, but was forced to retire leaving his dead behind. They had to be recovered, and Alexander now did what he might have done before. Learning from one of the prisoners of a pass over the mountains, he left Craterus with two infantry battalions and a few cavalry to keep Ariobarzanes occupied, and marched at full speed with the remainder of his force. At dawn on the second day he fell on the rear of the Persian position while Craterus, hearing the pre-arranged signal—a blast on the trumpet, assaulted the pass. The Persians, caught between two fires, were cut down or perished in their flight. Only a handful of horsemen escaped with Ariobarzanes, and Alexander had his revenge.

Fearing that the treasure at Persepolis might be plundered before his arrival, Alexander raced on across the Araxes, which his men had already bridged, and reached the city in time. The vast sum of 120,000 talents, accumulated over many generations, fell into his hands, together with 6000 talents from the treasury of Cyrus the First at nearby Pasargadae. Alexander remained in Persepolis for almost four months, until about the middle of May 330, making arrangements for the disposal of the Persian treasure and securing the heart of the Persian homeland. At the start of his stay, perhaps angered by the hostility of the inhabitants, he allowed his troops to loot, and many natives were killed.[15] But this was a passing phase. Once again he appointed a Persian satrap, for as the rightful ruler of Persia, as he claimed to be, he was seeking the cooperation of the Persian nobility, whose administrative talents he appreciated and needed.

The most controversial event that occurred during his stay was the burning of the vast complex of buildings—palaces, treasury, and audience-halls—that constituted the 'palace' of Xerxes. Even today its ruins, particularly the reliefs that flank the great double staircase leading up to the open audience-halls, permit us to envisage something of the grandeur that confronted Alexander.[16] The fire took place soon after the conclusion of a month-long campaign against the Mardi which began about 6 April.[17] The official version, given by Arrian, is that Alexander set fire to the palace deliberately, to punish the Persians for their crimes in Greece in 480. Many scholars accept this view of the incident; others argue that Alexander intended the conflagration to be a sign to the peoples formerly subject to the Persians that he had come as their deliverer.[18] But it is difficult to believe that Alexander, now bent on conciliating the Persians, deliberately recalled the 'war of revenge'. Such an act would be more credible at the beginning of his stay, when there was looting and massacre, but scarcely in May. Again, would Alexander, already in control of the subject peoples, risk alienating the Persian nobles in order to make a superfluous gesture to these peoples? Or can we believe that Alexander, unaware that the war in Greece had ended, sought to remind the loyal Greeks that he had not forgotten them?[19] Apart from the question of the effectiveness of the gesture, it cannot have taken seven or eight months for a vital message to reach Alexander. It seems altogether more reasonable to accept the version given by the 'vulgate' writers. According to them the fire came as the climax of a wild drinking-party at which the Athenian *hetaira* Thais suggested to Alexander, who was already drunk, that he should win favour among the Greeks by setting fire to the palace of the Persian king. If this is so, the official version will have been put out to account for an action of which Alexander, once he sobered up, was bitterly ashamed.

Darius had been joined at Ecbatana, the Persian summer capital, by Bessus and his Bactrians, Barsaentes, Nabarzanes, the commander of the Persian Guard, Artabazus, and other leading nobles. He had by this time assembled an army of 6000 foot and 3000 horse and had collected the sum of 7000 talents, and was now waiting to see what Alexander would do; if he advanced, Darius was prepared to retire to Bactria and fight on from there; if he remained in Persis, reinforcements could be brought to Ecbatana. By about the middle of May Alexander's intelligence had located Darius in Media and the king set off northwards. On the way he was informed that Darius was at Ecbatana, then that he had determined to fight, and lastly that his expected reinforcements had failed to arrive and that he intended to flee. Hurrying on, Alexander entered Ecbatana to find that Darius had indeed fled five days earlier. The king now discharged his Greek allies and the Thessalians, rewarding them handsomely; for Darius' flight had shown how weak his position was, and Alexander did not foresee the hard fighting that lay ahead of him in Bactria. They were given an escort to the coast, where Menes was instructed to arrange their transport to Euboea. A great number, however, chose to re-enlist as mercenaries. The League of Corinth remained in being and with it Alexander's position as *Hegemon*, but the 'war of revenge' was officially over and his task as 'Captain General' at an end. Henceforth he acted in the east as King of Persia and King of Macedon.

Before he set out after Darius, Alexander issued his orders for the disposal of the enormous wealth, totalling more than 180,000 talents, which the Persian treasuries had yielded. Parmenio was instructed to collect it and convey it to Ecbatana, where he was to hand it over to Harpalus, the Imperial Treasurer.[20] Arrian relates that Parmenio was then instructed to march from Ecbatana into Hyrcania through the territory of the Cadusians; but, if this is not an error, the order was subsequently countermanded, for Parmenio remained in Media, entrusted with the vital task of maintaining communication with the west. As Parmenio was now nearing seventy, this post need not be regarded as demotion, particularly as the type of warfare to be expected in the future called for a vigour and an adaptability that could not reasonably be expected of him. Although it is likely enough that Parmenio disapproved of Alexander's policy of appointing Persian governors and that Alexander was aware of his disapproval, there is no reason to suppose that Alexander had doubts concerning his loyalty. Had he distrusted him, he would never have given him so important a task in so strategic a position. Admittedly Callisthenes put out, surely with the king's approval, the story that Parmenio had been out-generalled at Gaugamela and had lost his nerve; but this was done after Parmenio's death and has no bearing on the relationship of the two men at this time.[21]

Alexander's next objective was the capture of Darius, who had taken the Royal Road leading by way of Rhagae (near Tehran) and the Caspian Gates to Parthia and the eastern satrapies.[22] The Persian king had a long start and Alexander spared neither man nor horse in his pursuit. Although it was now midsummer and he had his heavy infantry with him (for Darius was reported to have 2000 Greek mercenaries with him), he covered the 200 miles to Rhagae in only eleven days. There, hearing that his quarry had passed through the Caspian Gates, some 45 miles to the east, Alexander rested his troops for five days. Then in a single day's march he almost reached the Gates and in another passed through them and advanced as far as the edge of the desert, where he was told by deserters that Bessus and the other leaders had placed Darius under arrest. It was this information that sent him off on his final mad gallop, at first with cavalry and infantry, then later, when he heard that the Greek mercenaries had left the party, with cavalry alone. Near Shahrud at dawn on the fourth day he sighted the dust cloud that marked the fugitives, having covered some 250 miles in less than a week in scorching heat over ground that was mostly desert. On the approach of the small band of Macedonians—only 60 had kept up with Alexander—Nabarzanes and Barsaentes stabbed Darius and fled into the desert. When Alexander reached the waggon in which Darius lay, the Persian king was dead. His death was most opportune for Alexander, for in captivity he could only have been an embarrassment. Alexander now proceeded to act as his legitimate successor, and when Bessus and Barsaentes were captured they were punished for his murder. Meanwhile, he sent Darius' body to Persepolis to be buried in the tomb of the Achaemenid kings and appointed Oxyathres, the brother of Darius, to be one of his Companions, the only oriental to be so honoured.

THE CONQUEST OF THE NORTH-EAST

Bessus fled eastwards, making for his province of Bactria. His intentions were obvious to Alexander, but after the exertions of the past week immediate pursuit was impossible. Instead, in his usual methodical fashion, Alexander decided to secure his rear. Darius' mercenaries and most of the Persian leaders who had accompanied him had retired northwards to the Elburz mountains south of the Caspian sea, a region inhabited by the Tapurians. Dividing his army into two columns, one of which he entrusted to Craterus who had taken Parmenio's place as second-in-command, he carried out a rapid sweep of the countryside and the Tapurians submitted.

The Persian leaders gradually came in; Artabazus with several of his sons, including Ariobarzanes, then Phrataphernes, who had ruled Hyrcania and Parthia, and Autophradates, satrap of Tapuria, together with Nabarzanes. Pursuing his policy of reconciliation, Alexander pardoned them all, even Nabarzanes. How far the king was influenced by his gift of an attractive eunuch named Bagoas, we have no means of knowing.[1] Autophradates was restored to his satrapy, but Amminapes, who had been appointed to rule Hyrcania and Parthia, was not displaced. However, Phrataphernes was treated with honour and employed on important missions before replacing Amminapes as satrap of Parthia, as was Artabazus until his appointment as satrap of Bactria. Envoys from the mercenaries came too, but Alexander refused to bargain with men who had contravened the decision of the League of Corinth by serving with the Persian king and demanded unconditional surrender. The envoys agreed and Artabazus was sent to bring them in. To round off his conquests in the district Alexander conducted a brief and bloody campaign against the war-like Mardians to the west of Tapuria and made them too subject to Autophradates. On his return he found not only the mercenaries at his camp but also envoys from Sparta, Athens, Sinope, and Calchedon, who had been on their way to the court of Darius. In dealing with both groups Alexander showed that he still regarded himself as *Hegemon* of the League. Those mercenaries who had entered Persian service before the formation of the League were discharged; the remainder had to enter Alexander's service on the same conditions as before. Of the ambassadors those from Sinope and Calchedon, which were not member states of the League, were sent home, but the Athenians were detained under guard; so, too, were the Spartans, since Alexander had not yet given his decision about the punishment of Sparta.

At Zadracarta (Gorgan, formerly Asterabad), the capital of Hyrcania, Alexander gave his troops fifteen days' rest before marching through Parthia to Susia (Meshed) on the border of Aria. There he received the submission of the satrap, Satibarzanes. Alexander's policy of conciliation appeared to be working well and he confirmed Satibarzanes in his satrapy, leaving only forty mounted javelin-men under Anaxippus in the province. Their task, we may note, was to prevent looting by the Macedonians not, it seems, to keep watch on the natives. At Susia news reached Alexander that Bessus was wearing his tiara upright, the prerogative of royalty, and was calling himself Artaxerxes. He heard, too, that Bessus had gathered a large force of Bactrians and was expecting the Scythians of the steppes to join him. Accordingly, the king set out along the main road to Bactra, also called Zariaspa (the modern Balkh), the capital of Bactria. However, he was soon overtaken by a messenger bearing the news that Satibarzanes had massacred Anaxippus and his men and was mustering an army at the Arian capital, Artacoana, with the intention of joining Bessus. Alexander reacted swiftly. Leaving Craterus with the bulk of his forces, he took the Companions, two battalions of infantry, the archers, Agrianians, and mounted javelin-men and by forced marches reached Artacoana, some 70 miles away, in just two days. Astounded at the speed of the king's return, Satibarzanes fled to Bessus and his troops dispersed. Infuriated, doubtless, at the satrap's treachery, Alexander remained in Aria for a whole month, stamping out the revolt without mercy. Nevertheless, he did not abandon his policy of appointing Persian governors and appointed Arsaces to succeed Satibarzanes.

Alexander now abandoned his plan of marching by the main road to Bactria; instead, once Craterus had rejoined him, he turned south to Drangiana. Most probably, after the Arian revolt, he feared the threat to his communications if Drangiana and Arachosia, formerly governed by Barsaentes, were left unconquered. He may also have cherished the hope that Bessus, if given time, would make the same mistake as Darius and meet him in a decisive pitched battle. Barsaentes had fled to the Indians living west of the Indus and he apparently remained there until 326 when, on Alexander's approach, the Indians handed him over to Alexander, who put him to death for his part in the murder of Darius. Since he had pardoned Nabarzanes, it is clear that Alexander's attitude was determined by the willingness or unwillingness of the Persian leaders to accept him as Darius' successor.

At Phrada (usually identified with Farah)[2] in the province of Drangiana there occurred the 'conspiracy' of Philotas, which was to have far-reaching effects on relations between Alexander and his Macedonians.[3] A Macedonian named Dimnus had rashly invited his lover Nicomachus to join in a plot against the king but Nicomachus rejected the idea in horror and told his brother Cebalinus, who thought that Alexander should be informed. Cebalinus therefore asked Philotas for an audience with the king, but Philotas replied that Alexander was busy. When this happened again on the following day, Cebalinus approached the page in charge of the armoury and through him gained access to the king. Alexander took the story very seriously and sent a party to arrest Dimnus, but he drew his sword and was killed resisting arrest. Deprived of Dimnus' evidence, Alexander was even more perturbed and called a meeting of his senior officers. Craterus spoke against Philotas, and it was decided to put him on trial before the Macedonian assembly, that is the assembled troops, the customary procedure in cases of treason. The arrest was planned and executed with great care in order to prevent news of it reaching Parmenio. In the assembly Alexander accused Philotas of treason, and Philotas replied in his own defence. The assembly was then adjourned and, at the suggestion of Craterus, Hephaestion, and Coenus, torture was used to extract a confession from Philotas, who was then stoned to death according to Macedonian custom.

The only 'proof' of Philotas' guilt appears to have been his failure to arrange an audience for Cebalinus or to inform Alexander of what he had been told.[4] His defence, a reasonable one, was that he had not taken the matter seriously, attributing the story to the spite of a rejected lover. It has been argued that Alexander wished to rid himself of the hostile influence of Parmenio and Philotas—Parmenio's other two sons were already dead—and took this opportunity to remove Philotas or, more radically, that Alexander fabricated the 'plot' in order to incriminate Philotas. Although these suggestions cannot altogether be discounted, it seems more probable that there really was a plot against Alexander and that the king believed Philotas to be involved. If the king did believe this, Philotas had himself partly to blame.[5] He was a dashing cavalry commander, but arrogant and boastful, and notorious for the tasteless display of his new-found wealth. By his high-handed actions he had made many enemies among the Macedonian leaders, who must have resented being reminded that he was the son of the great Parmenio, and it is very likely that these enemies did not lose the opportunity to blacken Philotas' character by asserting that since Dimnus was a nobody he must be a mere tool. It would not be surprising if Alexander took their charges seriously, for some two years earlier, we are told, there had been rumours about Philotas' disloyalty which Alexander had discounted or disregarded. Since then his suspicions must have been aroused by the disclosures of Philotas' mistress, Antigone, who had told her friends how, when drunk, Philotas had boasted of his own and his father's achievements and had belittled Alexander's. The rumours had reached Craterus' ears and he had reported them (with gusto, we may be sure) to the king. As a result Antigone was instructed to report any further remarks of this kind.

We should remember that Alexander was suspicious of plots and ruthless in dealing with them, and it is perhaps significant that it was at this time that Alexander of Lyncestis, who had been kept in custody for almost four years on suspicion of treason, was brought to trial and executed. Alexander evidently now felt that his namesake, being of royal blood, might become a focus for plots against his own life. His suspicions may have been sharpened by a feeling of insecurity, engendered by Philip's treatment of him in 337 and increased by the unfavourable reaction of the Macedonians to his policy of reconciliation with the Persians. They resented, as he well knew, his employment of Persian satraps, and resented even more his adoption of certain elements of Persian dress and the introduction of the elaborate ceremonial of the Persian court, even if, at first at least, this was required only from his oriental subjects.[6] The case of Demetrius the Bodyguard well illustrates Alexander's feeling of insecurity and his skill in dealing with those who had incurred his suspicion. Demetrius, when accused of complicity in the 'plot' of Philotas, stoutly denied the charge and Alexander accepted his denial. Evidence of his guilt was clearly lacking. Nevertheless, soon after, Demetrius was removed from his position as Bodyguard and vanishes from our records.[7] On the other hand, Amyntas, commander of an infantry battalion, and his three brothers, who were close friends of Philotas, were all acquitted after a vigorous defence by Amyntas, despite the fact that one of the brothers had run off on hearing of Philotas' arrest.

There remained the problem of Parmenio. Alexander could not simply 'retire' him, and it was too dangerous to leave him in his present position astride the communications with the west; for he was popular with the troops and he could lay his hands on the Persian treasure. At any rate Alexander was taking no chances. He immediately dispatched Polydamas, one of the Companions, with urgent instructions to his generals in Media. Dressed in Arab costume and mounted on a dromedary, Polydamas covered the distance to Ecbatana, over 800 miles across desert country, in just over ten days—for it was vital that he arrive before news of Philotas' execution reached his father—and handed over the king's letters. They contained orders to put Parmenio to death, orders which were immediately carried out. It is certain that even under torture Philotas did not incriminate his father and that no charge was brought against Parmenio. Moreover, Alexander had suspended the custom that the relatives of conspirators must die. The execution of Parmenio was 'plain murder', as Tarn has bluntly put it.[8] We need not suppose that Alexander had no regrets; but where his own safety was concerned he did not hesitate.

It was now the very end of the year but Alexander, perhaps fearing the effect that idleness might have on the Macedonians, did not go into winter-quarters in 330–329. Instead, after founding a city which came to be called Prophthasia ('Anticipation') in evident allusion to the conspiracy, he advanced up the valley of the River Helmand, where he encountered a people called the Ariaspians, but surnamed 'Benefactors' because of the assistance they had given to Cyrus the First. To stress his connection with the founder of the Achaemenid dynasty, whose tomb he had visited at Pasargadae, he gave them their freedom. In Arachosia, departing from his usual practice, Alexander appointed as satrap a Greek or Macedonian, called Menon, and left him with 4000 mercenaries and 600 cavalry to reduce the province. Then he turned north, founded another Alexandria, almost certainly at Kandahar,[9] then crossed the mountains into the territory of the Paropamisadae. His troops suffered terribly from frostbite and snowblindness and many died. They were reduced to killing the mules for food and to catching fish in the rivers, and the losses might have been much greater had they not found shelter in native huts which were almost buried in the snow and revealed only by the smoke issuing from holes in the roof.

About this time came news that Satibarzanes had invaded Aria with 2000 Bactrian cavalry. But Alexander did not turn back. Instead he sent Artabazus and two Companions, Caranus and Erigyius, with a strong force and ordered Phrataphernes, now satrap of Parthia, to assist them. The trouble was soon over, for Satibarzanes fell in single combat with Erigyius and his followers scattered. Meanwhile Alexander had founded (probably at Begram) another city called Alexandria of the Caucasus—for the Macedonians thought of the Hindu-Kush as an extension of the Caucasus—and had appointed a Persian, Proexes, satrap of the Paropamisus.

Since reaching Bactria Bessus had recruited an army of 7000 Bactrians and Dahae and had laid waste the country north of the Hindu-Kush, expecting thereby to halt Alexander's advance. But he had underestimated Alexander's determination. Despite the lack of provisions the king marched on in deep snow, crossed the Hindu-Kush (by which pass, we cannot say), and 15 days after leaving Begram reached Drapsaca (Kunduz) in Bactria. However, he failed to make contact with Bessus, who retired north across the River Oxus (Amu Darya) into Sogdiana with the Sogdian barons, Spita-menes and Oxyartes, the Sogdians and Dahae. The Bactrians, how-ever, dispersed to their homes. The chief towns in Bactria, Bactra and Aornus (Tashkurghan, now officially also called Khulm) were taken without difficulty and the Bactrians submitted. A garrison was stationed at Tashkurghan and the faithful Artabazus was appointed satrap of the province. Then Alexander set off in pursuit of Bessus. The mighty Oxus was a formidable barrier but, as he had done on the Danube, Alexander filled hides with hay and crossed the river in only five days. Once again his speed disconcerted his opponents. From Spitamenes came a message that he had arrested Bessus and was ready to hand him over, if a small party was sent. Alexander accordingly dispatched Ptolemy to bring him in, but Spitamenes, not trusting Alexander, fled on Ptolemy's approach leaving Bessus behind. Ptolemy, therefore, brought him in, naked and wearing a wooden collar, as the king had ordered, and Alexander had him flogged before sending him to Bactra to be executed for the murder of Darius.[10]

Alexander now continued his advance through Sogdiana by way of Maracanda, the modern Samarcand, to the River Jaxartes (Syr Darya), which flows northwards to the Aral Sea. This river the Macedonians, perhaps misunderstanding their native informants, called the Tanais, believing that they had reached the Tanais, or Don, which flows into the Sea of Azov.[11] As the Tanais/Don was the recognized boundary between Europe and Asia, later writers on Alexander sought, dishonestly it would seem, to use the identification of the Syr Darya with the Tanais to prove that Alexander had con-quered all Asia. But we have no reason to suppose that the king him-self was guilty of deception. In the prevailing ignorance of the geography of the region it was natural that two great rivers flowing into inland seas should be identified.

On the Jaxartes Alexander stormed a mountain fortress, killing over two-thirds of the defenders, and gained control of Cyropolis

D

and the other forts which the Persians had built to ward off the
incursions of the Massagetae across the river. In these he established
garrisons. Bactria and Sogdiana now appeared to have been subdued
and Alexander summoned the barons to a meeting at Bactra. Perhaps
alarmed by this summons, the Sogdian leaders roused the people,
massacred the Macedonian garrisons, and prepared to defend the
forts. However, Alexander had little difficulty in capturing the forts
one after the other. Only at Cyropolis, where he had to bring up his
siege-engines, did he experience any real trouble; there the men were
massacred and the women and children enslaved, for Alexander had
resolved to teach the Sogdians a lesson.

ALEXANDER'
WORST
DISASTER

    Then came news that Spitamenes was besieging Maracanda.
Alexander evidently failed to realize that he had a national uprising
on his hands and sent only a small force, consisting of 60 Companion
cavalry, 800 mercenary cavalry, and 1500 mercenary infantry, to
deal with the situation.[12] The force appears to have been placed under
the command of a Lycian interpreter named Pharnuches, on the
assumption that negotiation rather than fighting was required.
Remaining on the Jaxartes, Alexander founded Alexandria Eschate
('Alexandria the Furtherest'), the modern Khojend, as a defence
against the Scythians who had assembled in force on the far bank of
the river. Irritated by their insults, Alexander decided to take the
initiative. He prepared rafts of hides for the crossing, and using his
catapults as field artillery, drove the enemy from the riverbank. Faced
for the first time by the Scythian 'desert tactics', in which the Scythian
cavalry circled round firing their arrows then made off before they
could be attacked, Alexander handled his attack with characteristic
skill. He covered the landing with archers and slingers, then sent
forward light cavalry until he was able to draw up the Companions
for the attack. When the heavy cavalry charged, supported by the
Agrianians and the javelin-men, the Scythians fled, losing 1000 killed
and 150 taken prisoner. Alexander set off after them and the victory
would have been even more decisive had he not been attacked by
dysentery (the result of drinking foul water) which necessitated his
being carried back to camp.

    Meanwhile the force sent against Spitamenes had met with dis-
aster. When it approached, the Sogdian leader retired and enticed the
Macedonians to pursue him to the edge of the desert where he was
joined by 600 Sacae horsemen. Baffled by the same tactics that
Alexander had successfully countered, the Macedonians managed to
withdraw to the River Polytimetus (Zarafshan). Then discipline
collapsed. The cavalry, seeing salvation on the far side of the river,
dashed into the water without waiting for the infantry and as the
infantry followed in disorder the Sacae attacked. The whole force was

surrounded and wiped out. Aristobulus tells a different story of an ambush and of the refusal of the Macedonian leaders to accept command at the critical moment. Whichever story is correct, this was the worst disaster that had befallen Alexander's forces and the king cannot escape responsibility for it, at least in part. He had sent a force that was inadequate for the task and had put in charge of it an interpreter, who can hardly be blamed for seeking to relinquish his command to more experienced officers at such a crisis.

No sooner had Alexander been informed of the fate that had overtaken this force and that Spitamenes was once again besieging Maracanda than he immediately sought to retrieve the position. He set out with a picked force and reached Maracanda, almost 180 miles from his starting-point, in three days and a night.[13] But again Spitamenes escaped, and Alexander had to be content with burying those who had died in the previous battle and with systematically devastating the Zarafshan valley to prevent Spitamenes from returning to Maracanda. Further campaigning was out of the question, for his troops had not taken up winter-quarters in the previous year and were in urgent need of rest. Accordingly, he left 3000 men to guard Sogdiana and returned to Bactra until the worst of the winter should pass. It was probably at this time that Alexander set about devising a new strategy to deal with this new kind of warfare. It was clear that he was no longer to have the opportunity to defeat the enemy in pitched battles, for he was faced by men who were highly mobile, who knew the country and who took refuge in the natural fortresses of the region or vanished into the limitless steppes. The phalanx was no longer so important; instead he required detachments of infantry and, more particularly, of cavalry operating under independent commanders. Alexander was already making use of Persian mounted javelin-men and probably Persian heavy cavalry as well, although this is not attested, and he now received large reinforcements of Greek mercenaries, totalling 19,000 horse and foot, whom he used particularly as garrison troops.[14] He seems, however, to have received no more drafts from Macedon until his return to the west.

To Bactra this winter came Stasanor, the recently appointed satrap of Aria, bringing his predecessor Arsaces, who had shown himself untrustworthy, and Barzanes, whom Bessus had made satrap of Parthia. Their fate is not mentioned, but presumably they were put to death. Other visitors to Bactra were envoys from the new Scythian king, who offered Alexander his daughter's hand, an offer he gracefully declined, and Pharasmanes, the king of the Chorasmians, who lived south of the Aral Sea. It may have been from Pharasmanes that Polycleitus, an eminent Thessalian who accompanied Alexander, learned of a lake of fresh water into which a great river flowed—a good description of the Aral, although Polycleitus calls the lake the 'Caspian'.[15] Alexander concluded an alliance with the Chorasmian king, but he refused his offer to guide him on an expedition to the Black Sea. He had in mind, he said, an invasion of India; when he returned to Greece, he would remember Pharasmanes' offer.

Although Artabazus had been appointed satrap of Sogdiana, the country was far from being subdued and early in 328 Alexander was informed that the inhabitants had taken refuge in their forts and were refusing to acknowledge Artabazus' authority. As soon as operations were possible Alexander advanced to the Oxus, where petroleum was discovered near his tent—probably the first occasion on which it had been seen by Europeans—and sacrifice offered to mark the miraculous event. Then he crossed the river into Sogdiana, where he put his new strategy into operation. To cope with the widely-scattered rebel forces he divided his army into five columns, which swept through the countryside, storming the fortified places and securing the surrender of the villages, before reassembling at Maracanda. Then, while Coenus and Artabazus set off towards Scythia in pursuit of Spitamenes, Alexander completed the subjugation of the province and Hephaestion established a network of fortified positions throughout the country.

Meanwhile Spitamenes had eluded his pursuers. With the help of the Massagetae he surprised a fort on the Bactrian border, massacred the defenders, and advanced on Bactra but did not venture to attack the city. Then Craterus appeared, pursued the invaders to the edge of the desert and killed 150 of them in a hard-fought battle. The majority, however, escaped. Where had Craterus been? For he is not one of the commanders of the four infantry battalions which were left behind to keep watch over Bactria and to complete its subjugation. Most probably he was at this time engaged in the conquest of Margiane to the west of Bactria and in securing Alexander's communications with Aria and was responsible for the foundation of Alexandria in Margiane (Merv).[16]

We now find Coenus stationed in Sogdiana with two battalions of infantry, his own and Meleager's, which had been serving with Craterus. The inference is plain: Craterus and Coenus had linked up during or after the pursuit of Spitamenes. Craterus now presumably returned to Margiane, while Coenus remained in Sogdiana with orders to intercept Spitamenes should he attempt to invade the province. His force included some newly-raised Bactrian and Sogdian light horse, a measure of Alexander's confidence in the pacification of the provinces. These were attached to the new satrap, Amyntas; for Artabazus, perhaps feeling that the task required a younger man, had requested and been granted permission to retire. Alexander himself took up winter-quarters at Nautaca.

Alexander had planned well. Wherever they turned, Spitamenes and his followers found themselves faced by Macedonian garrisons. Finally, Spitamenes, who had persuaded three thousand Massagetae to join him, resolved to risk a pitched battle against Coenus. In hard fighting 800 of Spitamenes' cavalry fell, and the Bactrians and Sogdians surrendered. The Massagetae fled to the steppes with Spitamenes but, on learning that Alexander was moving against them, they cut off his head and sent it to the king as a peace-offering. Spitamenes' family fell into Alexander's hands and was given characteristically honourable treatment; then, in 324 at Susa, his daughter Apame married Seleucus. It is perhaps ironical that the Seleucids, who ruled the largest portion of Alexander's empire, should be descended from the Bactrian patriot.

The war in Sogdiana was not ended with Spitamenes' death. Many of the inhabitants, including the baron Oxyartes, had taken refuge in the rocky fortresses in the east of the country. So, at the first hint of spring in 327, Alexander marched against the 'Sogdian rock' near Derbent. The rock was sheer on every side, provisions for a long siege had been laid in, and heavy snow assured the defenders of a plentiful supply of water while at the same time hampering the attackers. Nevertheless, nettled by the jibes of the Sogdians that he would need 'winged soldiers', Alexander called for volunteers to scale the rock. During the night 300 mountaineers, equipped with linen ropes and iron tent pegs for use as *pitons*, succeeded in making the perilous ascent although they lost thirty men in the process. When they reached the summit, Alexander bade the defenders look up and they would see the 'winged soldiers'. Astounded at the feat and unaware how few Macedonians held the summit, the tribesmen surrendered, Oxyartes and his family among them.

When Alexander saw Roxane, one of Oxyartes' daughters, he instantly fell in love with her, we are told, and 'deigned to marry her'. But, whatever the king's feelings towards Roxane may have been, it can hardly be doubted that the marriage, solemnized according to Iranian custom by the cutting of a loaf of bread, was intended to conciliate the Sogdian barons.[17] Oxyartes himself soon made his peace with Alexander and many others followed his example. But not all the leaders were convinced of the king's good intentions, and he found it necessary to besiege the 'rock' of Chorienes (who was also called Sisimithres) situated over a hundred miles east of Kunduz near Faizabad in Pareitacene. This was even more difficult of access than the Sogdian rock, since it was surrounded by a deep ravine and the summit could be reached only by a single narrow track. Undaunted,

Alexander set his army to work to fill in the ravine by hammering stakes into its sides and placing hurdles of osiers upon them, which were then covered with earth. When arrows began to reach the rock, Chorienes took fright and sent a herald requesting that Oxyartes be sent to him, and Oxyartes, pointing to his own treatment by Alexander, induced him to surrender. Thereupon Alexander not only gave him back his stronghold but made him governor of the surrounding district. Then, leaving Craterus to reduce the remaining rebels, Catanes and Austanes, and to conquer the territory east of the River Vakhsh, he returned to Bactra to prepare for the invasion of India.

I O

ALEXANDER AND THE MACEDONIANS

During the Iranian campaign Alexander's orientalism led to conflict between him and the Macedonians and also, it appears, to some extent between the older and younger Macedonians. In the summer of 328 Cleitus 'the Black', the commander of the Royal Squadron of the Companions, had been appointed to succeed Artabazus as satrap of Bactria. But he did not survive to take up his post, for at Maracanda in the autumn he was killed by Alexander. The incident took place at a drinking party at which both men had drunk too much of the local wine, and Alexander had provocation. So much is clear, but what sparked off their quarrel and what each man said is variously reported.[1] Arrian recounts a conversation in which Alexander's achievements were compared to those of the deified heroes, the Dioscuri, Castor and Pollux, and even of Heracles himself—an unlikely theme at this time—while in Curtius' version Alexander behaves exactly like a stage tyrant. Plutarch, who probably derived his information from Chares, the Court Chamberlain, tells a much more likely story, circumstantial and free from bias. According to this version a poem was recited—it was a composition of one of the minor poets who accompanied the expedition—in which those Macedonians who had been defeated by Spitamenes at the end of 329 were held up to ridicule. The older Macedonians protested, but Alexander and those around him urged the reciter to proceed. Cleitus could not contain himself; it was not right, he protested, for Macedonians, even if they had been unlucky, to be insulted in the presence of 'barbarians'. Alexander remarked that Cleitus by calling cowardice 'bad luck' was pleading his own case; whereupon Cleitus retorted that his 'cowardice' had saved the life of 'the son of Ammon' at the Granicus. The brawl continued with Alexander, now very angry indeed, warning Cleitus to desist and Cleitus shouting that the dead were lucky in not being alive to witness his adoption of oriental practices. Alexander, we are told, then remarked to the Greeks beside him that Greeks among Macedonians were heroes among beasts. Cleitus did not hear what was said—clearly Alexander intended it only as an aside—but suspected that it was derogatory and shouted to the king to speak out; otherwise, he jeered, he should not have invited free men to the banquet, but consorted with his 'barbarian slaves' who would do obeisance to his Persian garb.

Goaded beyond endurance, Alexander threw an apple at Cleitus and made for his dagger, only to find it missing; for one of his bodyguards had prudently removed it. Suspecting treachery, Alexander shouted for his Guards in the Macedonian dialect—a sign of great trouble—and ordered the trumpeter to sound the alarm. When the man refused, he struck him. Meanwhile Cleitus' friends had hurried him out of the tent and back to his quarters. However, he did not remain there but returned to the banquet chanting the verses from Euripides' *Andromache* (693ff.) in which the Greek custom of inscribing trophies with the names of kings is lamented. As Cleitus appeared in the doorway, Alexander snatched a spear from one of his Guards and ran him through. Then Alexander's anger left him. He attempted to pull the spear out of Cleitus' body in order to kill himself, but the Guards overpowered him and carried him forcibly to his tent. For three days he lay there, refusing to eat or drink until, we are told, he was persuaded by the soothsayers that the tragedy had been inevitable.

This incident figures prominently in the criticisms of Greek and Roman moralists, but there is no indication that the Macedonian leaders were much affected by it. Its importance lies chiefly in the insight it gives us into the various stresses in Alexander's headquarters and the resentment felt by some at least of the leading Macedonian at Alexander's policies; for it was not simply a personal quarrel. Cleitus, when drink loosened his tongue, gave vent to complaints which he and doubtless many other Macedonian officers had been bottling up for the past two years. During this time Alexander had been trying, as tactfully as possible, to combine his position as king of Macedon with that of Great King.[2] He evidently had two courts, one Macedonian and one Persian, each with their bodyguards, and he adopted only certain items of Persian dress, such as the diadem, not the tiara and the baggy trousers which marked out the Persian as a foreigner in Greek (and Macedonian) eyes in very much the same way that his 'breeks' marked out the Gaul in Roman eyes. Nevertheless, it was clearly difficult for Macedonians, accustomed as they were to regard their king as first among equals, to accept the adjuncts of a Persian court, particularly perhaps the eunuchs and the harem (whose existence we need not doubt), and the aura that surrounded the Great King. Fully as difficult for them to accept was the treatment as equals, or near equals, of 'orientals' whom they had defeated in battle and who were traditionally regarded as inferior to Greeks, let alone Macedonians. More understandable was the resentment they felt at the mystique that surrounded Alexander as 'son of Ammon', since this may well have been felt to involve the rejection of Philip as Alexander's father.

It would be excessively sceptical to doubt the genuineness of Alexander's grief at Cleitus' death, but his determination to pursue his 'policy of fusion' was unshaken. Certainly it cannot have been much later that he attempted to extend to Greeks and Macedonians the traditional Persian practice of *proskynesis*, by which those who entered the Great King's presence prostrated themselves before him.[3] For the Persians it is quite certain that this practice had no implications of worship. They did not consider their kings to be gods, and *proskynesis* was merely a ceremonial act acknowledging the superior position of the monarch. But Greeks and Macedonians prostrated themselves only before the gods and to them *proskynesis* did imply worship. Did Alexander, then, propose, by introducing this practice for Greeks and Macedonians, to have himself recognized as a god? Many scholars have held that he did, either because he desired divine honours for their own sake or to strengthen his position by becoming a divine king. But to become a divine king would not put an end to the opposition to his policies unless the Macedonians actually thought of him as a god, and it is not likely that Alexander was naïve enough to suppose that it would. It is much more likely that Alexander's intention was simply to further his policy of fusion by the introduction of a uniform court procedure for both Macedonians and Persians. He could not forbid the Persians to perform *proskynesis* without running the risk of their thinking that he was not a real king. The alternative was to explain to the Greeks and Macedonians that the ceremony did not involve worship, that it was a regular Persian court practice, and to persuade them to adopt it on formal occasions when Persians were present. For there is no evidence, nor any likelihood, that the Macedonians were expected to perform *proskynesis* on *every* occasion.[4]

Alexander decided to make the experiment with a picked group of Macedonians, Greeks and Persians, and it is likely that Hephaestion (the obvious man to do so) was given the task of explaining the position to the Macedonians and Greeks. At any rate he later claimed that Callisthenes had agreed to perform *proskynesis* and had gone back on his word. We are fortunate in having, preserved by Arrian and Plutarch, the account of Chares, the Court Chamberlain, who was undoubtedly present.[5] One evening after dinner Alexander handed a cup of wine to one of the party who made a libation at the altar, then drank from the cup and prostrated himself before the king. He then approached Alexander, who kissed him, thereby gracefully acknowledging in Persian fashion in response to the act of *proskynesis* that the man was his equal. The other members of the party followed the first man's lead and all went well until Callisthenes' turn came. Callisthenes took the cup, made a libation, then drank from the cup and came up to Alexander without first having prostrated himself. Alexander, who was talking to Hephaestion, did not notice the omission but Demetrius, one of his Companions, drew his attention to it, and the king refused to kiss Callisthenes. The philosopher thereupon left the banquet, remarking in a loud voice, 'Well, I shall go then, the poorer by a kiss', and the attempt to introduce *proskynesis* for Macedonians and Greeks was abandoned and never repeated. The Persians, of course, continued to perform the act on coming into the king's presence.

Callisthenes' refusal to prostrate himself has occasioned much surprise among historians, but unnecessarily. Even on the assumption that Alexander, for whatever reason, was seeking to secure recognition of his divinity, Callisthenes' action is quite intelligible. Certainly, he had propagated the 'noble lie' that Alexander was the son of Zeus, a belief which Alexander may have entertained and one which he undoubtedly encouraged. But this was a very different matter from asserting Alexander's divinity, and Callisthenes had never sought to spread the belief that the king was a *god*.[6] But if, as seems more probable, Alexander's aims were more practical, Callisthenes' opposition is no less easy to understand. Like the Macedonians and his fellow-Greeks, he doubtless regarded *proskynesis* as a 'barbarian' practice, ridiculous and degrading, which would depress them to the level of those who, as his uncle Aristotle held, should be treated like animals. It is credible enough that Callisthenes promised Hephaestion that he would perform the act and that when the time came for him to do so, he felt unable to go through with it.[7]

Callisthenes, who has been well described as 'a guileless antiquarian',[8] may have regarded the incident as trivial; for his uncle once remarked that he lacked common sense. Alexander, it is evident, took a different view of his refusal. He had counted on the introduction of *proskynesis* to help to bring the Macedonians and Persians together, and he did not forgive Callisthenes. His resentment is perhaps shown by an incident which is often thought to have occurred soon after.[9] One evening, when the philosopher had won great applause for an impromptu speech in praise of the Macedonians,

Alexander remarked that it was an easy matter to speak eloquently on such a theme. Why, the king asked, didn't he display his talent by speaking *against* them? Callisthenes fell into the trap. He criticized the Macedonians with vigour, attributing Philip's success (with some truth) to the divisions among the Greek states and quoting a verse from a tragedy to the effect that in times of dissension the utter villain gains honour. The Macedonians, not surprisingly, were enraged and Alexander sarcastically remarked that Callisthenes had given proof not of his eloquence but of his ill-will towards the Macedonians. It may be going too far to see this incident as part of a plan by the king to 'liquidate' Callisthenes, as some have argued,[10] but at the least we must conclude that Alexander considered him a dangerous man whose influence, apparently considerable with young and old, must be destroyed.

In the late spring of 327 there occurred the conspiracy of the Royal Pages.[11] One of the duties of these young nobles was to attend the king at the hunt and on one occasion a certain Page called Hermolaus had forestalled the king by killing a wild boar. For this offence Alexander had him whipped, according to the custom of the corps, and deprived of his horse. Hermolaus thereupon conspired with a number of his fellow Pages to kill the king, but the plot was detected and the conspirators arrested and put to death.

Although Arrian and Curtius[12] attribute purely personal motives to the conspirators, the extent of the plot—nine names are known—and the fact that by the standards of the corps Hermolaus' punishment was not excessive suggest that it was not simply an act of revenge. Indeed, in the speeches which Arrian and Curtius attribute to the Pages at their trial they claimed that they had found Alexander's policies intolerable, and it is reasonable to suppose that they were no less alienated by the events of the past two years than the older Macedonians. The suggestion that they saw themselves in the role of tyrannicides is by no means improbable.[13] But, although the background to the plot may have been political rather than personal, we are under no obligation to believe Ptolemy and Aristobulus when they loyally assert that Callisthenes, who had been the boys' tutor, had urged them to kill the king. Most writers, in fact, denied this and Alexander himself in a letter (which is demonstrably genuine), written immediately after the event to his generals in Pareitacene states that only the Pages were involved. Nevertheless, Callisthenes was arrested and in a letter to Antipater, which may or may not be genuine, Alexander made veiled threats against Aristotle and the Athenians, because of their connection with 'those who plotted against him'.[14] What happened to Callisthenes is a mystery. Ptolemy states that he was tortured and hanged, while Chares says that he was carried around with the army in captivity (a statement which Aristo-bulus confirms—or adopts) and that after seven months he died of natural causes, 'having become excessively fat and lousy'.[15] Chares adds that Alexander intended to have Callisthenes tried in the *Synhedrion* of the League of Corinth, presumably on a charge of having plotted against the *Hegemon*. However, this may be no more than an intelligent guess on his part; for he presumably knew that Callisthenes, being a Greek, was not subject to the jurisdiction of the Macedonian assembly. Even if Callisthenes' importance may have been exaggerated, it is difficult to credit that Ptolemy did not know how he died and equally difficult to suggest a convincing reason why he should lie. Chares, on the other hand, may have sought to excul-pate Alexander and have been followed by Aristobulus either for the same reason or because he did not know the truth. Possibly, since Arrian's account *need* not mean that Ptolemy said that Callisthenes was hanged immediately, Callisthenes may have been taken round with the army for several months before being executed.

Alexander, naturally suspicious as he was, will have found it only too easy to convince himself of the guilt of a man who was in close touch with the conspirators and who had recently made his attitude to *proskynesis*, and to what it implied, only too clear. He may even have credited Callisthenes with his own revengeful nature and, re-membering the incident when he encouraged the philosopher to abuse the Macedonians, have believed that Callisthenes bore him ill-will.

The effect of Callisthenes' arrest and death on Alexander's reputa-tion in antiquity has been greatly exaggerated. Undoubtedly it dealt a blow to the good relations that existed between Alexander and Aristotle, but this rift appears to have been temporary and, if the king did utter threats against his former teacher, they were never translated into action. Theophrastus, the Peripatetic philosopher and friend of Callisthenes, described the king as a man unable to bear prosperity, and we need not doubt that Alexander was not popular with the Peripatetics, although at least one of them wrote favourably of him. But it goes far beyond the evidence to talk, as Tarn does, of a 'Peripatetic portrait' of Alexander which formed the basis of Curtius' *History*.[16] The philosophic condemnation of Alexander, particularly by the Stoics, was directed against his outbursts of anger, his (alleged) drunkenness, and his orientalism. The Callisthenes affair was unimportant, except at the personal level. It is unlikely that Callisthenes was greatly lamented by the Macedonians, for he appears to have been somewhat arrogant and boorish; moreover, as Wilcken has reminded us, the military successes in Bactria and Sogdiana demonstrate that the hold which Alexander had on his army was largely unaffected by the events of 328 and 327.

THE INDIAN EXPEDITION

Under Darius I the Persian empire had reached the River Indus and
it is no surprise that Alexander, as Great King, should seek to extend
his empire to that point. But it is clear that his ambitions went beyond
this, and there is no agreement about his ultimate intentions in this
direction. That is a question best considered when we come to the
mutiny of his army on the River Beas, but this much we can say with
certainty: his march into India was no venture into the unknown.
Alexander had always endeavoured to inform himself about the
country that lay ahead—witness, for example, his use of lesser-known
routes—and by this time he must have discarded or revised whatever
Aristotle had told him about India. He may perhaps have found
something useful in the Persian archives, but this cannot have been
recent and doubtless he obtained more valuable information from
the native rulers. Sisicottus (Sasigupta), whose kingdom lay east of
Bactria, had joined him there, and Taxiles, the ruler of the country
between the Indus and the Hydaspes (Jhelum), had sent envoys to
him in Sogdiana in 329 or 328.[1] From them Alexander will have
learned of the feuds between the rulers in the west of India, and he will
doubtless have planned to exploit them.

It was early summer in 327 when Alexander left Bactria. To safeguard this important link in his communications he left a Macedonian, Amyntas, and gave him a strong garrison of 10,000 infantry
and 3000 cavalry, doubtless mercenaries for the most part but
perhaps including some Macedonians. Re-crossing the Hindu-Kush,
he came to the Alexandria he had founded early in 329. There he
replaced the governor of the city who had proved incompetent and
reinforced the city with native settlers and troops past active service.
This was to be the pattern for his other foundations. Then, appointing Tyriaspes, another Persian, satrap of the Paropamisus in place of

Proexes, who may have died, he descended to the valley of the River Cophen (Kabul).

As he approached the river he was met by Taxiles and the other Indian rulers he had sent for, and Perdiccas and Hephaestion with half of the army and the heavy baggage were dispatched with the Indians through the Khyber pass to the Indus, where they had instructions to bridge the river and await Alexander. With the other half of his forces the king embarked upon a campaign against the warlike tribes of Bajaur and Swat, north of the Kabul, to secure the route into India. Despite fierce resistance, city after city was taken, or surrendered. A hard-fought battle near Arigaeum (possibly Nawagai, the present capital of Bajaur) resulted, we are told, no doubt with some exaggeration, in the capture of 40,000 Indians and almost a quarter of a million cattle. The best of the beasts Alexander sent to Macedonia to improve the native stock. In Swat the Assacenians had concentrated their forces at Massaga, whose site has not been identified, and enlisted the aid of 7000 mercenary Indians. For three days they held out in the face of determined Macedonian attacks, during which Alexander was wounded, but on the fourth their leader was killed and the garrison surrendered. Later that night Alexander surrounded the hill to which the mercenaries had withdrawn and massacred them. So much is clear. Diodorus relates that the mercenaries had been given permission to leave the district and attributes the massacre to a gross breach of faith on Alexander's part. However, Arrian states that the mercenaries had agreed to join Alexander but were intending to desert and that it was to prevent this that the king put them to death. The truth is irrecoverable, for it is just as probable that Arrian's source, probably Ptolemy, was whitewashing Alexander as that Diodorus' source was blackening his reputation. Certainly it will not do to say, as Tarn does, that Alexander never cheated and to ascribe the agreement with the mercenaries to Cleitarchus' imagination.[2]

It was in Swat that the Macedonians came across the city of Nysa, inhabited by a people who differed from the other peoples of the region, perhaps being immigrants from the west or even descendants of Darius' mercenaries.[3] They worshipped a god, possibly Shiva, whom the Macedonians called Dionysus, perhaps because they saw ivy growing in the district. The identification will have been welcome to Alexander, since Dionysus had not proceeded beyond this point in his march eastwards and thus when Alexander advanced he would have surpassed the god. In the same way, when he captured Aornus, he will not have discouraged those who asserted that he had achieved what Heracles had failed to achieve. To foster the myth about Dionysus, Alexander allowed the Nysaeans as an honour to the god to retain their aristocratic form of government independent of the satrap.

Following his capture of Massaga, Alexander took Bazira (Bīrkōt) and Ora (Uḍe-grām) and garrisoned all three places. Then, entering Peucelaotis by the Malakand pass, he subdued the district before turning north again to besiege the 'rock' of Aornus, where the majority of the inhabitants of the region had taken refuge. This 'rock' was identified by Sir Aurel Stein in 1926 as Pīr-Sar, a flat-topped ridge over 7000 feet high with precipitous cliffs commanding the Indus more than 5000 feet below. At right angles to Pīr-Sar and separated from it by a deep ravine, 500 yards across and 600 feet deep, is an even higher ridge called Ūna-Sar, along which, as deserters informed Alexander, Pīr-Sar could best be attacked.[4] Guided by the natives, Ptolemy led a picked band of Guards and light-armed troops by a difficult path to the summit of Ūna-Sar, but when Alexander attempted next day to join him the difficult terrain combined with the fierce Indian resistance forced him to withdraw. During the night a messenger got through to Ptolemy with a message from the king. This instructed him to attack the tribesmen in the rear as soon as the main Macedonian force should approach, and although there was again hard fighting on the following day Ptolemy's help enabled Alexander to force his way up the slope and join his advance party. Then he advanced along Ūna-Sar only to find his way blocked by the ravine. The task ahead was formidable, but the king had no thought of giving up, for Aornus held a strategic position dominating the Indus and threatening his communications. On the following day he began the construction of a causeway across the ravine in the face of Indian attacks. These, however, became fewer as his slingers and siege-engines began to operate from the causeway, and in three days it was complete. As Alexander had calculated, the Indians were so astounded by his achievement that they requested a truce. Their intention was to escape during the night, but news of their plan reached the king who rushed the 'rock' at the head of his Guards and overcame the fugitives. Sisicottus, who had convinced Alexander of his loyalty, was left in charge of a garrison on the 'rock', subject of course to the satrap of the province, and Alexander marched north-east to complete the conquest of the Assacenians. Then, building some rough boats, he sailed down the Indus to Ohind, 16 miles above Attock, where Hephaestion had bridged the river in accordance with his orders.

At Ohind Alexander found that Taxiles, who had already made his submission, had sent 700 cavalry as well as a great many gifts in acknowledgement of his client status. His desire for friendship with

Alexander was largely due to the fact that he was at war with Porus, the powerful rajah whose kingdom lay east of the Jhelum, and with Abisares, the ruler of Kashmir. Undoubtedly, Alexander's task in the Punjab was made much easier by the absence of any united resistance, for he was able to defeat the Indian rulers one after the other with the help of their enemies. Porus, for example, was an enemy of his nephew, also called Porus, and with Abisares had recently undertaken an unsuccessful campaign against the Cathaeans and Oxydracae, independent tribes to the south of his kingdom. Crossing the Indus, Alexander advanced to Taxila, the capital of Taxiles' kingdom, situated some 20 miles north-west of the modern Rawalpindi at the meeting-place of the trade routes from Bactria, Kashmir, and the Ganges valley.[5] There he met Taxiles and granted him as much of the surrounding territory as he requested, for he needed his support against Porus. It was at Taxila that Alexander first encountered the ascetics, or Gymnosophists (naked wise men) as the Greeks called them. He was greatly interested in their doctrines and sent Onesicritus to persuade their chief, Dandamis, to accompany his army. In his book Onesicritus included a lengthy account of his meeting with the Gymnosophists and of their teachings which, however, bear a suspiciously close resemblance to those of the Cynics.[6] Dandamis would not accompany Alexander, but Calanus joined his entourage and returned with the king to the west. Calanus was a younger man and accounted rather lacking in self-control, a judgement not borne out by the manner of his death. For in Susa he fell ill and, despite Alexander's efforts to dissuade him, insisted on being burned to death on a funeral pyre. Few writers on Alexander failed to record how Calanus lay without flinching as the pyre was lit, the trumpets sounded, and the flames consumed him.

It was early in 326 when news reached Alexander at Taxila that Porus was encamped on the Jhelum with a large army, determined to oppose his passage. Coenus was sent back to the Indus with orders to dismantle the boats there and transport them in pieces (two or three according to size) to the Jhelum where they could be reassembled. Then appointing Philip, son of Machatas, satrap of the territory between the Indus and the Jhelum and leaving him in Taxila with a garrison, Alexander set out to meet Porus. It seems probable that he set up camp near the modern Haranpur, after marching due south over the Salt Range.[7] His first problem was to get across the Jhelum, swollen by the summer rains and the melting snow in the mountains, in the face of Porus' 200 elephants; for he was well aware that the horses would not remain on the rafts once they scented the elephants. It was necessary, therefore, to find a spot where he could embark his troops without the enemy detecting his intentions. Accordingly, he

feinted to cross at various points until Porus ceased to send out
forces to counter his movements and relied on messengers to give *STRATEGY.*
him sufficient warning to bring up his main force. At last Alexander
found a suitable place for a crossing, probably at Jalalpur, some 17
miles north of his camp, opposite a wooded island which would
screen his preparations for crossing and the initial stages of the
crossing itself. In the main camp preparations were made openly, as
if Alexander intended to cross at that point, and Craterus was left
there with some 8000 infantry, his own regiment of horse, and the
cavalry from Arachosia and Paropamisus. He was ordered, however,
not to attempt to cross unless Porus should withdraw *all* his elephants. Between the camp and the crossing point Alexander stationed
Meleager, Attalus, and Gorgias with their infantry battalions and an
unspecified number of mercenary horse and foot. Their orders were
to cross once battle had been joined. The forces under Alexander's
own command are known to have comprised the Royal Squadron
and four regiments of Companions, the Bactrian, Sogdian, and
Scythian horse, and 1000 mounted archers, together with two
infantry battalions, the Guards, archers, and Agrianians. Arrian's
totals, 6000 infantry and 5000 cavalry, seem certainly too low, perhaps an attempt by Ptolemy to enhance a victory that needed no
enhancing. Possibly figures of 9000 infantry and 6000 cavalry would
not be far out.

On the night before the crossing the weather was atrocious. There
was heavy rain and thunder, which effectively concealed the advance
to Jalalpur and the completion of the preparations. However, at
dawn the wind dropped and the rain eased so that the rafts and the
boats were able to set out. When they passed the island, they were
sighted by the Indian scouts who immediately galloped off to tell
Porus. When the Macedonians reached land, Alexander disembarked first, followed by the cavalry, only to receive an unpleasant
surprise; he had landed not on the eastern bank of the Jhelum but on
a large island separated from the bank by a narrow but deep channel.
Hurriedly he searched for a ford, for time was precious. At last he
found one and the troops managed to wade across, although the water
was almost up to their chins. Then, drawing up his forces in battle
order under cover of the mounted archers, Alexander gave orders for
the infantry to advance at their normal pace and rode ahead with his
cavalry and the archers. His object was surely not to defeat Porus'
entire force with his cavalry, as Arrian says, but rather to contain it
until his infantry should arrive.

When he learned from his scouts that a Macedonian force was
crossing the river, Porus did not know whether this was the main
attack or merely a diversion. Accordingly, he compromised and sent

his son with 120 chariots and 2000 cavalry to try to drive the attackers back into the river as they struggled ashore. But he was too late; Alexander was already across and his superior force made short work of the Indians. Four hundred Indian horsemen fell, including Porus' son, and all the chariots were captured.

News of this disaster soon reached Porus. It was now clear that this was no feint but that Alexander was across the river with a large force. Meanwhile Craterus was threatening to cross from the main camp. Faced with this dilemma, Porus made the correct decision. Leaving a small detachment, including a number of elephants, to keep Craterus at bay, he advanced against Alexander with the remainder of his forces—4000 cavalry, 30,000 infantry, 300 chariots and 200 elephants. On reaching a position favourable to cavalry manœuvres, he halted and deployed his troops. In the van he placed the elephants, 100 feet apart, and in the intervals between them but in their rear he posted his infantry, whose line extended beyond the elephants. This suggests that the figure of 200 given for the elephants may be an exaggeration. On either flank of the infantry rode the cavalry, shielded by the chariots.

When Alexander sighted the Indians, they were already moving into position and he halted to allow his infantry to come up. When they arrived, he gave them time to recover from their march and during the interval doubtless planned how to overcome the problem posed by the presence of the elephants in the Indian line. To advance by the centre would be to send his infantry to certain destruction. Yet at some stage they must tackle the elephants; for the battle could not be won by cavalry alone. Alexander's solution was to eliminate the Indian cavalry to prevent them attacking his infantry in the flanks and, it seems probable, to throw the Indian infantry and the elephants into confusion. He issued his orders accordingly: the infantry were not to engage until they saw the enemy ranks in disorder, while Coenus was to take his own cavalry regiment and Demetrius' regiment and ride towards the Indian right. There he was to remain out of sight in dead ground until the Indian cavalry on the right wing had ridden round to support the cavalry on the left, when he was to attack them in the rear. But how was Alexander to ensure that the Indians concentrated all their cavalry on their left? Not, as Tarn suggests, by enticing them to attack his force, inferior after Coenus' departure, but by concentrating *all* his cavalry (except Coenus' force) on his right wing. Including the Iranians, he would have a total of at least 4000 and perhaps 5000 in this sector, a local superiority of at least two to one. This would compel Porus to transfer his cavalry from the right to even the odds.

Alexander opened the attack by sending his mounted archers, 1000 strong, against the cavalry on the enemy left and before the Indians could recover launched the Companions at their flank. Meanwhile the Indians were assembling all their cavalry on this wing, as Alexander had planned, when Coenus took them in the rear, causing them to face both ways. The Indians did not wait to fight it out, but retired hastily to the shelter of the elephants. The Macedonian infantry now advanced to meet the beasts, which tore great gaps in their ranks. The Indian cavalry was emboldened to charge the Macedonian horse but once again was forced to retreat and, as the Macedonian forces encircled the Indians, the elephants began to inflict heavy casualties on their own side. As the beasts tired and the ring tightened, the Indian cavalry was almost wiped out and their infantry too suffered severely; when a gap opened up in the circle of the attackers, the surviving Indians took to their heels. Then Craterus and his men crossed the river and, taking over the pursuit from Alexander's weary troops, cut down the fugitives. The Indian losses are given by Arrian as 20,000 infantry and 3000 cavalry, which may well be substantially correct, but the Macedonian casualties, 80 infantry and 230 cavalry, including 20 Companions, are surely underestimated.

Porus was not among the dead—or the fugitives. Even when the battle was clearly lost he continued to resist until he was wounded, then retired slowly on his elephant. Finally, after almost killing Taxiles who had been sent to persuade him to surrender, he took the advice of an old friend, Meroes, and made his submission to Alexander. On being asked how he wished to be treated, Porus made the celebrated reply, 'Like a king', and Alexander treated him as one. Not only was Porus restored to his kingdom, but he received as much territory in addition. Our sources represent Alexander's generous treatment of the Indian rajah as stemming from his admiration for a gallant opponent but, while this view may accurately represent his feelings towards Porus, it does less than justice to his statesmanship. He knew that the Punjab could not be held by force alone, or at least not without more men than he could spare. He needed Porus to govern the territory east of the Jhelum, as Taxiles (subject to a satrap) governed that west of the river. Besides, Porus and Taxiles, although formally reconciled, were not likely to combine against him: each would act as a useful check on the other.

Immediately after the battle Alexander began the foundation of two cities, Nicaea on the site of the battle and Bucephala near Haranpur, from which he had set out to cross the river. For his favourite stallion, Bucephalas, now 30 years old, had died of exhaustion after the battle. At this time, too, he gave orders for the building of a fleet on which he planned, after his eastern campaign, to sail down the Jhelum to the Indus and thence to the sea.

STATESMAN SHIP.

Alexander gave his weary troops a month's rest, then set out east-wards. The weather was very bad, for it was now the height of the summer monsoon. Until he reached the River Hydraotes (Ravi) he encountered little opposition and many populous villages and towns surrendered to him. His victory over Porus had evidently convinced the natives that resistance was futile, and Abisares, the ruler of Kashmir, who had earlier planned to join Porus in opposing Alexander, now sent envoys with money and elephants to offer submission, pleading ill-health as a reason for not coming himself. In view of Abisares' previous attitude, Alexander sent envoys of his own to find out whether Abisares was telling the truth and, when they reported that he was indeed ill, permitted him to remain in office. Meanwhile news came that the 'bad' Porus had risen in revolt; for, now that Porus had become Alexander's ally, he feared his uncle's power. Hephaestion was sent to suppress the revolt and after accomplishing his mission handed over the conquered territory to the 'good' Porus.

East of the Ravi the tribesmen continued to submit until the Macedonians reached the territory of the Cathaeans (Kathas), foremost of the warlike Aratta (kingless) peoples of the Punjab. They had concentrated their forces at their capital Sangala, in the Amritsar district, and had taken up a strong position on a hill defended by a triple line of waggons. Only after two days of fierce fighting did the Macedonians succeed in storming the city. We need place little reliance on the reported Indian casualties of 17,000 dead and 70,000 captured, but the admitted Macedonian losses, 100 killed and 1200 seriously wounded, which are not likely to be overestimated, show how hard the Cathaeans had fought for their freedom. Sangala was razed to the ground and the territory of the Cathaeans bestowed upon those Indians who had surrendered. Two other cities, whose inhabitants had fled, were handed over to Porus to govern. This does not mean, as some have argued,[8] that Alexander was short of men, but merely that he wished to save his own troops for the campaigns that he planned east of the Hyphasis (Beas).

But on the Beas Alexander met opposition that proved insuperable, not from the enemy but from his own troops.[9] Knots of men gathered throughout the camp and voiced their unwillingness to go on. The army had marched a very long way since 334 and, although perhaps not more than half of the Macedonians can have fought in all the major campaigns, the majority of them must have endured the rigours of the Bactrian campaigns and the horror of the conflict with Porus' elephants. Their morale had been sapped by the burning heat and by seventy days of incessant rain. There were rumours, too, of great armies of Indians beyond the river possessed of hordes of the dreaded elephants. Most important, no one knew how far they were going, perhaps not even Alexander himself.

Can we deduce how far Alexander intended to advance?[10] Some scholars have maintained that he had in mind only a limited campaign, in the interests of trade or to safeguard Porus' kingdom. But his preparations do not suggest that he meant to turn back in the near future. The army which mutinied on the Beas comprised virtually all the men at his disposal: Coenus and Craterus, who had been left behind to collect provisions, had already rejoined and Porus had brought 5000 Indians and all his elephants during the attack on Sangala. Moreover, when Alexander returned to the Jhelum he found that some 5000 cavalry and at least 7000 infantry (Diodorus says 30,000) had arrived from Greece. These were surely intended to form part of the force that was to operate east of the Beas, had the army not mutinied. The order given by Alexander immediately after Porus' defeat for the construction of a fleet indicates that he had made up his mind to sail down the Indus to the sea. On the other hand, it need not mean that the voyage was to take place in the near future; not only would the timber require time to dry, but there was no need for Alexander to use his fleet immediately it was ready.

We must conclude, then, that Alexander meant to advance a considerable distance east of the Beas. But was his objective the eastern Ocean? In the speech which Arrian attributes to him at the Beas he implies that it was and asserts that the Ganges and the Ocean were no great distance away. But this would be the obvious thing for him to say on this occasion, and we have no means of telling which details, if any, in this speech are genuine. For it is assuredly not all authentic, since Alexander did not think, as he is made to say, that the Caspian sea was a gulf of the Ocean. Certainly he must long before this have discovered the falsity of Aristotle's belief that the Ocean could be seen from the summit of the Hindu-Kush.[11] Moreover, it is likely that Alexander knew something at least about the Ganges. Even if we reject the story, which occurs only in the 'vulgate', that Phegeus informed Alexander about the river and the tribes beyond it, the king must surely have inquired about the interior of India from Taxiles when he reached Taxila, the principal seat of Hindu learning, situated at the end of the great trade route from the East, to which scholars from all over India came to study. Porus, too, will not have been ignorant of the country east of the Beas. Finally, Nearchus wrote (what he could have learned only on this expedition) that the journey through the plains of India took four months.[12] All in all, it is difficult, if not altogether impossible, to believe that Alexander did not know in general, if not in detail, what lay ahead of him beyond the Beas.

His intention to advance, then, was not taken through ignorance, and he will not have expected to reach the Ocean, if he did intend to reach it, without hard fighting. On the other hand, the disunity of the Indian princes he had met so far will have encouraged him to believe that he could defeat his opponents *seriatim*, perhaps even with the assistance of those rulers he had already defeated or won over by diplomacy. It is sometimes assumed[13] that if he had gone on he would have been defeated. But Chandragupta, if he is correctly reported,[14] did not think so, and the speed with which this Indian ruler overthrew the kingdom of the Nandas suggests that the task which faced Alexander was less formidable than patriotic Indian historians would have us believe.

While we cannot, then, rule out the possibility that Alexander did intend to advance to the eastern ocean—he had, after all, overcome all obstacles so far and may have seen no reason why he should not continue to do so—there seems to me to be no evidence to support the statement that he was bent on reaching the eastern Ocean in pursuit of his desire for world conquest. It seems more likely that the considerations that influenced Alexander were military, that he proposed to continue his march until all effective resistance was at an end. This is Arrian's view[15]—whether it is backed by Ptolemy's authority is uncertain—and it seems to be supported by Alexander's evident intention to sail down the Indus to the sea.

A long silence followed Alexander's speech to his commanders until the veteran Coenus ventured to plead with him to return home. The applause that greeted Coenus' speech must have shown Alexander that his officers, like the men, had no stomach for further conquests. Next day, when a threat to call for volunteers failed to move the troops, he shut himself up in his tent like Achilles and remained there for three days, hoping for a change of heart. When this did not happen, he reluctantly accepted the inevitable but, to save face, offered sacrifice with a view to crossing the river. This, of course, proved to be unfavourable and amid general rejoicing Alexander announced his intention to turn back. As a memorial of his victorious advance he ordered the erection of twelve towers, one for each of the Olympians, 'as high as the loftiest siege-towers and even broader in proportion'. Then, assigning the territory west of the Beas to Porus, he returned to the Jhelum. At this time Coenus died and was given a magnificent funeral. That Alexander had forgiven his loyal but outspoken marshal, it would be rash to assert, but that Coenus' death was other than natural we have no reason to suppose.

By early November the great fleet was ready, 80 thirty-oared ships with horse transports and supply vessels, 800 in all, together with masses of smaller craft. The Phoenicians, Cypriots, Carians, and

Egyptians who had accompanied the expedition provided the crews. As admiral Alexander appointed his boyhood friend Nearchus, with Onesicritus as his second-in-command. On the ships were to travel the Guards, the Companions, the archers, and the Agrianians, perhaps because they had seen the hardest fighting. On the west bank of the river Craterus commanded a force of cavalry and infantry, while on the opposite bank Hephaestion led the bulk of the troops and the elephants. Philip, satrap of the territory west of the Jhelum, was to follow at three days' interval, evidently to mop up the Indians who escaped the forces of Craterus and Hephaestion; for Alexander had determined to subdue all opposition along the rivers down which he was to sail.

The day for departure came. As the troops embarked, Alexander sacrificed to the gods to whom he usually sacrificed and, on the advice of his seers, to the River Jhelum. Then, going on board his ship, he poured libations from a golden bowl to the same gods, to the Chenab and the Indus as well as to the Jhelum, to his goal the Ocean, to Poseidon, Amphitrite, and the Nereids, to his ancestor Heracles and his 'father' Ammon. Then he gave the signal to start. The trumpets sounded, the oars dipped in unison, and the ships got under way, followed down the river by crowds of Indians, singing their native songs and marvelling at the horses in the horse-transports.

The first stages of the voyage were peaceful enough and the tribes along the river submitted successively as Alexander put in at various places. Then he heard that the Malli (Mahlavas) and the Oxydracae (Kshudraka) were preparing to join forces to resist him. Alexander realized the danger and pushed on at full speed past the confluence of the Jhelum and the Chenab, where the fleet suffered severe damage in the whirlpools and the rapids, until it reached a point where the Chenab broadened out and the current became less swift. There he disembarked to carry out a brief campaign against the Indians who had not submitted, in order to prevent them from assisting the Malli. Then he rejoined his fleet on the borders of the Mallian territory, where the remainder of his army caught him up.

For his last major campaign Alexander had devised a bold and comprehensive strategy.[16] The Malli lived between the Chenab and the Ravi, the Oxydracae to the south of them. Alexander planned to cross a waterless desert, the Sandar-Bar, which protected the Malli on the west, then to move south and drive them and the Oxydracae into the arms of a force under Hephaestion which he had sent forward five days earlier. Ptolemy was to follow in the rear and intercept those Indians who tried to break back to the west.

With a picked force consisting of the Guards, archers, Agrianians, an infantry battalion, and half of the Companions, Alexander crossed

the desert, covering 50 miles in a day and a night, and took the first
town of the Mallians by surprise. Many of the Indians were caught
outside the walls and killed; the remainder fled into the town, but it
was taken in two assaults and the defenders butchered. Meanwhile
Perdiccas cut down the fugitives as they attempted to escape from a
second town. The massacre of the Mallians continued. Alexander
himself, after an all-night march, caught up with the stragglers as they
were crossing the Ravi and killed a great many of them, then he too
crossed and put to death or took prisoner still more. But the majority
escaped to a stronghold, only to be attacked by a force commanded
by Peithon and either killed or enslaved. Another group of Malli had
taken refuge in 'a city of the Brahmans', but here too their respite
was short-lived. For Alexander drove them first from the walls, then
stormed the citadel, where they fell fighting or were burned to death
in the houses they themselves in their desperation had set on fire.
However, it was at this time that the decline in Macedonian morale
became increasingly apparent, when the king had to lead the way up
a scaling-ladder in order to shame his troops into mounting the wall.

DECLINE IN TROOP MORALE

Detachments under Peithon and Demetrius, the cavalry leader,
were now sent back to scour the woods along the banks of the Ravi,
where some of the fugitives had taken refuge, and all who resisted
were put to death. The surviving Mallians, said to number some
50,000, had turned westwards again and recrossed the Ravi, prepared
to make a stand on the west bank. But such was the speed of Alexander's attack with his cavalry that they withdrew and, on the
approach of the infantry, fled to the strongest of the cities nearby.
Next day Alexander's men easily took the city wall and the defenders
were forced to retire to the citadel. Once again Alexander had to
mount the wall first, followed by Peucestas, Leonnatus, one of his
bodyguards, and an NCO named Abreas. Then the ladder broke
under the weight of the Guards who were trying to mount. As he
stood on the wall, Alexander was a conspicuous target for Indian
arrows. Characteristically, he leapt down *inside* the wall, and fought
off his attackers until the other three leapt down beside him. Abreas
was killed almost immediately, then the king was shot through his
lung by an arrow that pierced his breastplate. Peucestas protected
him on one side with the sacred shield of Ilium, while Leonnatus
guarded the other. Somehow or other they survived until a few of the
Macedonians, climbing on each other's shoulders or hammering
pegs into the mud wall, reached the top and jumped down into the
town. Then the gates were broken open and a wholesale massacre
ensued. Alexander was carried out on his shield half-conscious,
Perdiccas cut out the arrow with his sword and the king fainted,
stopping the haemorrhage.

The first report that reached the army and the fleet that awaited him at the junction of the Chenab and the Ravi was that Alexander was dead. Dismay succeeded grief as men wondered who was to take his place and lead them home. When news arrived that the king was alive, it was received with disbelief and even when a letter from him announced that he would soon arrive in the camp the men suspected that it had been composed by the officers. Accordingly, as soon as he was fit to be moved, Alexander sailed downstream, for he feared that the situation in the army might get out of hand. As his ship neared the camp, he ordered the awning under which he lay to be removed in order that the troops might see him. Even then they thought it was his corpse lying there, until he waved his hand. A great shout went up and, when he was carried ashore on a litter, mounted his horse and rode to his tent, then dismounted and walked a few steps, their joy knew no bounds. In a moving passage Arrian describes how the men ran to touch him, or gaze on him and bless him, while others garlanded him or threw flowers upon him. All was forgotten and for-given in their joy and relief at his survival.

IMP.
for attit.
of men.

When his friends reproached him for his foolhardiness, Alexander was angry, knowing, as Arrian rightly says, that their rebukes were deserved. Nevertheless, his leap had not been in vain, for it was probably this action as much as the capture of the town or his cam-paign of terrorism that led the surviving Mallians and the Oxydracae to send envoys making submission. They were subordinated to Philip, son of Machatas, the southern limit of whose satrapy was fixed at the meeting-place of the Chenab and the Indus. To garrison the country Philip was given a strong force of infantry, including the Thracians, and he was ordered to found an Alexandria and to con-struct dockyards at the junction of the rivers. The importance that Alexander attached to the Indus as a means of communication is shown by his foundation, a little further downstream, of another Alexandria and other dockyards.

COMMUNICAT
IONS.

The second half of his voyage to the sea was to involve no less fighting than the first. He came next to the kingdom of Musicanus, who had made no gesture of submission but now, surprised by the speed of the Macedonian advance, hastened to acknowledge his error. This secured his continuance in office, although his capital was fortified and a garrison installed to keep watch over the neighbouring tribes. The next ruler, Oxycanus, offered resistance but, when two of his towns were stormed and he was captured in the second of these, the remainder surrendered. Oxycanus was executed and the prisoners sold into slavery. A third king, Sambus, did not await Alexander, but fled across the Indus on hearing that his enemy, Musicanus, had been pardoned. However, the Brahmans inspired the populace with a fanatical hatred of the invader and there was clearly much bitter fighting about which Arrian is silent. Cleitarchus stated that 80,000 Indians were killed and large numbers sold into slavery, and in view of the slaughter that took place during the descent of the lower Indus he may not have exaggerated greatly.[17] News now came that Musicanus had revolted, and Peithon was sent to bring him in. Alexander himself dealt with the towns, destroying some and garrisoning others. The inhabitants were sold and Musicanus himself was hanged or crucified. The Brahmans, who here too had instigated the revolt, were executed.

By this time Alexander's plans for his return to the west were already made. This is clear from the fact that Craterus was now ordered to proceed through the Mullah pass into Arachosia and Drangiana to deal with the trouble that had been reported there and then to rejoin Alexander in Carmania. He was to take with him three battalions of infantry, some of the archers, and such Macedonians as were unfit for further campaigning, together with the heavy baggage and the elephants.

About the middle of July in 325 Alexander reached Pattala (perhaps on the site of Bahmanabad or Hyderabad), at the head of the Indus delta as it existed at that time, to find the city and the surrounding territory deserted. The governor of the district had earlier submitted to Alexander, but had now fled together with most of the natives. With unwonted clemency, perhaps connected with his need for settlers for Pattala, Alexander sent out troops to persuade the inhabitants to return, and most of them did so. The citadel of Pattala was fortified and, despite the attacks of the neighbouring tribesmen, wells were dug in the surrounding desert. Then the king gave orders for the construction of a harbour and dockyards which could accommodate a considerable fleet, for he had decided to make Pattala a major port.

From Pattala Alexander set sail down the western arm of the delta to the sea. At first he was unable to obtain any native pilots and several ships were damaged or wrecked in a violent storm; then, when they had taken refuge from the gale in a side channel, the fleet was left high and dry as the tide ebbed, much to the surprise of the Greeks and Macedonians, used as they were to the tideless Mediterranean. When the tide turned, they got a further surprise; for the onrushing water dashed the ships together and a number were lost. Near the mouth of the river Alexander discovered an island called Cilluta, where he left most of his ships before setting out to explore the passage to the sea. At the mouth of the river he sighted a second island standing out to sea, and at this island and at Cilluta he sacrificed to the gods to whom Ammon had ordered him to sacrifice, as a thank-offering for his successful voyage to the sea. Then, sailing out into the open sea, he made a sacrifice of bulls to Poseidon, and poured a libation. After this he threw into the sea the golden cup from which he had poured the libation together with the bowls, also of gold, in which he had mixed the wine for the sacrifice, before praying that the god would bring safe to the mouths of the Tigris and the Euphrates the fleet that he proposed to dispatch under the command of Nearchus. There is no reason to think that this was 'a great sacrifice of gratitude for the past', for Poseidon had nothing to do with the rivers down which the fleet had sailed. The sacrifice and the libation looked only to the future. The suggestion that these proceedings marked 'the proud and happy consciousness that he had reached a limit of the world' is equally untenable; for not only did Alexander sail only a short distance out to sea but, since Onesicritus, who wrote soon after Alexander's death, knew of the existence of Ceylon (Taprobane), so presumably did Alexander.[18]

Sailing back to Pattala, Alexander set out down the other arm of the delta to see which route was safer for his fleet. In his day—since then the shape of the delta has altered out of recognition—the eastern arm passed through a large lake near its mouth, which sheltered the channel from the south-west monsoon, and the king decided that the fleet should sail this way. Accordingly he rode along the coast with a small band of cavalry, selecting sites for wells to supply water for the fleet during its passage. Returning briefly to Pattala, he gave orders that part of the army should continue the work of digging wells, then returned to the lake. There yet another harbour and other dockyards were built and all necessary preparations, including the collection of four months' supplies—the expected duration of the voyage—were made. Alexander then returned to Pattala.

At this point it may be appropriate to outline Alexander's arrangements for the government of India. In the north-west Philip, son of Machatas, governed the most extensive and most important satrapy. At first he was appointed satrap of the territory between the Indus and the Jhelum with Taxiles subordinate to him. Later, since he is described in autumn 326 as 'satrap of the territory west of the Indus towards Bactria', he evidently also took over the region formerly governed by Nicanor. In the south the boundary of his province was fixed at the confluence of the Indus and the Chenab, but as he was also responsible for the territory of the Malli and the Oxydracae his rule extended as far as the Ravi and the Sutlej in the east. In late 325, when Philip was killed in a mercenary revolt, Taxiles was instructed, as a temporary measure, to take control of his satrapy with a Macedonian, called Eudamus, as general. However, at Alexander's death no arrangements had been made to replace him.

2.

To the east, between the Jhelum and the Beas, Porus was probably nominally satrap as well as king, but as Alexander left none of his own troops in this satrapy—although Hephaestion had built a city on the upper Chenab in which mercenaries were settled—he was virtually independent. This does not mean, as Tarn argued, that Alexander had decided to abandon his Indian conquests. The fighting along the rivers, the foundation of cities, the garrisons in the citadels, the building of dockyards, and the voyage of Nearchus all prove that Alexander was determined to link his eastern conquests with the west by sea as well as by land. Porus was still, technically at least, satrap and client king with, presumably, the right to call on other satraps for help, should he require it. To maintain Porus' loyalty Alexander doubtless counted not only on Porus' gratitude but also on the hostility of the other princes, especially Taxiles.

3.

The third satrap was the Macedonian Peithon, son of Agenor, who ruled the region bounded on the north by Philip's satrapy, on the south by the Ocean, on the west by Gedrosia and on the east by the Indus. Lastly, the important province of Paropamisus, which controlled the approach by land to India, was entrusted in late 325 to

4.

Alexander's father-in-law, Oxyartes. The previous governor, Tyriaspes, had been found guilty of misgovernment.

12

RETURN TO THE WEST

In a story which loses nothing in the telling Nearchus describes
Alexander's difficulty in choosing a leader for the naval expedition
and his reluctance to expose his friends and his fleet to danger. Yet it
is clear that the king had no doubts about the *feasibility* of the voyage.
What he feared was that on so long a voyage along so barren a
stretch of coastline the fleet would be unable to obtain provisions
and, more particularly, water; for the ships could carry only a few
days' supply. It was to be a voyage of discovery—Nearchus was
instructed to reconnoitre the coast, its harbours and nearby islands, to
explore any bays and report on any towns that existed, and to discover
the possibilities for agriculture—not a venture into the unknown.[1]

Indeed, Herodotus relates that in the reign of Darius I Scylax of
Caryanda had sailed down the Indus and along the coast as far as
Hormuz, where he turned south to circumnavigate Arabia and land
in the gulf of Suez. It will not do to argue, as some modern scholars
have done, that since no historian of Alexander even mentions
Scylax's name Herodotus was no longer read. For Nearchus' account
of his voyage bears unmistakable traces of Herodotean influence.[2]
Either Nearchus and Onesicritus kept silent about Scylax's voyage in
order to enhance the fame of their own achievement, or, if they did
mention it, subsequent writers did not think it important enough to
record.

Nearchus had planned to wait until the arrival of the north-east
monsoons about the middle of October, but the threatening attitude of
the natives forced him to advance his departure. About 21 September
he cut through the sand-bar at the mouth of the eastern channel of
the Indus and sailed west to 'Alexander's Harbour' near the site of
Karachi. There he had to wait for twenty-four days until the monsoons began.

Meanwhile, Alexander had set out with his army from Pattala at the end of August to march along the coast of the Makran. His intention was to support the fleet by digging wells and establishing dumps of provisions, and to subdue the Oreitae of eastern Gedrosia. But other less rational considerations also moved him to undertake this hazardous journey.[3] For his friend Nearchus attributes to him a desire to outdo Cyrus and Semiramis by leading a large army through country that had defeated them, and it is difficult to imagine that he is romancing. Indeed, this motive recalls Alexander's wish to emulate Perseus and Heracles by making a journey to Siwah. Alexander may well have felt that to achieve this superhuman feat would restore his reputation for invincibility, dented by the army's refusal to advance at the Beas. Whether he also planned to punish his troops for their contumacy by imposing upon them the hardships of this desert march seems more open to doubt.[4] But we need not hesitate to believe that Alexander was well informed of the risks involved, although he appears to have underestimated the difficulties facing a *large* force attempting to cross this waterless region. Possibly, too, the summer rains, on which he counted to fill the wells, had been less plentiful than usual.

The evidence for the size of Alexander's force is scanty. Plutarch states that he had 120,000 infantry and 15,000 cavalry, of whom only one quarter survived, and Nearchus, more credibly, says that he was accompanied by 120,000 fighting men at the start of the voyage down the Indus. Unfortunately, we do not know how many men were left behind in India or the exact number who followed Craterus by the inland route. Modern estimates of Alexander's army vary widely from 8000 to 70,000 men, with the higher figures being more probable. At any rate the lowest figures can be ruled out immediately, for in the territory of the Oreitae, when the bulk of his forces remained behind with Hephaestion, units totalling some 11,000 men accompanied Alexander.[5] We may be sure, then, that more (in all likelihood, many more) than 25,000 to 30,000 troops, plus a number of traders, women and children impossible to estimate, set out on the march.

On reaching the River Hab (Arabius), the eastern boundary of Oreitan territory, Alexander marched south to the coast, crossed the river and advanced through a desert region to the edge of the inhabited area. Dividing his cavalry into three groups, he systematically devasted the countryside and killed large numbers of the natives. The survivors fled to the Gedrosian border, where together with the Gedrosians they awaited Alexander's army at a defile, but on his approach they were deserted by their allies and submitted. Alexander could now be merciful, and the Oreitans were instructed to return to their homes without fear of punishment. To govern them he ap-

pointed Apollophanes and left Leonnatus with a strong force to put
the country in order and to take over from Hephaestion the task of
settling an Alexandria at Rhambacia, the Oreitan capital.[6] Leonnatus
had instructions also to collect provisions for the fleet at the nearby
port of Cocala. But the country was not pacified. Soon after Alexander's departure the Oreitae rose in revolt and, although they were
defeated in a great battle by Leonnatus in which they lost 6000 men,
the Macedonian casualties included the satrap, Apollophanes.

Meanwhile Alexander had entered Gedrosia. At first, despite the
shortage of food and water, he encountered no great difficulties. The
scientists who accompanied the expedition were able to observe the
flora and fauna and the Phoenician traders collected the gum of the
myrrh tree and roots of spikenard. Soon, however, he was forced to
leave the coast and march inland to skirt the southern spurs of the
Taloi range and to cross the Harrian pass. All this time the fleet
dominated his thoughts. He sent what provisions he could collect to
the shore, but his own men were so short of food that on one occasion
even the guards themselves broke the royal seal and distributed the
provisions. Alexander thought it advisable to pardon them—a
measure of their plight. Marches were made at night, but when they
extended well into the following day in order to reach the next stream
or waterhole, the lack of water and the scorching heat—the Swedish
explorer, Sven Hedin, recorded a shade temperature of 127° in the
region—imposed intolerable hardships on the marchers. Casualties
were very heavy among the baggage animals, which either died from
their exertions in the deep sand or were slaughtered by the troops for
food, a practice upon which Alexander thought it politic to turn a
blind eye. The waggons could not be dragged through the thick sand
and had to be burnt, and few of the men left behind regained the
main body. Ironically, when the army was encamped beside a stream
this was transformed by heavy rain in the mountains into a raging
torrent in a matter of minutes and many of the camp followers were
drowned; the soldiers escaped with their arms alone, some not even
with these. Then, to make matters worse, the guides lost their way in
the featureless desert where the wind had obliterated all landmarks.

Throughout this long agony Alexander displayed his great qualities
of leadership. He led the way on foot and shared the hardships
equally with the men. He drank no more than they did and on a celebrated occasion, when some of the troops had found a little water in
a creek and brought it to him in a helmet, he took the helmet and
poured out the water on to the sand. 'So extraordinary was the effect
of this action', comments Arrian, 'that the water wasted by Alexander
was as good as a drink for every man in the army.' At length the army
reached the coast again at Pasni, marched along the seashore to

Gwadur, then followed the regular route inland to Pura, the Gedrosian capital, in the Bampur district. Exactly sixty days had elapsed
since they left the territory of the Oreitae.

No sooner had Alexander reached Pura than he dismissed Apollophanes from his position as satrap of Gedrosia for failing to carry out
his orders, presumably to forward supplies to the army. It soon trans-
pired that he had acted precipitately when a dispatch arrived from
Leonnatus containing news of his victory over the Oreitae and of
Apollophanes' death in the battle. But was Alexander's haste due to a
desire to find a scapegoat for what had undoubtedly been a major
disaster in which thousands had perished?[7] The chief support for
this view comes from the (later) executions of Abulites and his son,
Oxathres, satraps of Susiana and Pareitacene respectively. The
official reason for their deaths was that Abulites had abused his
office, but Plutarch[8] relates that he had sent Alexander money
instead of provisions and adds the detail that Alexander killed
Oxathres with his own hand. In view of the tendency of the official
account (Ptolemy–Arrian) to exculpate Alexander, Plutarch's version
cannot be dismissed out of hand and the suspicion must remain that
Alexander was still, in Susa, seeking a scapegoat for a disaster for
which he was largely responsible and which seriously damaged his
reputation for invincibility.

At Pura the troops enjoyed a much-needed rest before marching
on by way of the Bampur and Halil Rud valleys to Carmania, where
supplies from Parthia and Aria awaited them together with camels
and transport animals. At Gulashkird Alexander was rejoined by
Craterus and the remainder of the army. They had marched by way
of the Mullah pass, Kandahar, and the lake of Seistan through
Arachosia and Drangiana, and brought with them the leaders of the
revolt which they had suppressed.

The revolt in Drangiana was by no means the only trouble in the
empire. Over five and a half years had elapsed since Alexander had
left Persepolis in pursuit of Darius, over four and a half since he had
crossed the Hindu-Kush into Bactria. In the interval the government
of the empire had gone on; tribute had been collected, reinforcements
sent east to Alexander, and orders relayed back. But as month succeeded month and Alexander continued to advance, his satraps were
encouraged to act more and more independently. Armies of mercenaries had been enrolled, subjects ill-treated or put to death, and
temples robbed. Worse still, far from stopping the wrongdoing, the
generals left behind in Media—Heracon, Agathon, the Thracian
Sitalces, and Coenus' brother, Cleander—had joined in, while
Harpalus, the Imperial Treasurer, had lived in royal splendour at
Babylon with his successive Greek mistresses, Pythonice and Glycera.

In fact, when the former died, he had erected a temple and an altar to Pythonice Aphrodite.[9] Yet the upheaval should not be exaggerated; by no means all the satraps had proved disloyal. Phrataphernes, the satrap of Parthia, for example, had sent his sons to Carmania with provisions, while Atropates, the Median satrap, had arrested a noble, Baryaxes, for attempting to seize power in the province. Nevertheless, the situation was serious.

Alexander must have acted without delay, for the four generals reported to him in Carmania according to his instructions with some six thousand of their troops. At the same time came representatives of the Medians to accuse them. The generals were arrested and tried for pillaging temples and ill-treating the inhabitants. Cleander and Sitalces were put to death either in Carmania or a little later in Persis, while Heracon, after being acquitted of the charge of oppression, was subsequently found guilty of plundering the temple at Susa and he, too, was executed. The fate of Agathon is unknown, but may be conjectured. Six hundred of their followers, who were implicated in their crimes, were also put to death. Having arrested this important group of generals, Alexander could now issue his decree to all his other generals and satraps to disband their armies of mercenaries.[10]

We have no reason to doubt that the four men had been guilty of the crimes with which they were charged, but Alexander's treatment of Cleomenes raises the suspicion that he did not act simply out of concern for his subjects' welfare. For Cleomenes, a Greek from Naucratis, who had usurped satrapal powers in Egypt, had been guilty of flagrant oppression of the natives; yet Alexander confirmed or at least tolerated his position and took no action against him. Indeed, after Hephaestion's death some months later, he wrote Cleomenes a notorious letter, which is beyond doubt genuine, in which he offered to pardon him for his past crimes and give him a free hand in the future, if he erected shrines at Alexandria in honour of Hephaestion.[11] The speed with which Alexander summoned the generals, from whom the greatest danger might be expected, suggests that fear for his own position may have been a powerful motive. Together they formed a formidable group, particularly if they had the backing of Harpalus and the money he controlled. Alexander's suspicious nature, sharpened by the experiences of his youth, had made him increasingly sensitive to the possibility of plots, and all our sources remark on his readiness to listen to informers. His very debt to these men for carrying out so promptly his order to kill their commander, Parmenio—an order which, I suspect, Alexander would have preferred not to have to give—may even have prejudiced him against them. To fear for his position and concern for his subjects

E

we should perhaps add a third motive, possibly more potent. For Curtius (X.1.7) relates that Alexander remarked that the generals' accusers had overlooked the gravest charge of all, despair of his own safety. They had, in other words, doubted his invincibility. Even if the remark is not authentic, it accords well with Alexander's character; for his self-confidence had kept pace with his success.

To celebrate his conquest of India and his army's escape from the Gedrosian desert, Alexander now offered sacrifice and held athletic and artistic contests. Doubtless the celebrations went further than this and gave rise to the story in the 'vulgate' writers that Alexander's progress through Carmania was a week-long Bacchanalian revel in which the king imitated Dionysus, travelling with his Companions in a waggon laden with jars of wine, while his drunken soldiers followed, singing and playing lyres and flutes.[12]

It was in Carmania that Alexander's fears for the safety of his fleet were set at rest. Nearchus tells, in truly epic fashion, of his landing at Harmozeia (Hormuz) at the mouth of the River Anamis, of his encounter with a straggler from Alexander's army, his march inland with a few companions and his meeting with the king. Nearchus stresses Alexander's anxiety for the fleet, not merely or principally for his old friend. At first Alexander did not recognize Nearchus and his companions; then, when he did, he thought that they were the sole survivors and wept. But did he weep for the loss of the men or for the failure of the enterprise, the blot on his record? When he learnt the truth, that all his ships, except four, were safely anchored at Hormuz, Alexander's joy was unbounded. He offered sacrifice for the safe arrival of the fleet, and athletic and artistic contests were held and a great procession took place, with Nearchus at its head.[13]

Nearchus had an enthralling tale to tell. He had left Karachi with the monsoon about the middle of October. Sailing along the coasts of Arabitan and Oreitan territory, he met Leonnatus at Cocala, where the sailors enjoyed a brief spell ashore while the damaged vessels were repaired; ten days' provisions were taken on board and malingerers among the sailors were replaced by some of Leonnatus' soldiers. At the mouth of the Hingol they came across a tribe of Stone Age savages, whose hairy bodies were clad in the skins of animals or large fish and who used their claw-like nails to tear open fish and even the softer types of wood. They had no iron, but hardened the tips of their spears in the fire.

The real difficulties of the fleet began when they reached the 'Fish-Eaters' who inhabited the coast of Gedrosia; for their supply of corn soon ran out and they had to depend on what they could obtain from the natives. So severe were their privations that Nearchus dared not let the crews ashore for fear they might desert. As their name implies, the 'Fish-Eaters' lived mainly on fish, caught in nets as the tide receded—for they had no boats—and eaten raw; for meal they used fish ground down. The richer among them lived in huts built of the bones of stranded whales. They evidently had a few sheep, for the mutton that Nearchus obtained tasted of the fish on which they were fed. Apart from mutton, the diet of the sailors consisted of dates and the 'hearts' of date-palms, although on one occasion they caught a few goats and on another seven camels found in a deserted village were slaughtered and eaten.

The voyage was not without its adventures, and Nearchus does not underestimate his part in them. Near an island sacred to the Sun a ship and its crew were lost without trace, and Nearchus compelled his unwilling sailors to land in order to disprove the local legend that all who set foot on the island vanished. At another time the expedition encountered a school of whales whose water-spouts terrified the men. But Nearchus ordered them to row towards the monsters, shouting and blowing bugles; thereupon, to their great relief, the frightened whales dived and came up astern without doing any damage.

When the fleet reached Carmania with its trees, its vines, and its abundance of corn and water, their troubles were at an end. One crisis remained. When they sighted Ras Mussendam, the eastern tip of Arabia, Onesicritus wanted to sail direct to it. However, Nearchus overruled him. They had been ordered, he said, to sail along the coast and observe the harbours and watering-places. So the fleet sailed on into the Persian Gulf and anchored by the River Anamis. Alexander was reluctant to expose his friend to further danger, but Nearchus begged to be allowed to complete the voyage and the king agreed that he should carry on to Susa.

On the way back to the coast Nearchus and his party came into conflict with various bodies of natives; for Tlepolemus, the new satrap, had not yet established his authority. When Alexander arrived in Carmania, the ruler of the province had been Astaspes, but he had been deposed (immediately, it would seem) and executed, allegedly for a wish to revolt during Alexander's absence in India. Possibly he was a scapegoat for the Gedrosian disaster. His successor, a Macedonian named Sibyrtius, cannot have governed Carmania for long before being appointed satrap of Gedrosia, including the land of the Oreitae, and Arachosia. In Gedrosia Apollophanes had been succeeded by a Greek named Thoas, but Thoas had since died, as had Menon, the governor of Arachosia. That Alexander should have entrusted this vast and disparate satrapy to a man whom none of our sources has previously mentioned is worthy of remark. Possibly he felt that recent events pointed to the need for an overall command to coordinate the administration and, where necessary, the military operations of the whole area, and saw in Sibyrtius a man possessing the necessary ability and loyalty.[14]

Early in 324 Alexander advanced into Persis by the main road to Pasargadae, leading the Companions, the fittest of the infantry, and a few archers. With his customary solicitude for his men, he sent the remainder under Hephaestion by the route along the sea-coast, where provisions were plentiful and the climate milder. At Pasargadae Alexander was very distressed to find that the tomb of Cyrus, whom he particularly honoured, had been broken into and all its contents removed except the golden sarcophagus containing the body of Cyrus and the divan on which it stood. Even the sarcophagus had been damaged in an unsuccessful attempt to remove it and the body thrown out. Aristobulus, who has left us a detailed description of the monument which tallies closely with its extant remains, was instructed to repair the damage and restore the tomb to its original condition, then to wall up the entrance and seal it with the royal seal. The Magi who guarded the tomb were interrogated, but even under torture they neither admitted their own guilt nor implicated others, and Alexander let them go free.[15]

Nevertheless, this crime may have led to another. On entering Persis, Alexander had found that the satrap, Phrasaortes, had died and that Orxines, a rich and distinguished Persian, had assumed control of the province. Soon after, Orxines was put to death on Alexander's orders. The official reason for his execution, given by Arrian, was that he had rifled tombs and put Persians to death without cause. Curtius, however, tells a different story, which seems preferable. According to this, Orxines' death was the result of his refusal to enrich Bagoas, the eunuch favourite of the king; for Bagoas, in revenge, bribed men to testify that Orxines had been responsible for plundering Cyrus' tomb.[16]

To succeed Orxines Alexander appointed Peucestas, a native of Mieza, on whom he had recently conferred a signal honour by creating him a Bodyguard in addition to the existing seven. This honour was his reward for his part in saving the king's life in the Mallian town, but his appointment to the satrapy he probably owed principally to his oriental mode of life. As satrap he adopted Persian dress and learnt the Persian language, the only Macedonian to do so, thereby earning the approbation of the Persians and of Alexander, and the disapproval of his fellow Macedonians.

It must have been about this time that Harpalus fled from Babylon with 6000 mercenaries and 5000 talents from the imperial treasury in the company of his mistress Glycera. Although he had been a boyhood friend of Alexander and had not suffered for his flight to Greece in 333, he knew that on this occasion he could expect no mercy for his misdeeds. He had seen the fate of various satraps and of the generals, whose removal had deprived him of possible allies; if he obeyed Alexander's order to disband his mercenaries, he would be left defenceless. Accordingly, instead of complying and awaiting the inevitable summons, he decided to make for Athens, where he had been granted citizenship for his assistance to the city during the famine of 330–326 and where he might perhaps hope to find support in challenging Alexander.[17]

Shortly before reaching Susa in February 324 Alexander was reunited with his fleet. Nearchus had completed his mission to explore the shores of the Persian Gulf as far as the mouth of the Euphrates and had sailed up the Pasitigris to meet the king. Once again games and sacrifices marked Alexander's relief at Nearchus' safe arrival and his joy at the success of the venture. At Susa an impressive ceremony was held to mark the end of the Indian campaign; for Leonnatus too had now returned. The men who had distinguished themselves were decorated, while Hephaestion and the other Bodyguards received golden crowns. Crowns of gold, too, were bestowed upon Peucestas and Leonnatus for their part in saving Alexander's life in India and upon Nearchus and Onesicritus for their historic voyage.

Alexander was now free to look to the future, and another ceremony, more lavish and more important, brought to a climax his policy of fusing Macedonians and Persians into a single race. The festivities, for which Chares doubtless made the arrangements and which he described in detail, lasted five days and leading tragic and comic actors, Indian conjurors, and musicians of every sort took part.[18] The ceremony itself took place in Alexander's great tent. This was nearly half-a-mile in circumference and held a hundred couches—Agathocles' tent, the largest building in Sicily, could hold only sixty. It was supported by 30-foot columns 'gilded and silvered and studded with precious stones', and luxuriously furnished with expensive carpets and curtains worked with gold. In this splendid setting Alexander and Hephaestion and 90 of the leading Macedonians and Greeks married in Persian fashion the noblest of the Medes and Persians. Alexander's second wife—he remained married to Roxane—was Barsine, the eldest daughter of Darius, while Hephaestion married her sister Drypetis, since Alexander wished their children to be cousins. According to Aristobulus, Alexander then took a third wife, Parysatis, the daughter of Artaxerxes III, wishing no doubt to link his monarchy with both branches of the Achaemenid house. Craterus' eminence was marked by his marriage to Amastrine, a niece of Darius, while Perdiccas became the son-in-law of Atropates, the wealthy satrap of Media, and Ptolemy and

Eumenes married the daughters of Artabazus. To all the brides Alexander gave generous dowries. But despite the honour that the king had done the Macedonian bridegrooms by this joint ceremony, few of them sympathized with his ideas and most of them made haste to rid themselves of their Persian wives at his death. A notable exception was Seleucus, the founder of the Seleucid dynasty, who had married Apame, Spitamenes' daughter.

At the same time Alexander gave wedding gifts to those Macedonians, 10,000 in all, who had previously 'married' native wives. This had nothing to do with his 'policy of fusion', which was confined to Macedonians and Persians, but was designed to improve his relations with his troops. That these relations stood in need of improvement is shown by another incident which took place soon after. Alexander, we are told, judged the time opportune for settling the debts of the army but, when he ordered a list of these debts to be made, only a few soldiers came forward to enter their names, for they suspected that the king wanted to find out who had been extravagant. Remarking merely that they should never suppose that their king told anything but the truth (!), Alexander ordered that the debts, which were found to amount to the surprising sum of nearly 10,000 talents, should be paid simply on the production of an IOU.

The soldiers' distrust of their ruler was heightened by the arrival at Susa of the 30,000 young Iranians, whom Alexander called his 'Successors'.[19] In 327 he had arranged for them to be taught Greek and to be trained as soldiers in Macedonian fashion, as part of his policy of treating Macedonians and Persians as equals; there may, however, be some truth in Curtius' suggestion that they would be hostages for the good behaviour of their parents during his Indian campaign. Wearing Macedonian clothing and carrying Macedonian equipment, they now proceeded to give a dazzling display of their skill and discipline, much to the annoyance of the veterans who suspected that Alexander intended to replace them with these young 'war-dancers', as they resentfully termed them. Their suspicions were natural, particularly in view of Alexander's name for the Persians, but probably unjustified. It is hardly conceivable that Alexander intended to rely entirely on Asiatic troops, and in 327 his relations with his men had not been such as to lead us to suppose—as recruitment of 30,000 Iranians in 324 might perhaps have done—that his object was to create a body of troops on whom he could depend to carry out his orders without question. More probably he intended in 327 no more than to make provision for a time when Macedonian infantry might become scarce and might need to be husbanded even more.

The growing discontent with his orientalizing policy did not deter Alexander from carrying out a reorganization of his Companion

cavalry which had the effect of increasing the non-Macedonian
element. Ever since 329 a limited, but growing, number of distinguished orientals had served in the Companions. Now, according to
Arrian, Alexander formed a fifth regiment (*hipparchy*), consisting
mainly, if we accept a probable emendation of Arrian's text, of
orientals.[20] This must mean that the eight (or more) regiments into
which the Companions had been grouped had at some stage been
reduced to four. This has been thought to have taken place after the
march through Gedrosia and to have been, in part at least, the result
of the losses sustained there. This is very probably correct; only we
must beware of thinking that the losses among the Companions were
anything like 50 per cent. For it seems likely that the four (and later
five) regiments formed after the return to the west consisted (nominally) of 1000 troopers each. At any rate Hephaestion's regiment was
to be known after his death as 'Hephaestion's *Chiliarchy*', presumably
because it was a unit of 1000 men. At the same time as the fifth
regiment was formed, the most distinguished young Iranians were
enrolled in the special squadron (*Agema*) and armed with Macedonian
spears instead of their native javelins.

13

ALEXANDER AND THE GREEKS

Since 331 Alexander had had no cause to concern himself with the affairs of the Greek states. The failure of Agis' revolt had reinforced the lessons of Chaeroneia and Thebes; at Corinth, Chalcis, and Thebes Macedonian garrisons kept watch, while behind them, in Macedonia, stood Antipater at the head of a powerful army. In a few states, Sicyon, Pellene in Achaea, and Messenia, tyrants ruled in the Macedonian interest and with Macedonian backing, but most were controlled by politicians who, from conviction of self-interest, pursued policies if not of cooperation at least of acquiescence in the *status quo*.[1] Demosthenes had kept Athens out of the revolt and, although she had once again built up a formidable navy, it seemed as if only a threat to her vital interests could produce a reversal of her present policy.

Early in 324 Alexander was himself responsible for creating such a threat, when he announced to his assembled troops at Susa his intention of ordering the Greek states to recall their exiles, except those convicted of murder or sacrilege.[2] The states vitally affected were Aetolia and Athens: The Aetolians had expelled the inhabitants from the Acarnanian town of Oeniadae and occupied it, while the Athenians had in 365 seized Samos and established cleruchies there.

Why did Alexander choose this particular moment, when Harpalus might be conjectured to be making for Athens with a considerable force of mercenaries and a large sum of money, to issue his Exiles Decree? Was it an act of disinterested generosity? On the surface it might seem so, for many of the exiles had been driven from their homes and condemned *in absentia* by the oligarchic regimes that governed in the Macedonian interest. A closer examination of the situation, however, raises doubts whether the welfare of the exiles was uppermost in Alexander's mind. The decree seems rather to have

been the king's method of solving the pressing problem of the existence of masses of exiles and mercenaries, a problem caused largely by
his own policies;[3] for many of the exiles had taken service with
Darius and by no means all of them had chosen to continue as mercenaries with Alexander after he had abandoned his original policy
of treating them as traitors to the Greek cause. Again, not all the
mercenaries who had been settled as 'volunteers' in cities in the East
were content to remain there. We hear, for example, quite by chance
of one band of 3000 who left their posts and made their way back to
their homeland.[4] The number of these homeless men who roamed
Asia, a menace to peace and security, was greatly increased by Alexander's order to his satraps to disband their private armies. This
threat to law and order had overflowed into Greece; for at Taenarum
in Sparta an international market in mercenaries had come into
being, and at the beginning of 324 a regular ferry service from Asia
to Greece seems to have been established by the Athenian Leosthenes.

Alexander's handling of the problem was typically shrewd.
Nicanor, who later became the son-in-law of Aristotle, was dispatched to Greece to make the proclamation of the Exiles Decree at
the Olympic Games which in 324 began at the end of July.[5] News of
his mission was evidently well publicized, for Diodorus (18.8.5)
relates that 20,000 exiles flocked to Olympia to hear the announcement. In his message Alexander explicitly disclaimed responsibility
for the banishment of the exiles and claimed credit for their restoration. He had written to Antipater, he announced, instructing him to
compel the cities to receive back their exiles. Formally, Alexander
was no doubt correct in attributing their exile to the city authorities,
but in the final analysis he was as much responsible for this as he had
been for the destruction of Thebes in 335, when the decision had
been taken by the *Synhedrion* of the League of Corinth.

True, there were certain drawbacks in this solution. It meant that
the pro-Macedonian oligarchies in the cities would be faced with an
influx of potentially hostile citizens, although Alexander might hope
that the returning exiles would be grateful to him personally for their
restoration. Nor can he have been blind to the problems, revealed to
us in the extant inscriptions from Mytilene and Tegea, to which
claims for the restoration of the exiles' property would give rise.[6]
More important for Alexander's relations with the Greeks, the Exiles
Decree was an infringement of the terms of the League of Corinth,
which forbade any interference in the internal affairs of the member
states; for there is no evidence, despite assertions to the contrary,[7]
that Alexander troubled himself to go through the motions of consulting the *Synhedrion*. His action, in fact, only made explicit what
had long been the case, that he was not the executant of the League's

decrees, but its master. The greatest danger from Alexander's point of view lay in the reaction of Aetolia and, especially, of Athens, the key to any resistance in Greece to Macedon. No doubt he believed, and in this he was clearly correct, that Athens would fight for Samos only if all attempts at negotiation failed and that, if the worst happened, Antipater would be able to deal with any outbreak.

For the present the decree might be expected to reduce the number of mercenaries on whom Harpalus might draw, one reason perhaps why Alexander made his intention known to his troops several months before the Olympic Games. In the event Harpalus caused little trouble in Greece, at least to Alexander. After a necessarily long and circuitous journey, he reached the Piraeus shortly after Nicanor's arrival in Greece. But, although he was an Athenian citizen, he was refused admittance to Athens, for the Athenians feared him at the head of an army. Thereupon he took his forces to Taenarum and left them there together with the bulk of his treasure and all but three of his thirty ships before returning to the Piraeus. This time he gained admittance to the city. In the face of demands for his extradition from Antipater, Philoxenus, and Olympias, the Athenians compromised. They did not give Harpalus up but kept him under open arrest and deposited on the Acropolis the 700 talents he had brought with him. Some time later Harpalus managed to escape—doubtless he was assisted, but by whom is no longer clear—collected his troops, ships, and money from Taenarum, and sailed to Crete, only to be murdered there by one of his officers. In Athens he left behind him a legacy of trouble. After his escape half of the 700 talents was found to be missing and, following an inquiry by the Areopagus that dragged on for six months, a number of leading politicians, notably Demosthenes and Demades, were declared to have accepted bribes. Those named were then tried; Demosthenes, Demades, and one or two others were convicted and fined and when they could not pay went into exile.

Alexander's dominance threatened not only the political independence of the Greek states, but their religious freedom as well. Plutarch and Aelian, clearly drawing on a common source, state that he wrote to the Greeks requesting them to grant him divine honours.[8] Since none of the historians of Alexander mentions this request—there is, however, a lacuna in Arrian's text at this point—the statement is sometimes rejected but, in my view, wrongly.

We can catch just a glimpse of the debate about the grant of divine honours to Alexander that late in 324 divided Athenian politicians along lines, it seems, rather of policy than of religious conviction. The orators Pytheas and Lycurgus waxed sarcastic at Alexander's expense, Demades warned the Athenians not to lose the earth by guarding the heavens (a reference, evidently, to Samos), while Demosthenes, after opposing the proposal, is said to have remarked, 'Let Alexander be the son of Zeus, and of Poseidon too, if he wants to be.' Elsewhere in Greece we hear only of the ironical utterance of the Spartan Damis who said, in true Laconic style, 'Since Alexander wants to be a god, let him be a god.'

That the Greek states did grant divine honours to Alexander is certain, and should never have been denied; for Arrian[9] relates that in the spring of 323 envoys from the Greek states arrived at Babylon, wearing crowns, and crowned Alexander with crowns of gold. The gift of a gold crown, it is true, does not mark out the recipient as divine; we need only recall those bestowed on the Bodyguards at Susa. But the decisive point, often overlooked, is that the envoys themselves wore crowns. This indicates the recognition of Alexander as divine. When Arrian remarks that they came 'like sacred envoys indeed (ὡς θεωροὶ δῆθεν) to honour a god', he is not denying that the envoys acknowledged Alexander's divinity; he is implying sarcastically that Alexander was no god. For he goes on to comment, 'and yet Alexander's end was near'. How could Alexander be a god, for gods were immortal and Alexander clearly was not? Like the contemporary historian Appian and the biographer Plutarch,[10] Arrian did not hold with the worship of rulers: rulers were men.

Nevertheless, we must agree that the arrival of the *theoroi* does not *prove* that Alexander issued a request that he be worshipped. It is a legitimate argument that the initiative may have come not from the king but from his supporters in the cities, bent on winning the king's favour and embarrassing their opponents. However, since Arrian implies that envoys came from a number of Greek states, this argument requires us to suppose that the idea of granting Alexander divine honours occurred to his supporters in the various cities independently, or that they collaborated more successfully than Greeks usually did. We must suppose, further, that his supporters took it upon themselves to act in this important matter on their own initiative without consulting the king. This presupposes a great deal and it seems to me altogether more likely that the initiative came from Alexander. The failure of the Alexander-historians to mention a request is not decisive against its existence—they are silent, too, about the *granting* of divine honours—but it is possible that the king may have made his wishes known to his supporters more informally. It makes little difference to his attitude to divinity which method he pursued.

Regarding Alexander's motives for desiring divine honours, we are, as usual in any question of motive, reduced to conjecture. The theory, frequently advanced, that Alexander sought deification from the

Greeks in order to obtain the right to interfere in their internal affairs to enforce his Exiles Decree has been completely exploded and need not detain us.[11] There is no connection, not even a temporal one, between the decree and the grant of divine honours. Nor is it plausible to suppose that Alexander sought to become the god of his empire.[12] So far as we know, the request (if he issued one) was confined to the cities of mainland Greece—certainly the *theoroi* are expressly said to have come from Greece—and affected neither Macedonia nor Asia, where he may indeed already have been receiving worship from the Ionian League and certain cities, such as Ephesus.[13] It seems likely that Alexander considered that his achievements surpassed those of any other mortal, as well he might, and that in asking, formally or informally, for divine honours he was seeking recognition of these achievements. A similar attitude of mind surely underlies his approval of the painting of the court artist Apelles which depicted him wielding a thunderbolt. Some scholars have found it impossible to believe that the king 'sat' for such a portrait, but the truth of the statement is strongly supported by the issue of the very rare 'Porus' decadrachms. These coins, or rather medallions, of which only three specimens are extant, must have been issued, at Babylon, in the last year of the king's life and they, too, show him on the reverse holding a thunderbolt.[14]

For the Greeks, or at any rate for some Greeks (for we need not suppose uniformity of belief), the barrier between gods and men had never been impassable. In myth Heracles is the outstanding example of a mortal who achieved immortality through suffering and toil, while in historical times the Samian oligarchs had in 404 set up altars, made offerings and sung paeans to the Spartan Lysander in gratitude for their restoration. Indeed, at the wedding festivities at Aegae in the same year Philip had had his image carried in a procession together with those of the twelve gods of Macedonia, an act which, at the very least, came close to claiming divine honours.[15]

How far Alexander was influenced by these Greek precedents, particularly perhaps by the events at the end of his father's reign and the apotheosis of his ancestor Heracles, we have no means of telling, but consciousness of his own greatness and of what he had achieved was probably the most important factor. To this we may add the effect of the visit to Siwah and the position he enjoyed as Great King. While we cannot *know* how Alexander was affected by the happenings at Siwah, it seems likely that he cherished the belief that he was the son of Ammon or Zeus; certainly mocking references to his 'father' roused him to fury, and in the letter to the Athenians about Samos, which appears to be genuine, he referred to Philip as his 'so-called' father.[16] To be the son of a god was, of course, not the same as being a god, but it did set Alexander apart from other men. Again, while the Persians did not worship their rulers and Alexander must have known that they did not, the pomp and reverence which surrounded him as Great King introduced a mystique into his position which we cannot altogether discount.[17]

14

THE LAST TWELVE MONTHS

At the beginning of the summer of 324 Alexander decided to follow the example of the Persian kings and withdraw from the scorching heat of Susa to the summer palace at Ecbatana, the modern Hamadan, in the mountains. First, however, he resolved to satisfy his 'longing' to visit the Persian Gulf. Leaving Hephaestion to lead the main part of the army to the Tigris, he embarked with the hypaspists and part of the Companion cavalry on the fleet and sailed down the River Eulaeus to the sea. His purpose was evidently to explore the possibilities for trade in the region, for it must have been at this time that he founded an Alexandria, later called Charax, between the mouths of the Eulaeus and the Tigris to handle exports from Mesopotamia.[1] Then, as he sailed up the Tigris, he destroyed the weirs which the Persians had built as a defence against attacks from the sea; they were, he said, unnecessary and, as he himself demonstrated, ineffective.

After being joined by Hephaestion and his force, Alexander continued up the river to Opis. There he summoned his troops to an assembly and announced his intention of repatriating those veterans who through age or wounds were unfit for further service, promising them a magnificent bounty. At this pronouncement the smouldering resentment of the Macedonians flared up into open mutiny. More convinced than ever that their king was seeking to get rid of them and replace them with the 'Successors', they shouted to him to discharge them all and carry on with the help of his 'father'. This mocking reference to Ammon brought a swift response from Alexander, conscious of his good intentions and, allowing for all exaggeration in our sources, clearly more irascible than at the start of the expedition. Leaping down from the platform on which he stood, he ordered his guards to arrest the ringleaders and march them off to execution.

Then, remounting the platform, he bitterly attacked the men for their ingratitude. His father Philip, he said, had civilized Macedon and made it master of the states of Greece; but his own achievements were far greater. Starting with a load of debt, he had led them into Asia, he had won satrapy after satrapy, city after city, not for himself but for them. They, not he, had gained wealth and position, although no man had suffered more wounds than he had. Their debts had been paid, and no questions asked. As for the dead, they had received fitting honours and their dependants had been suitably cared for. He had intended, he concluded with bitter sarcasm, to send home only those past fighting; now they could all go and tell their fellow-countrymen that they had abandoned their king among the barbarians. 'This news will surely win you praise on earth and reward in heaven. Go!'

For two days Alexander shut himself up in his palace, taking no food and refusing to see anyone. However, the Macedonians made no move to submit. Then, on the third day, Alexander played his trump card. He issued orders for Persians to be enrolled in the Macedonian units and for these to be called Persian Companions, with a Persian *agema*, and Persian hypaspists, and allowed only his Persian 'kinsmen' to kiss him. This move produced the desired result. The Macedonians rushed to the palace and refused to leave until Alexander forgave them. Alexander had won. He came out, weeping, and in response to the complaint that he was allowing only Persians to kiss him declared, 'I make you all my kinsmen', and permitted all who wished to kiss him. To mark the end of his differences with his men and, by implication, the reconciliation of the Macedonians and Persians, Alexander held a great feast at which 9000 were present. With Alexander sat the principal Macedonians, next came the most distinguished Persians, then the leaders of 'the other peoples', and Alexander prayed not for 'the brotherhood of man', as Tarn has so eloquently misinterpreted him, but for 'harmony and partnership in rule between Macedonians and Persians'.[2]

Alexander now proceeded with his original plan to send home those veterans who were unfit for further service, giving them not only their arrears of pay but payment for the time of their journey home and adding a bonus of a talent for each man—a magnificent bounty, indeed. Such openhandedness was characteristic of Alexander—his mother Olympias is said to have reproached him for it[3]—but on this occasion the king may well have intended his generosity to encourage others to enlist. To avoid trouble in Macedonia, Alexander told the men to leave behind the children they had had by native women, promising to bring them up and train them in Macedonian fashion, and to bring them to Macedonia when they were grown up.

To conduct them home Alexander appointed Craterus (with
Polyperchon as his second-in-command, since Craterus was in poor
health), an appointment which convinced the men, we are told, that
the king had their welfare at heart. While this may have been so, we
may suspect that Alexander had other reasons for his choice than
Craterus' undoubted abilities and his popularity with the troops. Not
only did Craterus lack sympathy for his orientalizing policy but he
and Hephaestion were bitter enemies, and his presence blocked the
advancement of Hephaestion, Alexander's dearest friend and a
wholehearted supporter of his policies, to the position of second-in-
command.

Craterus was ordered on his arrival to take over Antipater's
functions as ruler of Macedonia, Thrace, and Thessaly, and as
Alexander's deputy in his capacity as *Hegemon* of the Corinthian
League. Antipater was to join Alexander, bringing fresh drafts of
Macedonian troops to replace the veterans who had returned home.
Why did Alexander decide to replace Antipater at a time when
Greece was in a ferment over the Exiles Decree and the question of
granting divine honours to Alexander? Arrian[4] regards the change as
being due to Alexander's desire to put an end to the long-standing
quarrel between the regent and Olympias, but modern research has
rightly found this reason inadequate. Tarn and Wilcken hold that
Alexander's new policy of promoting the unity of the Greek states—
as they interpret the Exiles Decree—required a new man; for Antipater's policy was too 'oligarchic'.[5] This seems based on a misinter-
pretation of the Decree which, it is clear, was just as unpopular with
the Greeks as Antipater's 'oligarchic' policy. More persuasive is
Badian's suggestion[6] that Alexander's reason for removing Antipater
was his suspicion that, as his mother kept telling him, Antipater had
during his absence in India built up a position in Macedonia and
Greece that threatened his own. Such a motive would accord with
Alexander's nature, always suspicious and made more so by the
conduct of the generals and the Harpalus affair. But it is far from
certain that he had determined to put Antipater to death. Removed
from Macedonia, the regent was no threat, as Parmenio in Media
had been, and Alexander was no butcher.

His intention to 'liquidate' Antipater would not be proved, even if
the regent had feared such a fate and taken measures to prevent it.
But did he take precautions? Certainly Plutarch relates that he
entered into treasonable negotiations with the Aetolians, although he
makes no mention of the Athenians. But, as Griffith has pointed out,[7]
Antipater would naturally deal with the protests of the Aetolians
against the provisions of the Exiles Decree, and such contacts could
be misunderstood or misrepresented in the light of the rumour put

about after Alexander's death that he had been poisoned by Antipater's son Iolaos at his father's instigation. Again, had Antipater
determined to resist Alexander, would he have sent his elder son
Cassander to Alexander's court early in 323 and so made him a
present of a valuable hostage? However, as Badian rightly stresses,
the slow progress made by Craterus needs to be explained; for,
leaving Opis in August or September 324, at Alexander's death in
June 323 he had not advanced beyond Cilicia. Had Antipater refused
to leave Macedonia, and did Craterus deliberately avoid a trial of
strength with him? Or can another explanation be found for the
delay? Griffith suggests that Alexander may not have wished the new
recruits to meet the veterans and hear unfavourable stories from
them. Alternatively, we might suppose that the slow progress is
sufficiently explained by Craterus' ill-health and perhaps also by the
condition of the troops, some of whom may have been in poor shape.
The army would, of course, spend several months in winter-quarters.
It seems clear, too, that the new recruits were not required for the
forthcoming Arabian expedition, and Alexander may have told
Craterus to take his time, particularly as Antipater might be supposed
to have a good deal to do before leaving Macedonia. On the whole
the evidence that Antipater so feared Alexander's summons that he
resorted to treason seems inconclusive.

At Ecbatana Alexander appears to have enjoyed a well-earned
rest, for we hear only of athletic and artistic contests and of his
drinking with his friends. But doubtless he was occupied with planning his Arabian expedition and the other projects which he set on
foot immediately on his return to Babylon. During his stay in the
Median capital the King suffered a terrible personal loss when
Hephaestion, whom he had raised to the post of Chiliarch or Grand
Vizier, a post which marked him out as second man in the empire,
died from excessive drinking. Hephaestion's promotion was probably
the result not so much of his military and administrative abilities,
considerable though these were, as of the affection that Alexander
felt for his boyhood friend and of Hephaestion's complete devotion
to his policies. We need not hesitate to believe that they saw themselves as Achilles and Patroclus; indeed, the violence of Alexander's
grief at his friend's death suggests that they had been lovers. Some of the
more bizarre manifestations of his grief, the hanging of Hephaestion's
doctor, for example, and the razing of the temple of Asclepius at
Ecbatana, we may reasonably attribute to the hostility, or the
partiality, of historians towards the two men.[8] But we have no reason
to reject the statements, made by all our sources, that Alexander lay
for three days without food and that he decreed general mourning
throughout the East. Indeed, we should probably accept the

unsupported statement of Diodorus (17.114.4) that he ordered the sacred fires to be extinguished throughout the empire, an action taken by the Persians only on the death of their king. To preserve Hephaestion's memory, he ordered that the cavalry regiment which he had commanded should continue to be called 'Hephaestion's Chiliarchy', although Perdiccas must have succeeded to this command and to Hephaestion's position of Grand Vizier.[9]

But this was not enough to assuage the king's sorrow. He resolved to erect a lasting memorial to his friend at Babylon and entrusted the task to Deinocrates, the Rhodian architect who had planned the city of Alexandria in Egypt. If the story is true, that Alexander had earlier declined his offer to convert Mount Athos into a monstrous memorial to him, Deinocrates must have welcomed this opportunity to display his talent for colossal sculpture.[10] Diodorus (17.115) has preserved a detailed description of the monument.[11] It rested, he tells us, on a foundation 200 yards square and reached a height of about 200 feet. There were five storeys, each smaller than the one below, a shape clearly influenced by the Babylonian ziggurats. The exterior walls were elaborately ornamented. On the bottom course were depicted in gold the prows of 240 triremes, bearing kneeling archers and marines larger than life size. Above these stood flaming torches over twenty feet high on which perched eagles with outspread wings, looking down at serpents which gazed up at them. On the third storey was portrayed an animal hunt, and on the fourth a Centauromachy. Above these stood alternate golden lions and bulls, while on top of the five storeys were set Macedonian and Persian arms, symbolizing the union of the two peoples and not, as Diodorus thought, their respective victories and defeats. On the summit of the whole edifice stood hollow Sirens within which singers could be concealed to sing a lament for the dead man. That Alexander should have approved of such a monument as this, costing 10–12,000 talents, is indicative of the strength of his feelings. It is no surprise after this that Alexander should have resolved to institute a cult of the dead Hephaestion. Accordingly, he dispatched envoys to Siwah to ask his father Ammon whether he should honour him as a god or as a hero. Meanwhile Perdiccas was ordered to convey the corpse to Babylon, where a magnificent funeral was planned. No fewer than 3000 competitors were hired to appear in the most lavish athletic and artistic contests yet held.

Recovering at length from his grief, Alexander embarked upon a campaign against the Cossaeans, a tribe of nomads living in the mountains north of Susa. They had been accustomed to exact tribute from the Persian kings as they passed through their territory and had made no gesture of submission to Alexander. They found, as others before them had found, that mountain fastnesses and winter conditions were no protection against Alexander. Within forty days they were forced to submit, after suffering many defeats and seeing their country devastated, in order to secure the release of their captives. Among them Alexander founded a number of cities at strategic points to hold down the country and to encourage the Cossaeans to abandon their brigandage and follow a settled existence.[12]

News of Alexander's victorious return from India had by now reached the west and, as he advanced towards Babylon, he was met by envoys from the states of Europe and Africa offering congratulations.[13] From Africa came Libyans and, possibly, Carthaginians and Ethiopians, from Italy Bruttians, Lucanians, and Etruscans, and from the far west of Europe, according to some accounts, Gauls and Spaniards. No one knew the extent of his ambitions and the friendship or neutrality of the master of the east was worth securing, in case he should have in mind a campaign against the west. The presence of Carthaginian envoys would not be surprising, for Cyrene was already an ally of Alexander and a great empire might well seem a likely target for his ambition or his resentment. Moreover, Carthaginian envoys had been captured in Tyre, and support for the Greek cities in Sicily would afford a plausible pretext. The Lucanians and Bruttians had even better reason to secure Alexander's goodwill, since his brother-in-law, Alexander of Epirus, had fallen to the dagger of a Lucanian deserter in 331–330 during his war against them. The hardest question to answer is whether the Romans sent envoys. Cleitarchus, not the best of witnesses, stated that they did and may have claimed to have seen them, but against this we must set the silence of Ptolemy and Aristobulus, which some have considered decisive.[14] However, the Romans, who had concluded an alliance with Alexander of Epirus less than ten years earlier and who were now involved in a bitter struggle with the Samnites, may have sought to conclude an alliance with Alexander or at least to secure his non-intervention. Nevertheless, certainty is impossible. Alexander will doubtless have welcomed this massive recognition of his prestige and power, but if specific requests were made to him we know nothing of them.

Alexander had crossed the Tigris and was approaching Babylon when he was met by the priests of Marduk. They begged him not to enter the city at this time for, they said, they had received an oracle from the gods prophesying that, if he did, misfortune would befall him. Alexander, however, suspected that their advice was not disinterested; for the rebuilding of the temple of Marduk which he had ordered during his first visit to the city had made little progress and meanwhile the priests enjoyed the revenues from the temple estates normally expended on repairs to the fabric of the temple and on sacrifices. Accordingly he refused to postpone his entry. However, he did try to fulfil their further request, that he enter the city from the east, but the purpose of the priests soon became apparent when the marshes made it impossible for him to advance eastwards. Nevertheless, Alexander did not abandon his intention of entering the city and passed into Babylon by the western gate. Naturally, his death occurring soon after was interpreted as confirmation of the oracle.

That Alexander should have attempted to comply with the priests' second request is characteristic of the regard in which he held seers and priests as interpreters of the will of the gods. The same attitude of mind is revealed in two incidents which occurred a little later. On one occasion, when Alexander was sailing in the marshes, his hat and diadem were blown off and the diadem came to rest on the reeds near the tombs of the Assyrian kings—a bad omen. One of the sailors swam out to recover it and to keep it dry bound it round his head. The sailor was rewarded with a talent, but was then executed on the seers' advice since he had worn the diadem.[15] Then one day, when Alexander had left the royal throne vacant, a man, perhaps an escaped prisoner, sat upon it and, according to some accounts, put on the royal robe and the diadem. He, too, was put to death on the advice of the seers.[16] Plutarch, indeed, depicts the king in his last months as surrendering himself completely to superstition, but his picture is clearly exaggerated.

Certainly, during this period Alexander displayed quite remarkable energy. No sooner had he entered Babylon than he intensified his preparations for the Arabian expedition, which had begun some months earlier. Orders for the reconnaissance of the coast of Arabia must have been sent from Ecbatana, if not earlier, as had orders for the construction of a fleet. When Alexander reached Babylon, he found there not only the ships which Nearchus had commanded but another fleet of some fifty vessels, mostly thirty-oars, already arrived from Phoenicia. They had been sawn into sections, taken overland to Thapsacus, reassembled, and sailed down the Euphrates. Still more ships were being constructed at Babylon from the cypresses that abounded in the district, for Alexander realized, at least partly, the magnitude of the enterprise.

He had sent out no fewer than three separate captains in thirty-oared vessels to explore the coast and the offshore islands. Archias had reached Bahrein (Tylus), while Androsthenes carried out a detailed investigation of the Gerrhaean coast and Bahrein, clearly with a view to their settlement. His report has perished but traces of it can be seen in Theophrastus' *History of Plants*. The last of the three, Hieron of Soli, had orders to sail right round the peninsula to

Heroopolis on the Red Sea, but on reaching Ras Mussendam he prudently returned to report to Alexander that the coast of the peninsula was almost as long as the coast of India. About the same time Anaxicrates was dispatched from Egypt to circumnavigate the peninsula from the west but, although he succeeded in rounding Bab el Mandeb, he was compelled to turn back off Hadramaut through lack of water.[17]

The reason given by Alexander for his expedition, that the Arabs had sent no embassy to do him honour, is rightly regarded by Arrian as a mere pretext. There is a good deal of truth in his view that Alexander had an insatiable thirst for extending his possessions; at any rate it is inadequate, if not positively wrong, to say, as Tarn does, that he had in mind 'primarily a naval expedition and voyage of exploration'. While it is true that on this occasion Alexander planned to accompany the fleet, a considerable army was an integral part of the force and his objective was nothing less than the conquest of Arabia, or at least of the coastal regions. We have it on the excellent authority of Aristobulus that the king was well aware of the wealth of the country and that the size of Arabia, so far from being a deterrent, was a stimulus to his ambition. Aristobulus also tells us that one of the motives for the expedition was the refusal of the Arabians to worship him as a third god alongside Uranus and Dionysus—an irrational motive paralleled by those put forward for the visit to Siwah and the march through Gedrosia. Nevertheless, the conquest of Arabia was part of a magnificent plan to link India with Egypt. The fine harbours in the Persian Gulf were to provide shelter for his fleets and sites for cities, and the offshore islands were also to be settled. The vast harbour capable of holding a thousand ships which Alexander had begun to construct at Babylon was surely meant to accommodate merchant ships as well as warships, and trade was to flow freely from one end of the empire to the other.[18]

The discovery that the Persian Gulf was an inlet from the Ocean had led Alexander to doubt that the Caspian sea was a lake, as Herodotus and his tutor Aristotle had believed. Might it not be, as many had thought, a gulf running in from the northern Ocean, balancing the Persian Gulf on the south? Shortly after leaving Ecbatana, therefore, Alexander had sent Heracleides to Hyrcania with orders to fell timber and build warships to explore the Caspian. However, it was not, we may conjecture, simply a disinterested passion for geographical discovery that led him to dispatch Heracleides, but rather a desire to find a connection in the north between India and the heart of his empire. Unfortunately, Alexander's early death led to the cancellation of the mission, and when Patrocles was sent by Antiochus I to explore the Caspian about 284–283 he reported that it was a gulf, and this report was generally taken to be true until the four-teenth century.[19]

While the ships were being built at Babylon and the great harbour was being excavated, Alexander was not idle. As the prosperity of Assyria depended upon the Euphrates, the Persian kings had pre-vented too great a flow in the summer by the construction of the Pallacopas canal, which drained off the excess water into the marshes and canals in the south and thence into the Persian Gulf. At the beginning of winter the outlets from the Euphrates into the Palla-copas were blocked up to prevent the level of the Euphrates from falling too far and leaving insufficient water to irrigate the Assyrian plain. However, these outlets, being cut through soft mud, were not entirely satisfactory in preventing the outflow of water. Hence Alexander, finding a spot some 4 miles below the junction where the ground was stony, constructed outlets at that point and so prevented the seepage. Then he sailed on down the Pallacopas to the lakes, where near the Arabian desert he built and fortified yet another Alexandria, probably to guard against incursions by the Bedouin tribesmen, and settled in it some of his mercenaries, some volunteers, and men unfit for service.

On his return to Babylon Alexander found that Peucestas, the satrap of Persia, had arrived with 20,000 native troops, mostly archers and slingers, together with some of the neighbouring Tapur-rians and recently-conquered Cossaeans. From Caria and Lydia came the respective satraps, Philoxenus and Menander, both bring-ing armies, presumably reinforcements from Macedonia, as were the cavalrymen who arrived at this time with Menidas.[20] Alexander now carried out what was destined to be the final reorganization of his army. He abandoned the principle of a purely Macedonian phalanx and incorporated in it the newly-arrived Persians. In each column of sixteen men, the smallest unit of the phalanx, the three leading positions were occupied by Macedonian NCOs, while another Mace-donian NCO brought up the rear; the remaining twelve positions were filled by Persians armed with bows or missile javelins. This flexible combination was perhaps designed only for a campaign in which no large-scale battles were to be expected, and it is most unlikely that it represented Alexander's final thoughts on army organization; but his early death prevented the new formation from being put to the test.

It was during this period that envoys arrived from the Greek states. They came, we may be confident, not to congratulate Alex-ander on his successful campaigns in the east and on his safe return, as Arrian conjectures, but among other matters to state their case against the implementation of the Exiles Decree.[21] The only indication of their reception is the letter written by Alexander to the Athenians about Samos from which Plutarch preserves an extract. From this it appears virtually certain that Alexander recognized the Athenian claim to the island. At any rate at his death two or three months later nothing had been done to remove the Athenian settlers. In fact, they remained on the island until Perdiccas restored it to the Samians in the following year.[22]

Soon after the arrival of the Greek envoys the *theoroi* whom Alexander had sent to Siwah returned, bearing the god's reply. It was not lawful, proclaimed Ammon, to sacrifice to Hephaestion as a god, but sacrifices might be made to him as a hero. The king, we are told, welcomed the god's decision and henceforth Hephaestion received worship as a hero, a cult that in Athens at least outlasted Alexander's reign. It was now that the king wrote his notorious letter to Cleomenes, ordering very large and costly shrines (hērōa) to be erected to Hephaestion in the city of Alexandria and on the island of Pharos.[23] A magnificent state funeral was held, to which contributions were made by the neighbouring cities by order of Alexander and by the leading Macedonians of their own volition. This they did doubtless in an attempt to placate the king, not out of affection for Hephaestion; for he had been generally disliked by his fellow-Macedonians.[24] Alexander himself offered the first sacrifice and no fewer than ten thousand victims were slaughtered. Then the period of official mourning came to an end.

It was now late in May, and the time for the expedition to start was drawing near; the army was due to march on 4 June and the fleet to set sail on the following day. On 29 May Alexander made the customary offerings for a successful outcome and sacrificed as his seers directed, then distributed victims and wine to his troops. In the evening a great feast was held in honour of Nearchus, who was again to command the fleet. When Alexander had left and was about to go to bed Medius, one of his most trusted Companions, invited him to a smaller, and wilder, party. At this party Alexander drank heavily, as he quite often did, and after bathing slept until dinner. Then he dined again with Medius and drank late into the night but, feeling the onset of the fatal fever, broke off drinking and after a bath slept where he was in the bath-house. On 31 May he had to be carried on a litter to perform the usual sacrifices, a duty he continued to perform until his illness made it impossible; then he gave his officers instructions about the Arabian expedition. In the evening he was carried from the palace on the west bank of the Euphrates across the river to the gardens. The healthier situation seems to have helped, for next day he talked and played dice with Medius and gave orders for his officers to meet him on the following morning. Despite a high fever during the night, he talked with Nearchus and the other leaders about the forthcoming voyage, and although his fever continued unabated he did the same on the next three days. On 6 June, although he was still able to perform his daily sacrifice, he ordered the generals to wait in the courtyard and the other officers to bivouac in front of the gates until morning. But on the 7th his illness was so serious that it was thought advisable to carry him back to the palace and when the officers arrived he was already beyond speech. His condition gradually deteriorated during the next two days. When the troops, suspecting that the king was already dead and that his death was being concealed from them, forced their way into the room where he lay, he could only raise his head with difficulty and give them a sign of recognition with his eyes as they filed past. On the night of 9–10 June five of his Companions and the two Greek seers, Cleomenes and Demophon, sought the help of the gods. After an all-night vigil in the , temple of the god, called Sarapis in the *Diary* but more probably Marduk, they inquired whether they should bring Alexander to the temple. But the god replied that it would be better if he remained where he was. Hence it was in the palace of Nebuchadnezzar that Alexander died towards evening on 10 June 323.[25] He was not yet 33 years old.

This is, in essence, the account of Alexander's last days given by Plutarch and Arrian, who both cite the *Diary* as their authority. From this it would seem that the cause of his death was a malarial fever which, as Schachermeyr has recently suggested, may have developed into leukemia.[26] However, a rumour soon circulated— inevitably, one might think, in view of his sudden and premature death—that Alexander had been murdered. It was alleged that Cassander, Antipater's son, had brought with him from Macedonia a deadly poison which was administered by his brother Iolaus, Alexander's cup-bearer. The instigator, of course, was said to be Antipater, whose relations with Olympias (and Alexander) were bad and who, in view of the summons to Court, had reason to fear for his life. Granted that Alexander was murdered, Antipater is the obvious suspect and a *prima facie* case could be established against him. But the use of poison cannot be established from the scanty data that the *Diary* provides; we may suspect (although I do not) that Alexander was systematically poisoned by doses of strychnine, but we cannot hope to prove it.[27] However, the fact that the testimony of the *Diary* can reasonably be advanced as proof that the king was poisoned does not encourage us to accept the hypothesis that the *Diary* was composed soon after his death, probably by Eumenes, at the behest of a group of generals who had arranged for him to be poisoned, for the express purpose of demonstrating that his death was natural.[28]

Even if the *Diary* is a 'forgery', which I regard as unproven, it may have been composed for reasons other than the concealment of crime, and the evidence for the formation of a junta by the generals before Alexander's death is far from conclusive. Admittedly, we cannot rule out the possibility that murder was committed and the lack of evidence may mean only that the conspirators covered their tracks skilfully; but it is equally likely that there was no plot.

15

ALEXANDER'S PLANS

The forthcoming Arabian expedition dominated Alexander's thoughts right up until his death. But was this to be his last major expedition? Did he intend at its conclusion to settle down to the tasks of administration and consolidation? It seems unlikely. Certainly there was a general expectation in antiquity that Alexander would undertake further conquests, even if there was no agreement about the details. At the beginning of the seventh book of his *Anabasis* Arrian tells us that 'some historians' said that Alexander intended to sail round Arabia and Africa and enter the Mediterranean to conquer Carthage and North Africa. Other writers, he adds, attributed to him the further project of sailing through the Black Sea and the Sea of Azov to campaign against the Scythians, while others again asserted that he had in mind to attack Sicily and Italy, spurred on by the growing power of Rome. Plutarch, too, writes of Alexander's intention to circumnavigate Arabia and Africa and enter the Mediterranean through the straits of Gibraltar, although he says nothing explicitly about conquest. Curtius, on the other hand, relates that Alexander proposed to complete the conquest of the coast of 'the Orient'—he presumably refers to the Arabian expedition—and then to embark upon a campaign against Carthage *from Syria*. This was to be followed by a voyage to Spain and along the northern coast of the Mediterranean as far as Epirus. For this expedition, we are told, 700 septiremes were to be built at Thapsacus and taken to Babylon—scarcely a convenient base for an expedition from Syria![1]

In fact, we need not take these speculations seriously. Arrian evidently thought that the 'plans' given by his sources did not represent Alexander's intentions. What these were he declined to guess. Nor can we suppose that Plutarch and Curtius preserve authentic information that escaped Arrian.

However, the plans given by Diodorus in the eighteenth book of his *History* are another matter.[2] The setting is circumstantial and Diodorus' source is almost certainly the reliable historian, Hieronymus of Cardia, whose patron was Eumenes, Alexander's chief secretary, who of all men ought to have known the truth. Alexander, we are told, left behind notebooks (*hypomnemata*) containing a number of plans. These plans Perdiccas, to whom the king on his death-bed had handed his ring, considered extravagant and expensive and wished to have annulled. But, fearing to act on his own authority, he presented them to the assembled Macedonians at Babylon for their verdict.

The most important plan was one to construct 1000 warships, larger than triremes, for a war against the Carthaginians and the other inhabitants of the western Mediterranean. For this a road was to be built along the coast of north Africa and harbours and dockyards were to be constructed in the eastern Mediterranean. Many historians, perhaps a majority, have considered the plans genuine and have credited Alexander with the project of large-scale western conquests.[3] A minority, notably Tarn and Hampl, have contended strenuously that they are pure invention, but their arguments, Tarn's in particular, must in many cases be rejected.[4] Still, the plans have disquieting features, which their defenders tend to minimize.

In itself the plan for the conquest of the west is not impossible to accept; perhaps, given the confidence and ambition of an Alexander, it is not even improbable. If such an expedition was planned, the number of ships envisaged is not unreasonable when one thinks of the combined strength of the navies of Carthage, Syracuse, the Etruscans, and Athens, whose relations with Alexander at this time were, to say the least, strained. On the other hand, it is not convincing to argue that the figure of 1000 warships given in the plans derives any support from Aristobulus' statement that Alexander began the construction of a harbour at Babylon to accommodate 1000 warships.[5] The plans ought not, one would think, to refer to projects already under way and the harbours for the expedition are explicitly said in the plans to be situated in the Mediterranean. Indeed, it is hardly going too far to say that, if the plans are not genuine, the harbour at Babylon may have suggested the figure of 1000.

But it is rather the other plans which give rise to doubts. Apart from the plan for western conquest, Diodorus mentions four others: temples were to be erected, three in Greece, three in Macedonia, and a particularly magnificent one to Athena at Ilium; Hephaestion's memorial was to be completed; a pyramid was to be built in honour of Philip; lastly, there was to be a transfer of population from Asia to

Europe and from Europe to Asia and cities were to be formed by the incorporation of villages.

There is nothing in the plan to build temples to excite disbelief. The cost involved, a total of 9000 talents for those in Greece and Macedonia, was less than the sum to be spent on Hephaestion's memorial, while the existence of temples at Delos, Delphi, and Dodona need not have prevented Alexander from planning to erect others there. The temple at Ilium, as we know from Strabo,[6] had already been promised, a circumstance which makes us wonder why the temples at Sardes and Babylon (to Bel), which Alexander proposed to build, are not mentioned. But little can be made of omissions, even so odd an omission (it seems to us) as the Arabian expedition, since Diodorus expressly states that he lists only the plans that he thinks most important.

Alexander had founded many cities in his lifetime and doubtless intended to found many more, while the transfers of population between Europe and Asia are expressly attributed to his desire to unite the two continents. This may be regarded as an extension of his 'policy of fusion', which during his life does not seem to have extended beyond Macedonians and Persians. That Alexander should have planned to increase the number of Greek settlers in Asia is not surprising; indeed, we might expect this; but that Alexander should seriously have contemplated transferring Asiatics to Greece is very difficult to believe. For Greece was already overpopulated, and it was only a short time since Alexander had issued his Exiles Decree which had the effect of adding many thousands to the population of the country. Did Alexander really believe that a further increase, this time of the despised 'barbarians', would promote harmony between the peoples?

Then we have the plan to erect a memorial to Philip 'of the same size and the same shape as the pyramid of Cheops'. We are not told where this monument was to be built, but it is usually assumed that its site was to be Aegae. Where else, indeed, would a memorial to Philip make any sense? One wonders what the population of Macedonia would have thought of this exotic edifice. Why erect a monstrous *pyramid* to honour a Macedonian king? It is quite beside the point to call attention to the memorial to Hephaestion which was influenced by the Babylonian ziggurats.[7] Hephaestion had at least shared Alexander's enthusiasm for his orientalizing policy and his memorial was being built in Babylon, not in Macedonia.

Yet, although one may have doubts about the authenticity of the plans given by Diodorus, it is perhaps correct to say that these doubts (particularly in my own case about the pyramid for Philip) do not constitute proof that they are not Alexander's plans. But what are we to make of the inclusion in the plans of the project for the completion of Hephaestion's memorial? It is this item, as Badian has very acutely observed,[8] which constitutes the greatest obstacle to believing that the plans preserved by Diodorus are entirely genuine. For the memorial had certainly been begun and in the eight or nine months since Hephaestion's death must have been well advanced. How, then, can its completion be called a 'plan'? What place has it in a list of future projects?

The intrusion of this item alone, apart from what I would regard as suspicious elements in others, is sufficient to cast doubts on the authenticity of the plans as a whole. Yet it is likely that Alexander did have plans for the future and that he committed these plans to writing. Indeed, it would be surprising, disturbingly so, if we heard nothing of them. Moreover, it is impossible to believe that the very circumstantial account of the proceedings at Babylon is pure invention. Hieronymus appears to have been a reliable and honest historian, and he had every opportunity to learn the facts from his patron, Eumenes. We may take it as a fact that Perdiccas read to the Macedonians what purported to be genuine plans of Alexander. Only slightly less certain is Badian's conclusion, that what Perdiccas read was Alexander's plans suitably touched up.[9] Few people would know the contents of the notebooks; only the leading Macedonians and Eumenes who, as chief secretary, would have the plans in his possession—and Eumenes was Perdiccas' ally. It is perhaps significant that the plans as given by Diodorus are all, with the exception of that for the pyramid for Philip, extensions of known policies of Alexander. Perdiccas' motive, it is suggested, was to prevent the production at some convenient time in the future of plans which could plausibly be represented as Alexander's, perhaps particularly by the absent Craterus. To stop this, 'Alexander's' plans must be produced and cancelled, and their rejection must be made certain by the inclusion of unpopular items and the alteration of others. It follows that we cannot know in detail what Alexander planned. He may well have had in mind an attack upon Carthage, on which he is said to have declared war after the capture of Tyre,[10] but of this we cannot be sure; that he planned the conquest of Spain and Italy is even more open to question. Nothing supports the widely-held belief that Alexander aimed at world conquest, either in the east or in the west.

The story of these plans, as Badian has justly said, belongs not to the history of Alexander but to that of his Successors. Nevertheless, it throws some light on what his Macedonians thought of Alexander. There is no suggestion that they rejected the plans because they suspected that they were not authentic; their rejection was based on the difficulty and extravagance of the projects. We may take it, then, that the Macedonians believed that Alexander was quite capable of planning projects such as these, which though 'extravagant' were not out of character. As the Macedonians knew their leader much better than we shall ever know him, this fact must be allowed its due weight.

16

LOOKING BACK

That Alexander set out on his expedition with the intention of spreading Greek culture throughout the Persian empire has been a cardinal belief of some eminent scholars. Wilcken, for example, repeatedly writes of his 'mission'. Nevertheless, this belief seems to me mistaken. No one will dispute that the inhabitants of Asia (or at least the upper strata among them) were to some extent Hellenized as the result of Alexander's conquests; but that is a very different matter from saying that Alexander consciously aimed at promoting this.

His attitude to the Greeks affords no support for this view. In 334, it is true, he set out from Macedonia as *Hegemon* of the Corinthian League to lead a 'crusade' against the Persians. But the 'crusade' was an inheritance from his father and Philip, it seems probable, saw the Corinthian League as a convenient means of securing the support, or at least the good behaviour, of the Greek states during his absence. We have no evidence that Alexander's attitude differed from his father's, and his treatment of the Greek cities of Asia Minor from an early stage in the campaign suggests that it did not. In effect, they exchanged one master for another, enjoying neither more nor less freedom than they had done under the Persians, even if they were technically not subject to the satrap of the province.

In issuing his Exiles Decree in 324 Alexander went far beyond the powers he possessed as *Hegemon*. There is undoubtedly much truth in the view that this autocratic action showed the effect of his position as Great King; for the man who is reported to have described the fighting in Greece as a 'war of mice'[1] is not likely to have been troubled by the feelings of the Greeks. But he revealed the same cavalier attitude to his position as *Hegemon* in the first year of the campaign, when he allowed Greek mercenaries serving with the Persians at Miletus to join his forces despite the decree of the

Synhedrion that mercenaries who fought for Persia should be regarded as traitors.[2] Again, at the beginning of 331 Alexander sent the Chian traitors under guard to Elephantinē, although only twelve months earlier he had stated in an edict to the citizens of Chios that these men would be tried in the *Synhedrion*.[3]

That Alexander sincerely admired Greek literature and 'music' we may readily believe, but it does not follow that he was determined to convert other peoples. If he held athletic and artistic contests in Egypt, this is more reasonably to be attributed to the mundane desire to provide relaxation for his troops (as he had already done at Soli in Cilicia) than to any idea of paving the way for the introduction of Greek culture. What other form of entertainment could he have been expected to provide?

One of the chief methods by which, it is suggested, Alexander forwarded the process of Hellenization was by the foundation of cities. Plutarch attributes to him no fewer than seventy[4] and, although some were without doubt later foundations which attached themselves to his name, he clearly did found a considerable number. It is noticeable, however, that the only city he certainly founded in the western portion of the empire—the case of Alexandretta is doubtful[5]—is Alexandria in Egypt. Arrian records no other foundation until Alexandria of the Caucasus in 329. Some, such as Alexandria in Egypt, Alexandria–Charax at the head of the Persian Gulf, and Pattala, were surely intended to become great trading centres. But, if it is too sweeping to call the others, as Welles does,[6] 'fortified camps and nothing more', one of their main functions was certainly to safeguard communications and to dominate the surrounding countryside. Most, in fact, were situated at strategic points, and some at least will have functioned as administrative centres as well. The idea that they were to promote Hellenization, or at least settled government, need not be ruled out, but it was probably not the principal factor in their foundation. Some of the larger cities at least may have been given Greek democratic institutions—magistrates, a Council, and an assembly—but excavation has not so far revealed the existence of such fundamentals as theatres, gymnasia and market-places. We know little of their population, but it is clear that Greek mercenaries were settled in many or all of them, together in some instances with Macedonian veterans unfit for further service, and natives. However, the presence of Greek mercenaries does not prove that the promotion of Greek culture was an important reason for their foundation. Alexander used whatever material he had to hand, and Greeks could be spared in a way that Macedonians could not. In the same way the garrisons in the west consisted mainly of Greek mercenaries. In this matter, as in others, Alexander was guided by practical considerations, not by a consciousness of possessing a 'mission'.

As an administrator Alexander did not follow any large overriding plan; on the contrary, he was thoroughly pragmatic. It was not admiration for democracy that led him to put down the oligarchies which the Persians had favoured, but the expectation that this policy would win him the gratitude of the majority of the inhabitants. Nor did he follow the advice of Isocrates and Aristotle to give the Greeks a privileged position at the expense of the Persians.[7] He was not a great innovator but, in general, he retained the existing system of government with its simple, if not altogether satisfactory, division into satrapies. Even in Caria, where Ada was recognized as queen and no satrap was appointed, there was no real change, since the Carian rulers in the fourth century had been largely independent. In Egypt, where Alexander did make radical changes in the Persian system, the overriding reason for the highly elaborate division of civil and military commands was the need for security, to prevent any individual from gaining sole control of a rich and defensible province.

Even after the battle of Gaugamela made him the ruler of the Persian empire Alexander did not introduce any fundamental change of policy. Instead of appointing Macedonians to govern the satrapies, he appointed or, where possible, reappointed Persian governors, and continued to do so until the supply of loyal Persians ran out. These Persian satraps appear to have been placed on precisely the same footing as their Macedonian counterparts. Whether this arrangement differed from the previous Persian system depends on whether the *strategi* (mentioned in some provinces, but not in all) and the financial officials, where they existed, were independent of the governor. The probability is that they were not, and that there was no change. In any case the *strategi* would have effective control of the troops, and the financial officers would serve, as they had done under the Achaemenids, to keep an eye on the satraps. The whole system depended for its efficient working on the close supervision of the ruler or the loyalty of his subordinates. It was Alexander's long absence in the east which gave the satraps and the generals their opportunity for misgovernment, particularly after the murder of Parmenio. In India Alexander had, of necessity, to make new arrangements. Again he adopted a simple system of allowing the native rulers to govern their own kingdoms, merely adding to these the territory of those princes who did not submit. These native rulers, however, he made subject to Macedonian governors, except Porus who was both monarch and satrap of the country east of the Jhelum. In fact, he was an independent ruler since no Macedonian troops were left behind in his territory.

F

In finance, since the professed aim of the expedition meant that the Greek cities of Asia Minor had to be treated as independent of the satraps, there was necessarily change. Philoxenus was accordingly appointed to receive the contributions which the cities, as members of the Corinthian League, were required to make. Coeranus' appointment was similar—to deal with the tribute of the cities of Phoenicia. However, Alexander retained the idea of a central treasury, and Harpalus' functions after 330 do not appear to have differed materially from those of the Persian Imperial Treasurer. Justin (XIII.1.9) states that only 50,000 talents remained in the treasury at Alexander's death, and it is commonly asserted that Alexander broke with the Achaemenid policy of hoarding and put into circulation the bulk of the 180,000 talents captured in the central Persian treasuries. Justin's statement may seem credible enough when we recall the (possibly exaggerated) statements in the Alexander-historians of the king's lavish expenditure; but, since in the same sentence he puts Alexander's income from the tribute of his empire at no less than 30,000 talents per annum (to which we must add booty and gifts, substantial in some instances), it may be doubted whether Alexander did, in fact, turn the bulk of his treasure into coin.[8] Moreover, although vast amounts of coin were certainly issued by the western mints, no substantial quantity of coins which can be attributed to any mint east of Babylon has been found.[9] However, whether the Persian treasure provided the means or not, Alexander's currency was an important instrument of trade and government. At the beginning of his reign he had taken the important decision to abandon his father's standard for silver and to adopt the heavier standard of the widely-circulating and highly-regarded Athenian coinage. Hence, during his reign twenty silver drachms bearing the head of the young Heracles were equal in value to one gold stater bearing the head of Athena. This gold and silver coinage, with its multiples and divisions of the drachm and the stater, provided a uniform currency throughout at least the western portion of his empire and circulated more extensively than even the Persian or the Athenian coinages had done.

Alexander's measures to improve the irrigation of Mesopotamia and to develop the coast and islands of the Persian Gulf highlight his concern for the economic wellbeing of his empire. One of his main motives for undertaking the Arabian expedition was clearly economic; for Aristobulus expressly states that Alexander was aware of the prosperity of the country and, as the voyages of Hieron and Anaxicrates make clear, he was bent on linking Egypt with Mesopotamia and thus with India and the remainder of his empire. But Alexander's interest in trade does not date only from 324, but goes back at least to the foundation of Alexandria in Egypt. Nearchus' voyage, too, was intended to discover suitable landing places for trading vessels, and it might even be argued that the development of trade was *a* motive (although not *the* motive) for the invasion of India. We know that Gorgus, a mining expert who accompanied Alexander, published a book (or a pamphlet) on gold and silver mining in the kingdom of Sopeithes east of the Jhelum, while in Greece his engineer Crates was given the task—prevented by the opposition of the Boeotians themselves—of draining Lake Copais.[10]

But if there is no doubt that Alexander was much concerned with the economy of his empire, it seems much less certain that Aristotle had inspired him with a passion for disinterested inquiry. While it is true that numbers of scientists accompanied him and that the information they sent back to Greece was of the greatest value to Greek science, the initiative may have come from Aristotle rather than from his pupil. Again Heracleides' expedition to explore the Caspian is just as likely to have had a practical as a scientific purpose. The tendency to depict Alexander as a philosopher and a scientific inquirer has probably been overdone. It is more likely that he was concerned primarily with practical matters and that he was as little an abstract thinker as a 'missionary'.

As a politician, too, Alexander was pragmatic. He was not concerned with the 'Brotherhood of Man' or the 'Unity of Mankind'. His 'policy of fusion', it must be emphasized, was confined to Persians and Macedonians (and Greeks who had settled in Macedonia). It can be argued that the employment of Persian satraps, like the introduction of Persian troops into the army, was a matter of necessity, to remedy a shortage of Macedonians, but this is not altogether convincing. There were certainly Greeks or Macedonians whom Alexander might have used to govern provinces, even if they were perhaps less competent than Persians, while the shortage of Macedonian troops has almost certainly been exaggerated,[11] and Greek mercenaries were to be had. It is very probable that Alexander's reason for using Persians was his perception that the empire was best governed with the cooperation of the ruled and that the Persian nobles were best able to secure this.

Alexander was by no means insensitive to the feelings of the Macedonians, even if he was determined to have his own way. He appears to have made strenuous efforts to avoid giving offence or at least to lessen the resentment which his policy caused. In the mixed dress which he adopted he eschewed the more offensive Median elements, the tiara, the long-sleeved woollen *candys*, and the baggy trousers. He maintained separate courts for Macedonians and Persians, and when writing to correspondents in Europe and Asia he is said to have sealed his letters with different seals. Again, he did not select Persians as Court Chamberlain or Grand Vizier (Chiliarch). It is evident, too, that Macedonians continued to fill the top positions in the army, and even in the final reorganization at Babylon the Macedonians in the platoons were NCOs, the Persians privates. His political tact is shown, also, in his acceptance of defeat in his attempt to introduce *proskynesis* for Greeks and Macedonians.

Nevertheless, it is clear that Alexander became increasingly impatient of criticism and suspicious of plots against himself. Even Tarn admits that the Alexander of 324 was not the Alexander of 334. This was certainly not the effect of oriental luxury, as Curtius would have us believe, although the mere fact of his being Great King may have been partly responsible for the change in Alexander. It was rather that the physical and mental strain of years of constant campaigning and what Badian has well called 'The Loneliness of Power' were now taking their toll.[12] For Alexander appears to have had few close friends, and perhaps confided fully only in Hephaestion. This may explain Alexander's violent reaction to his death; for it is only after this that what has been termed his megalomania becomes apparent with the letter to Cleomenes, the monument to Hephaestion, and perhaps his request for deification.

That Alexander was a drunkard devoid of self-control is, of course, a figment of the rhetorical or philosophic imagination, an unwarranted generalization from the murder of Cleitus, particularly on the part of the Stoics, a school never noted for its common sense. But Alexander's admirers, ancient and modern, do him no service by denying that he drank heavily. The Macedonian court was only superficially Hellenized, and heavy drinking was characteristic of the Macedonian nobility. Alexander remained a Macedonian; he did not become a Greek—despite his education. In the same way Alexander's removal of possible rivals at the start of his reign must be seen in its Macedonian context. It was because he saw his security was threatened that he acted ruthlessly, as he did later in executing the generals in 324. In their case, however, as in his search for a scapegoat for the Gedrosian disaster, his conduct is probably determined partly by his vast ambition, his desire to be thought invincible. These men had betrayed Alexander's trust, as Harpalus had done—for there is no reason to suppose them guiltless—and they must pay the penalty, not so much for their offences against Alexander's subjects as against Alexander himself. He was a supreme egoist, determined to be the greatest ruler, and first and foremost his actions were determined by the interests of *his* empire.

A brief mention of Alexander's military achievements will suffice, for his generalship has almost always received the recognition it deserves and it would be perverse to attempt to be original about this topic. From the very first campaign in the north Alexander revealed the resource and determination that he was to display throughout his Asiatic campaigns. Tyre and Aornus spring to mind. He seems to have been convinced of his invincibility, to have convinced his troops of this, and to have imposed this conviction upon the enemy. Plutarch is not very wide of the mark when he remarks that Alexander's spirit rendered his ambition invincible over obstacles both human and non-human.[13] Nothing roused him so much as a challenge.

Alexander had the good fortune to inherit a great army, well trained and well officered, but even the best tools will not produce good results in the hands of a poor craftsman. His decision to neutralize the superior Persian fleet by depriving it of its bases was perhaps a gamble, but having taken the gamble he resisted the temptation to pursue Darius' defeated forces after Issus and later to abandon the siege of Tyre. Tactically, his qualities are seen to best advantage at Gaugamela, where the enemy had an overwhelming superiority in cavalry, and on the Hydaspes, where the elephants posed an entirely novel problem. But more impressive even than his performance in the major battles is the skill with which he adapted himself to the changed conditions of guerrilla warfare in Bactria and Sogdiana, where he first encountered the cataphracts, the mailed horsemen of the steppes. To cope with these new conditions we find him introducing mounted archers and combining light infantry with his cavalry. It is clear that Alexander was rarely advancing into unknown territory, but that he had taken care to find out from captives or deserters what lay ahead. Garrisons were established at strategic points in his rear and reinforcements continued to reach him in the far east apparently without difficulty.

Alexander the general, like Alexander the man, had his faults. The most obvious was his tendency to take undue risks, a tendency which almost cost him his life at the Granicus and again at the Malli town. Perhaps this was an inevitable consequence of leading from the front, but we may suspect that for a general he liked the thrill of battle too much. Occasionally he was too bold or careless, most notably at Issus when he allowed Darius to get in behind him, a blunder which the quality of his troops enabled him to retrieve brilliantly, but a blunder notwithstanding. The march through Gedrosia was perhaps not so much a military error as an example of his determination to achieve what no man had achieved. Here again, as he always did in adversity, Alexander displayed the highest qualities as a leader, enduring all the hardships that his troops had to endure, so that it is easy to understand how he retained their loyalty all the way from the Hellespont to the Beas. There their refusal to advance further was not an indication that they had lost confidence in Alexander, but simply reflected their war-weariness and the debilitating effects of the monsoon rains. This mutiny must be accounted the result of a mis-calculation on Alexander's part—again, perhaps, a victory for the non-rational element in his nature. But such instances are very few. One final point: it is clear that the Indian campaign, particularly in its later stages, was marked by a series of massacres. There is no point in denying this, but Alexander's conduct should be seen in the light of the attitude towards 'barbarians' prevailing in his day and in the centuries that followed. No Macedonian (or Greek) would have thought Alexander deserving of condemnation for his treatment of the Indians, just as few Roman senators thought the conduct of their leaders in Spain disgraceful.

It was the extent of his conquests that gained for Alexander the title of 'The Great', and some have seen in him no more than a great conqueror, a great 'robber' who destroyed the Persian empire without putting anything in its place. But this neglects the measures he took to secure the economic well-being of his empire—the creation of a uniform currency, at least in the west, the founding of cities, the irrigation schemes, the voyages of discovery. Military genius and administrative capacity he certainly possessed. His statesmanship we can scarcely judge. With his death his 'policy of fusion' came to an end, and in the absence of an agreed and capable successor—something, admittedly, for which Alexander may be held respon-sible—the break-up of his empire was inevitable. Whether he could have held the empire together had he lived is an intriguing—and insoluble—question.

Agis defeated and killed at Megalopolis in Arcadia (?September).
Macedonians occupy Babylon (?mid-October) and Susa (mid-December).

330 Persepolis occupied and sacked (?mid-January).
Expedition against the Mardi (about 6 April–6 May), followed soon after by burning of the 'palace'.
Alexander sets out for Ecbatana (mid-May).
Murder of Darius by Bessus (late July). Bessus assumes position of 'Great King'.
'Conspiracy' of Philotas. Murder of Parmenio.

329 Spring: Alexander crosses Hindu-Kush into Bactria.
Macedonians cross River Oxus and Ptolemy captures Bessus.
Alexander advances to Samarcand on River Jaxartes and engages Scythians north of river (mid-summer).
Spitamenes revolts.

329–328 Alexander winters at Zariaspa (Balkh).

328 Execution of Bessus.
Visits of Scythian envoys and Chorasmian king, Pharasmanes.
Campaign against Spitamenes.
Alexander murders Cleitus the Black at Samarcand (autumn).

328–327 Spitamenes defeated and murdered by his followers.
Alexander winters at Nautaca.

327 Early spring: Capture of 'Sogdian Rock' and marriage of Alexander and Roxane, daughter of Bactrian baron.
Capture of 'Rock' of Chorienes.
The 'Pages' Conspiracy'. Arrest of Callisthenes and subsequent execution.
Summer: Alexander recrosses Hindu-Kush, and campaigns in Bajaur and Swat. He visits Nysa, supposedly founded by Dionysus, in the Kabul valley, and captures Aornos (Pir-Sar).

326 Alexander advances to Taxila.
May: Battle of the River Hydaspes (Jhelum) against Porus.
Alexander advances to the River Hyphasis (Beas) where the troops mutiny. Return to the River Jhelum.
November: Departure from Nicaea for the Indian Ocean.

325 Massacres of Indian tribes. Alexander seriously wounded among the Malli.
Revolt of mercenaries in Bactria.
July: Alexander reaches Pattala.
End August: Alexander leaves Pattala to return to west.
Meets near disaster in Gedrosian desert (?September–October).
21 September: Nearchus leaves mouth of Indus. Waits for three weeks near Karachi.
?December: Nearchus meets Alexander near Gulashkird. Receives orders to proceed to Susa.
Executions of generals and satraps.
Flight of Harpalus to Greece.

324 January: Alexander reaches Pasargadae. Finds tomb of Cyrus
     plundered.
     Late February: Alexander reaches Susa to be joined by Nearchus.
     Holds mass marriages. Issues Exiles Decree and ? requests deification
     from Greek states.
     Arrival of the 'Successors'.
     July: Harpalus arrives at Athens.
     Between 31 July and 4 August: Proclamation of Exiles Decree at
     Olympic Games.
     Mutiny at Opis. Craterus appointed to lead veterans home and
     succeed Antipater.
     ?October: Death of Hephaestion at Ecbatana.

324–323 Winter campaign against Cossaeans.

323 Alexander returns to Babylon (spring). Visits of Greek envoys acknow-
     ledging Alexander's divinity. Memorial for Hephaestion begun.
     Alexander explores Pallacopas canal. Preparations for Arabian
     expedition.
     Arrival of Antipater's son, Cassander, at Babylon.
     29 May: Alexander falls ill and dies on 10 June.

NOTES

Modern works frequently cited in the notes are given by author's name and short title. They are listed in full in the Bibliography. The following abbreviations are used for the most commonly cited ancient authors:

Arr. = Arrian, *Anabasis Alexandri*
Diod. = Diodorus Siculus
Curt. = Quintus Curtius
Plut. = Plutarch, *Alexander*
Just. = Justin

Periodicals are abbreviated as follows:

AC = *Antiquité Classique*
AHR = *American Historical Review*
AJA = *American Journal of Archaeology*
AJP = *American Journal of Philology*
AUMLA = *Journal of the Australasian Universities Language and Literature Association*
CP = *Classical Philology*
CQ = *Classical Quarterly*
CR = *Classical Review*
G & R = *Greece and Rome*
GRBS = *Greek, Roman and Byzantine Studies*
HSCP = *Harvard Studies in Classical Philology*
JDAI = *Jahrbuch des deutschen archäologischen Instituts*
JEA = *Journal of Egyptian Archaeology*
JHS = *Journal of Hellenic Studies*
JNES = *Journal of Near Eastern Studies*
JOEAI = *Jahreshefte des Österreichischen archäologischen Instituts*
PACA = *Proceedings of the African Classical Associations*
PCPhS = *Proceedings of the Cambridge Philological Society*
SPAW = *Sitzungsberichte des Preussischen Akademie der Wissenschaften, Phil.-hist. Klasse*
TAPA = *Transactions of the American Philological Association*

Chapter 1: The sources

1. See R. A. Todd, 'W. W. Tarn and the Alexander Ideal', *The Historian*, **27** (1964), 48ff.

2. The fragments are collected by F. Jacoby, *Die Fragmente der griechischen Historiker* (cited as *F.Gr.Hist.*) IIB, nos. 117–53, with a commentary in IID (Berlin, 1927, 1930), and trans. by C. A. Robinson Jr., *The History of Alexander the Great* vol. i (Providence, R. I., 1953).

Lionel Pearson, *The Lost Histories of Alexander the Great* (New York, 1960) is indispensable for serious study of all the primary sources. See also E. Badian's review of Pearson in *Gnomon*, **33** (1961), 660ff.

3. T. S. Brown, 'Callisthenes and Alexander', *AJP* **70** (1949), 225ff. (= Griffith, *Main Problems*, 29ff.).

4. T. S. Brown, *Onesicritus, A Study in Hellenistic Historiography* (Berkeley, 1949). On the date of his book see Hamilton, *Commentary*, 127 (on Plut. 46.4).

5. Arrian, *Indica*, ch. 40, 6.

6. R. M. Errington, 'Bias in Ptolemy's History of Alexander', *CQ* N.S. **19** (1969), 233ff.

7. See, however, C. B. Welles, 'The reliability of Ptolemy as an historian', *Miscellanea Rostagni* (Torino, 1963), 101ff.

8. Forgery: L. Pearson, *Historia*, **3** (1954–5), 249ff. (= Griffith, *Main Problems*, 1ff.), and A. B. Bosworth, *CQ* N.S. **21** (1971), 112ff.

Babylonian chronicle: A. E. Samuel, 'Alexander's Royal Journals', *Historia*, **14** (1965), 1ff.

9. J. R. Hamilton, 'Cleitarchus and Aristobulus', *Historia*, **10** (1961), 449ff.; F. Schachermeyr, *Alexander in Babylon* (Wien, 1970), Anhang.

10. E. N. Borza, 'Cleitarchus and Diodorus' account of Alexander', *PACA*, **11** (1968), 25ff., doubts whether the dependence of Diodorus on Cleitarchus has been proved.

11. See A. E. Wardman, 'Plutarch and Alexander', *CQ* N.S. **5** (1955), 96ff., and Hamilton, *Commentary*, xxiii–xxxiii and lx–lxii.

12. See C. B. Welles' Introduction to the Loeb edition, vol. 8, and R. Drews, 'Diodorus and his Sources', *AJP*, **83** (1962), 383ff.

13. E. I. McQueen gives a general survey in *Latin Biography* (Ed. T. A. Dorey), London, 1967, 17ff. On Curtius' date see especially G. V. Sumner, 'Curtius Rufus and the *Historiae Augusti*', *AUMLA*, **15** (1961), 30ff., and H. U. Instinsky, 'Zur Kontroverse um die Datierung des Curtius Rufus', *Hermes*, **90** (1962), 379ff.

14. See, more fully, the Introduction to Hamilton, *Commentary*.

15. J. R. Hamilton, 'The letters in Plutarch's *Alexander*', *PACA*, **4** (1961), 9ff.; id., *CQ* N.S. **5** (1955), 219ff.

16. See my Introduction to Arrian: *The Campaigns of Alexander*, trans. A. de Selincourt (Penguin Books, 1971).

In an important article ('Arrian's Literary Development', *CQ* N.S. **22** (1972), 163ff.) A. B. Bosworth has vigorously challenged the generally accepted view that Arrian wrote the *Anabasis* after the end of his career in the Roman imperial service. He argues that it was a work of Arrian's youth and suggests a date between A.D. 115 and 120 for its composition. Although Bosworth demonstrates the weakness of the case for a late date, his own positive arguments do not seem to me compelling and I retain (with some hesitation) the usual view.

17. P. A. Brunt, 'Persian Accounts of Alexander's Campaigns', *CQ* N.S. **12** (1962), 141ff.

Chapter 2. The Macedonian homeland

1. *Philippics* 3.32.

2. K. J. Beloch, *Griechische Geschichte*, 2nd ed. (Berlin, 1927), IV. 1. 1–9; C. F. Edson, 'Early Macedonia' in *Ancient Macedonia i* (Thessaloniki, 1970). cf. Plut. 51.6.

3. See S. Casson, *Macedonia, Thrace, and Illyria* (Oxford, 1926), chs 1–2.

4. On the king's powers see E. Badian's salutary remarks in *HSCP*, **72** (1968), 197f.

5. Tarn, *Alexander*, II. 138.

6. G. T. Griffith, 'The Macedonian Background', *G & R*, **12** (1965), 134 ff.

7. Tod, *GHI*, nos. 91 and 111.

8. Diod. 16.8.6.

9. On the date (perhaps 352) see G. T. Griffith, 'Philip's Early Intervention in Thessaly', *CQ* N.S. **20** (1970), 73ff.

10. Jacoby, *F.Gr.Hist.* no. 72, Fr. 4. The fact that Thucydides (2.100) refers to the Macedonian infantry in 430 as 'a great mass of barbarians' would seem to rule out Alexander I as the creator of the phalanx.

11. See G. T. Griffith, *PCPhS*, **4** (1956–7), 3ff.; F. E. Adcock, *The Greek and Macedonian Art of War* (Berkeley, 1957), 26.

12. Brunt, *JHS*, **83** (1963), 34ff.

13. R. D. Milns, 'Philip II and the Hypaspists', *Historia*, **16** (1967), 507ff.

14. See E. W. Marsden, *Greek and Roman Artillery* (Oxford, 1969), 60.

15. Theopompus (Jacoby, *F.Gr.Hist.* no. 115), Fr. 225B, as interpreted by A. Momigliano, *Athenaeum* N.S. **13** (1935), 14.

16. Arr. 4.13.1; Curt. 8.6.3–6.

Chapter 3: The young Alexander

(For this chapter see, especially, Plut. chs 3–8)

1. Plut. 3.8; Diod. 16.22.3; Tod, *GHI*, no. 157.

2. Plut. 3.8.

3. See E. R. Dodds' Introduction to his 2nd ed. of Euripides' *Bacchae* (Oxford, 1960).

4. Pausanias 8.7.7.; Diod. 19.11.8; Tarn in *CAH* 6.480f.

5. Athenaeus 12.557b.

6. For the evidence, if not for the conclusions, on Alexander's attitude to sex see Tarn, *Alexander*, II.319ff.

7. Plut. 4.11; 39.5. On the ball-players see S. Dow, 'The Athenian honors for Aristonikos of Karystos, Alexander's *sphairistes*', *HSCP*, **67** (1963), 77ff.

8. W. Jaeger, *Aristotle*, 2nd ed. (Oxford, 1948), 120ff.

9. Plut. 8; Isocrates, *Epistle* 3. See Philip Merlan, 'Isocrates, Aristotle, and Alexander the Great', *Historia*, **3** (1954–5), 60ff.

10. As reported by Plutarch, *Moralia* 329b. See on this whole topic V. Ehrenberg, *Alexander and the Greeks*, 62ff., and Badian, *Historia*, **7** (1958), 432ff., 440ff. (=Griffith, *Main Problems*, 294ff., 302ff.).

11. For this hymn see Jaeger, loc. cit., D. E. W. Wormell, *Yale Classical Studies*, **5** (1935), 61ff., Lowell Edmunds, *GRBS*, **12** (1971), 383ff.

12. *Meteorologica* 2.1.10.

13. See, especially, Wilcken, *Alexander*, 66, 80, 260.

Chapter 4: Crown prince

1. Plut. 9.1.

2. Badian, *Historia*, **7** (1958), 442, n. 71.

3. Just. 9.1.8.

4. Diod. 16.86. For a modern analysis see W. K. Pritchett, *AJA*, **62** (1958), 307ff.

5. For what follows see C. Roebuck, 'The Settlements of Philip II with the Greek states in 338 B.C.', *CP*, **43** (1948), 86ff.

6. For the background see Diod. 16.89.3 and Just. 9.5. The main evidence for the provisions of the League consists of a speech, *On the Treaty with Alexander*, attributed to Demosthenes (no. 17) but delivered in the late 330s by a bitter opponent of Macedon (see G. L. Cawkwell, *Phoenix*, **15** (1961), 74ff.), and two fragmentary inscriptions. The first of these (text and commentary in Tod, *GHI*, no. 177 and H. H. Schmitt, *Die Staatsverträge des Altertums*, Band III (München, 1969), no. 403) contains portions of the oath sworn by the Greek states in 337, the second (text and commentary in Schmitt, op. cit., no. 446) fragments of the constitution as remodelled by Antigonus and Demetrius in 302.

In general, I follow Wilcken's interpretation (*Alexander*, 43ff.). For a recent discussion of the problems involved see T. T. B. Ryder, *Koine Eirene* (Oxford, 1965), 102ff., 150ff.

7. (Demosthenes) 17, paras. 8, 15, 10. Tod, *GHI*, no. 177, lines 11–12.

8. Representatives: Tod, *GHI*, no. 177, lines 24–35. Arbitrators: Tod, *GHI*, no. 179, lines 3–5. Judicial powers: Diod. 17.73.5; Curt. 6.1.19f.

9. On the remainder of this chapter see, especially, E. Badian, *Phoenix*, **17** (1963), 244ff.

10. Plut. 10.1–5 (the only evidence).

11. Diod. 16.93–4; *P.Oxy.* no. 1798 = Jacoby, *F.Gr.Hist.* no. 148. For the crucifixion cf. Just. 9.7.10.

12. *Politics* 1311ᵇ2; Plut. 10.6; Just. 9.6.4ff.

13. By C. B. Welles on p. 101 of the Loeb Diodorus, vol. 8.

14. Suidas s.v. *Antipatros*.

15. Diod. 16.92.5, 95.1. For an altar to Zeus Philippius at Eresus see Tod, *GHI*, no. 191, and for the cult of Philip see Habicht, *Gottmenschentum*, 12ff.

16. For a recent discussion see Kraft, *Alexander*, 11–42, who accepts that Pausanias had a purely personal motive. He anticipates some of the points made in this paragraph.

A. B. Bosworth, 'Philip II and Upper Macedonia', *CQ* N.S. **21** (1971), 93ff., regards the story of the assault on Pausanias as an invention, put about by Alexander and Olympias in order to allay rumours of parricide; for to reveal the truth, that Pausanias and the Lyncestian brothers had murdered Philip for political reasons, would have been to disclose the dangerous division between Upper and Lower Macedonia. But, apart from other difficulties, it is hard to credit that Aristotle sought 'to vindicate his former pupil' by giving currency to a falsehood of this sort.

17. Just. (9.6.5–8) is also confused, since he writes that Pausanias suffered this indignity in his early youth (*primis pubertatis annis*), but appears to envisage no long interval between this event and the murder of Philip.

Chapter 5: King Alexander

(Sources: Arr. I.1–11; Diod. 17.1–16; Plut. 11–15.6; Just. XI.1–4)

1. Polyaenus 8.60. The exact date is not known. The chronology of the events related in this paragraph is uncertain. Probably they occurred late in 335; see J. R. Ellis, 'Amyntas Perdikka, Philip II and Alexander the Great', *JHS*, **91** (1971), 21, and Badian, *Ehrenberg Studies*, 41–2.

2. Persuasively argued by Ellis, op. cit., 15ff.

3. See Arr. I.17.9; 20.10.

4. Deduced by Tarn (*Alexander*, II.339) from Plut. 14.6, who relates that Alexander visited Delphi at this time and forced the Pythia to declare him 'Invincible' (cf. Diod. 17.93.4), and a Delphic inscription (Dittenberger, *SIG*³ 251H) recording such a donation between autumn 336 and spring 335. On the coins see C. Seltman, *Greek Coins*, 201.

5. On Alexander's 'longing' (*pothos*) see Ehrenberg, *Alexander and the Greeks*, ch. 2 (=Griffith, *Main Problems*, 73 ff.). Both H. Montgomery, *Gedanke und Tat* (Lund, 1965), 191ff., and Kraft, *Alexander* 81–118, are critical of his conclusions.

6. King Agesilaus of Sparta observed in 394 that he was being driven out of Asia Minor by 10,000 'archers' (Plut. *Ages.* 15).

7. Aeschines III. 239ff.

8. Just. XI.2.8. cf. Arr. I.7.3.

9. For details see Hamilton, *Commentary*, 32 (on Plut. 13.1).

10. For the state of Alexander's finances see Bellinger, *Coinage*, 35ff.

Chapter 6: The conquest of Asia Minor

(Sources: Arr. I.11–II.3; Diod. 17.17–29; Curt. III.1; Plut. 15.7–18.4; Just. XI.5.6–7.16)

1. *Iliad* 2.701. cf. Herodotus 9.116.

2. See H. U. Instinsky, *Alexander der Grosse am Hellespont* (Godesberg, 1949), and the reviews by F. W. Walbank, *JHS*, **70** (1950), 79f., and H. Strasburger, *Gnomon*, **23** (1951), 83ff.

3. Diod. 17.17.2. cf. Just. XI.5.10. See also W. Schmitthenner, 'Ueber eine Formveränderung der Monarchie seit Alexander dem Grossen', *Saeculum*, **19** (1968), 31ff., especially 34ff., who connects the action with the obsolete Greek heroic symbolism of conquest.

4. On the various numbers for Alexander's army see the table in Brunt, *JHS* (1963), 46. For discussion see Brunt, op. cit., 32ff., and Marsden, *The Campaign of Gaugamela*, 24ff.

5. By Polyaenus 5.44.

6. See G. T. Griffith, *PCPhS*, **4** (1956–7), 3ff.

7. On the equipment and organization of the Hypaspists see Milns, *Historia*, **20** (1971), 186ff. He argues, on the basis of Curt. V.2.3, that the strength of a battalion was 500 until late in 331.

8. e.g. Brunt, *JHS*, **83** (1963), 27ff.

9. Berve, *Alexanderreich*, I.155ff.

10. Tarn, *Alexander*, II.137ff. For a complete list see Berve, *Alexanderreich*, I.31.

11. Fuller, *Generalship*, 147ff.; E. W. Davis, 'The Persian Battle Plan at the Granicus', *Studies Caldwell* (Chapel Hill, 1964), 34ff.

Diodorus' account of the battle (17.19ff.) differs from Arrian's in two important (and irreconcilable) details—(1) the battle takes place at dawn on the following day. (2) the Macedonians cross unopposed and engage the Persians on the further bank. For criticism of this improbable version see Davis, op. cit., 40ff.

12. For Alexander's treatment of the Greek cities of Asia Minor Badian's article in *Ehrenberg Studies* (37ff.) is fundamental.

13. See Badian's arguments, op. cit., 46ff.

14. Tod, *GHI*, nos. 184, 185.

15. On Alexander's routes in Asia Minor see Freya Stark, 'Alexander's March from Miletus to Phrygia', *JHS*, **78** (1958), 102ff., and *Alexander's Path from Caria to Cilicia* (London, 1958).

16. Fuller, *Generalship*, 200ff.

17. See Pearson, *Lost Histories*, 36ff., with Badian's comments in *Gnomon*, **33** (1961), 661.

18. On the Persian counter-offensive see A. R. Burn, *JHS*, **72** (1952), 81ff., and Badian, *Hermes*, **95** (1967), 174ff.

19. *Moralia* 339d–f.
20. Diod. 17.29.2.
21. See, on Alexander's motive for visiting Gordium, E. A. Fredricksmeyer, *CP*, **56** (1961), 160ff.

Chapter 7: Issus and its aftermath

(Sources: Arr. II.4–III.6; Diod. 17.29–53; Curt. III.2–IV.8; Plut. 18.5–30.14; Just. XI.8–12).

1. Xenophon, *Anabasis* I.2.20. See the photograph in Green, *Alexander the Great*, 120, or in Schachermeyr, *Alexander* (Tafel V).

2. For the battle of Issus and the events preceding it see Arr. II.7–11; Diod. 17.35–4; Curt. III.9–11; Plut. 20.1–6. Polybius (XII.17–22) severely criticizes Callisthenes' version. The best modern account is Fuller, *Generalship*, 155ff.

3. 2000 escaped with Darius, and two groups of 8000 and 4000 escaped independently. See pp. 69–70.

4. Diod. 17.48.2. For these events see Badian, *Hermes*, **95** (1967), 175ff.

5. Aeschines, *Against Ctesiphon*, 164.

6. Arr. II.17.

7. Diod. 17.39.2. G. T. Griffith, 'The Letter of Darius at Arrian 2.14', *PCPhS*, **14** (1968), 33ff., argues in favour of accepting Diodorus' statement.

8. On the Tyrian 'Heracles' see Arr. II.16, and B. C. Brundage, 'Heracles the Levantine: A Comprehensive View', *JNES*, **17** (1958), 225ff.

9. Described at length by Arr. II.16–24; Diod. 17.40–6; Curt. IV.2–4; cf. Plut. 24.5–25.3. See also Fuller, *Generalship*, 206ff.

10. For the complicated story of the Persian embassies see Hamilton, *Commentary* 76–7.

11. e.g. Wilcken, *Alexander*, 111.

12. This fact is recorded only by Pseudo-Callisthenes (I.34.2), which is in general pure fiction, but, since Alexander is attested by hieroglyphic texts to have borne some of the royal titles (details in Wilcken, *Alexander*, 114f.), it is probably correct.

13. I follow Arrian and Plutarch in putting the foundation *before* the journey; Ptolemy (Arr. III.4.5) expressly states that Alexander returned to Memphis by a direct route across the desert. C. B. Welles, *Historia*, **11** (1962), 271ff., however, accepts the version of Diodorus and Curtius, who put the foundation on the return journey from Siwah, largely because Alexandria's 'birthday' was celebrated on 7 April. His arguments are answered by P. M. Fraser, 'Current problems concerning the early history of the cult of Sarapis', *Opuscula Atheniensia*, **7** (1967), 23ff., at p. 30.

14. For the crimes and the punishment of the tyrants of Eresus, see Tod, *GHI*, no. 191.

15. Tod, *GHI*, no. 192.

16. For a description of the oasis and the temple see H. W. Parke, *The Oracles of Zeus* (Oxford, 1967), 196ff. He also discusses Alexander's visit.

17. For Greek knowledge of Ammon see C. J. Classen, 'The Libyan God Ammon in Greece before 331 B.C.', *Historia*, **8** (1959), 349ff.

18. Arr. III.3–4; Diod. 17.49–51; Curt. IV.7.5–30; Plut. 26. 11–27.11; Strabo 17.1.43 = Callisthenes Fr. 14(a). For a recent discussion of the sources see Kraft, *Alexander*, 48–67.

19. Tarn, *Alexander*, II, 354.

20. As suggested by Badian, *Hermes* **95** (1967), 179f.

21. For what follows see Badian, *Ehrenberg Studies*, 54ff.

22. Menes: Arr. III.16.9. On *hyparchos* see Tarn, *Alexander*, II.173, n. 1.

23. For details of types and mints see Bellinger, *Coinage*, 26ff., 48ff.

Chapter 8: The year of decision

(Sources: Arr. III.7–22; Diod. 17.54–73; Curt. IV.9–V.13; Plut. 31–43; Just. XI.13–15)

1. For the preliminaries to Gaugamela see, especially, Marsden, *The Campaign of Gaugamela*.

2. For the date of the battle see my note to Plut. 31.8. On the battle see Fuller, *Generalship*, 163ff.; Burn, *JHS*, **72** (1952), 85ff.; Marsden, op. cit., 40ff.; and G. T. Griffith, 'Alexander's Generalship at Gaugamela', *JHS*, **67** (1947), 77ff.

3. Suggested by Griffith, op. cit., 82ff., and Marsden, op. cit., 58ff., respectively.

4. Plut. 34.1 (the only evidence).

5. Arr. III.16.4; VII.17.1. However, Herodotus states (I.181) that the temple existed until his day; see How and Wells' note on this passage, and for a solution Schachermeyr, *Alexander in Babylon*, 55ff. (with plans on pp. 58–9).

6. So Tarn, *Alexander*, II.109 and Wilcken, *Alexander*, 141, respectively.

7. See, on this last point, Griffith, *PCPhS*, **10** (1964), 35ff.

8. Almost 15,000 in all. For details see Diod. 17.65.1 and Curt. V.1.40–2.

9. As Milns has demonstrated in *GRBS*, **7** (1966), 159ff.

10. Argued by Milns, *Historia*, **20** (1971), 188ff.

11. Arr. III.16.7–8. His later statement (VII.19.2)—given as a mere report (*logos*)—that they were sent back in 323 is incorrect.

12. I follow E. N. Borza, 'The End of Agis' Revolt', *CP*, **66** (1971), 230ff., in preferring Curtius' dating (VI.1.21) to Justin's (XII.1.4). The latter is defended by G. L. Cawkwell, 'The Crowning of Demosthenes', *CQ* N.S. **19** (1969), 170ff.

13. Burn, *JHS*, **72** (1952), 90f., regards the conquest of Persis as a surprising and brilliant move; *contra* Badian, *Hermes*, **95** (1967), 189.

14. Diod. 17.68.1, Curt. V.3.17; Arr. III.18.2 has 40,000 infantry and 700 cavalry. For the campaign see Fuller, *Generalship*, 226ff., based on the survey by Sir Aurel Stein, who identified the Gates with the pass at the head of the valley Tang-i-Khas. This is now confirmed by J. Hansman, 'Elamites, Achaemenians, and Anshan', *Iran*, **10** (1972), 101ff., at p. 118f.

15. Diod. 17.70.2, Curt. V.6.6. The incident is ignored by Arrian.

16. The 'palace' is described by Olmstead, *Persian Empire*, 272ff., and Donald N. Wilber, *Persepolis* (London, 1969). For the reliefs see, e.g. Sir Mortimer Wheeler, *Flames over Persepolis*, and, if at all possible, E. F. Schmidt, *Persepolis*, 2 vols. (Chicago, 1953, 1957).
The ancient sources for the event are Arr. III.18.10ff., Diod. 17.70–2; Curt. V.6–7; Plut. 38.

17. Curt. V.6.12, 'About the (evening) setting of the Pleiades'. See Hamilton, *Commentary* 99 (on Plut. 39.1), where the approximate date of the setting should read '6 April', not '20 April'.

18. e.g. G. Wirth, 'Dareios und Alexander', *Chiron*, **1** (1971), 133ff., especially 149ff.; Tarn, *Alexander*, II.47f., ' a political manifesto to Asia'.
E. N. Borza, 'Fire from Heaven: Alexander at Persepolis', *CP*, **67** (1972), 233ff., argues that the 'palace' was deliberately set on fire since Persepolis was 'the symbol of the *ancien régime* in Asia' (p. 243).

19. So Badian, *Hermes*, **95** (1967), 186ff. See, however, Borza, op. cit., 240ff. (cf his note to Wilcken, *Alexander*, 145), and G. Wirth, *Historia*, **20** (1971), 620f.

20. For the fate of this treasure see p. 162.

21. See Hamilton, *Commentary*, 89.

22. On Alexander's route see G. Radet, *Mélanges G. Glotz* (Paris, 1932), II.767ff., and A. F. von Stahl, *Geographical Journal*, **64** (1924), 312ff.

F*

Chapter 9: The conquest of the north-east

(Sources: Arr. III.23–IV.7, IV.15–22.2; Diod. 17.74–83; Curt. VI–VII, VIII.3–4; Plut. 44–9, 56–8.4; Just. XII.1–5)

1. Badian, *CQ* N.S. **8** (1958), 144ff., has shown that Bagoas was not an invention, as Tarn asserted (*Alexander*, II.319ff.).

2. Although Tarn, *The Greeks in Bactria and India*, 2nd ed. (Cambridge, 1951), 14, n. 4, identifies it with Nad-i-Ali in modern Seistan.

3. The sources are Arr. III.26.1–4; Diod. 17.79–80; Curt. VI.7–VII.2; Plut. 48–9.

4. See Schachermeyr, *Alexander*, 266 ff., Berve, *Alexanderreich*, II, no. 802, Badian, *TAPA*, **91** (1960), 324ff.

5. For the remainder of this paragraph see Plut. 48.

6. See Hamilton, *Commentary*, 120–1, and especially H. Berve, *Klio*, **31** (1938), 135 ff. (=Griffith, *Main Problems*, 103ff.), at pp. 148ff.

7. On Demetrius see Badian, *TAPA*, **91** (1960), 334ff.

8. Tarn, *Alexander*, I.64. For the custom see Tarn, *Alexander*, II.270–2. Badian, op. cit., 332ff., rejects Tarn's view that the murder was an act of regrettable necessity; but Parmenio was not merely a Macedonian officer, he was Alexander's second-in-command.

9. Tarn, *The Greeks in Bactria and India*, 2nd ed., 470ff., maintains that it was founded at Ghazni, but Wheeler's arguments (*Flames over Persepolis*, 65ff.) are decisive in favour of Kandahar, the generally accepted identification.

10. Bessus was executed for the murder of Darius, not for assuming the upright tiara; see Badian, *CQ* N.S. **8** (1958), 146, against Tarn, *Alexander*, I.70.

11. Since Tanais is derived from a native word *tana, meaning water; see J. R. Hamilton, 'Alexander and the Aral', *CQ* N.S. **21** (1971), 110, n. 5.

12. Arr. IV.3.7; 5.2–6.2.

13. C. Neumann, 'A Note on Alexander's March-Rates', *Historia*, **20** (1971), 196ff., refutes Milns' claim (*Historia* (1966), 256) that such a rate is impossible.

14. On the use of Persian cavalry see Griffith, *JHS*, **83** (1963), 72ff., and for details of reinforcements Curt. VIII.10.11–12.

15. See my article mentioned in n. 11.

16. For the evidence see Schachermeyr, *Alexander*, 515, n. 187.

17. Although the ritual may also be Macedonian, as Curtius (VIII.4.27) claims; see M. Renard and J. Servais, 'A propos d'un mariage d'Alexandre et de Roxane', *Antiquité Classique*, **24** (1955), 29ff.

Chapter 10: Alexander and the Macedonians

(Sources: Arr. IV.8–14; Curt. VIII.1–2, 5–8; Plut. 50–5; Just. XII.6–7.3. There is a lacuna in the text of Diodorus)

1. The murder is related by Arr. IV.8–9; Curt. VIII.1–2; Plut. 50–1. For an analysis of their versions see Brown, *AJP*, **70** (1949), 236ff. (=Griffith, *Main Problems*, 40ff.)

2. On what follows see Plut. 45, Diod. 17.77.4–7 (with Welles' notes), Curt. III.3.23ff., VI.6.1–11.

3. For the view that *proskynesis* involved simply blowing a kiss see F. Altheim, 'Proskynesis', *Paideia*, **5** (1950), 307, and E. J. Bickerman, 'A propos d'un passage de Chares de Mytilene', *Parola del Passato*, **8** (1963), 241.

4. The view adopted here is basically that advocated by Balsdon, *Historia*, **1** (1950), 371ff. (=Griffith, *Main Problems*, 179ff.). See, further, Brown, op. cit., and Hamilton, *Commentary*, 150ff. However, Badian (*Classical World* **65**, no. 2

(Oct. 1971), 43) considers that 'the implications of the obvious Greek interpretation must have been recognized and accepted'.

5. Plut. 54.3; Arr. IV.12.3, who also relates as a *logos* (IV.10.5–11.9) a debate between Callisthenes and Anaxarchus on the merits of deification. In this version it is the favourable reaction of the Macedonians to Callisthenes' objections that leads Alexander to abandon *proskynesis*.

6. See Badian's comments in *Gnomon*, 33 (1961), 661.

7. Arrian (IV.12.2) relates as part of the *logos* that Leonnatus laughed at a Persian bowing clumsily. This may be true and may account for the check to his career (so Badian, *TAPA*, **91** (1960), 337), but the incident occurred after Alexander had ordered the abandonment of *proskynesis*.

8. Brown, *AJP*, **70** (1949), 247.

9. Plut. 53.3–6. In Plutarch's narrative, admittedly, it precedes Callisthenes' refusal to perform *proskynesis*; see Hamilton, *Commentary*, 147–8.

10. See Brown, loc cit., and Schachermeyr, *Alexander*, 318 ff.

11. Arr. IV. 13–14; Curt. VIII. 6–8; Plut. 55.

12. So Tarn, *Alexander*, I.81 and Wilcken, *Alexander*, 170.

13. Schachermeyr, *Alexander*, 315ff.

14. For the letters see Plut. 55.6 and 55.7, and on their authenticity J. R. Hamilton, 'Three passages in Arrian', *CQ* N.S. 5 (1955), 219ff., and id., *PACA*, **4** (1961), 15f.

15. Arr. IV.14.3 (Ptolemy and Aristobulus); Plut. 55.9 (Chares).

16. Tarn, *Alexander*, II.96ff. His arguments are demolished by Badian, *CQ* (1958), 144ff., and E. Mensching, *Historia*, **12** (1963), 274ff.

17. See Hamilton, *Commentary*, lxi–ii.

Chapter 11: The Indian expedition

(Sources: Arr. IV.22.3–VI.20; Diod. 17.84–104.2; Curt. VIII. 9–IX.10.3; Plut. 58.5–66.3; Just. XII.7.4–10.7)

1. Arr. IV.30.4, Curt. VIII.11.25 (Sisicottus); Diod. 17.86.4, Curt. VIII.12.4 (Taxiles). See, in general, R. Andreotti, *Saeculum*, **8** (1957), 143.

2. Tarn, *Alexander*, II.53–4.

3. See Tarn, *Alexander*, I.90, and G. Woodcock, *The Greeks in India* (London, 1966), 21ff. For the emulation of Dionysus and Heracles as a motif see P. A. Brunt, *G & R*, **12** (1965), 209.

4. Stein's book, *On Alexander's Track to the Indus* (London, 1929), 128ff., is important for this whole chapter. The (tentative) identification of Bazira and Ora is also due to Stein; see pp. 30ff., 58ff. For the Aornus campaign see also Fuller, *Generalship*, 248ff. (with photographs).

5. See Sir John Marshall, *Taxila*, 3 vols. (Cambridge, 1951). Taxiles was the ruler's official name; his own name was Ambhi. 'Porus', the Paurava monarch, was a similar name.

6. See, especially, Strabo 15.1.63ff., and, more briefly, Arr. VII. 2.2–4, Plut. 65. For an analysis of their doctrines see T. S. Brown, *Onesicritus*, 39ff. M. Hadas, *Hellenistic Culture* (New York, 1959), 178ff., points out the popularity of the story of Calanus' death.

7. See Fuller, *Generalship*, 180ff., Burn, *G & R*, **12** (1965), 151ff., J. R. Hamilton, 'The Cavalry Battle at the Hydaspes', *JHS*, **76** (1956), 26ff. Sources: Arr. V.8.4–18.5; Diod. 17.87–8; Curt. VIII.13.5–14.33; Plut. 60.1–10.

8. e.g. Tarn, *Alexander*, II.275, n. 5. See, in reply, Schachermeyr, *Jax Festschrift*, 128, n. 17 128 (= Griffith, *Main Problems*, 142), n. 17.

9. On the mutiny see Arr. V.25–8; Diod. 17.93–5; Curt. IX.2.1–3.19; Plut. 62.1–4.

10. For detailed references to this paragraph and the following see Hamilton, *Commentary*, 170ff. Add G. Wirth, 'Nearchos, der Flottenchef', *Acta Conventus XI 'Eirene'* (1971), 627ff.

11. *Meteorologica* I.13.15.

12. In Strabo 15.1.12.

13. e.g. by Tarn, *Alexander*, I.99, Wilcken, *Alexander*, 186, A. K. Narain, *G & R*, **12** (1965), 156.

14. Plut. 62.9. On Chandragupta see Narain, op. cit., 161ff.

15. V.24.8.

16. Fuller, *Generalship*, 259ff.

17. I do not see how Tarn, *Alexander*, I.103 (followed by Narain, op. cit., 160) can call the Mallian campaign 'unique in its dreadful record of mere slaughter'.

18. Both quotations are taken from Wilcken, *Alexander*, 196. On Onesicritus' knowledge of Ceylon see Jacoby, *F.Gr.Hist.*, no. 134, Fr. 12 (=Strabo 15.1.15) and Fr. 13 (=Pliny, *NH*, 6.81), and on the date of his book, Hamilton, *Commentary*, 127 (on Plut. 46.4).

Chapter 12: Return to the west

(Sources: Arr. VI.21–VII.6; Diod. 17.104.3–108.2; Curt. IX.10.4–X.1; Plut. 66.4–71.1; Just. XII.10.8–11.4)

1. Arrian, *Indica* 20 and 32.11. See, also, G. Wirth, *Nearchos*, 630ff.

2. Herodotus 4.44.1 (Scylax). The influence of Herodotus is stressed by Pearson, *Lost Histories*, 118ff.

3. For his motives see Arr. VI.24.3; Strabo 15.1.5 (=Nearchus Fr. 3a,b); 15.2.4f., and H. Strasburger, 'Alexanders Zug durch die gedrosische Wüste', *Hermes*, **80** (1952), 456ff.

4. So Badian, *JHS*, **81** (1961), 21 (=Griffith, *Main Problems*, 211).

5. Details in Hamilton, *Commentary*, 184. For Alexander's army among the Oreitae see Arr. VI.21.3.

6. On its location see my article in *Historia* (forthcoming).

7. For this view see, especially, Badian *CQ* N.S. **8** (1958), 148ff., and *JHS*, **81** (1961), 16ff., especially 21. Note also the execution of Astaspes.

8. Plut. 68.7.

9. Athenaeus 13.594–5; Plut. *Phocion*, ch. 22.

10. Diod. 17.106.3.

11. On Cleomenes' misdeeds see Pseudo-Aristotle, *Oeconomica*, 2.33, and Pseudo-Demosthenes, 56.7ff. For the authenticity of Alexander's letter (Arr. VII.23.8) see Hamilton, *CQ* N.S. **3** (1953), 157 (=Griffith, *Main Problems*, 241).

12. See, especially, Plut. 67, Curt. IX.10.24ff.

13. Arrian, *Indica* 33–6. For Nearchus' story see *Indica* 21–32.

14. It is perhaps worth mentioning that Alexander's judgement was proved correct. Sibyrtius retained his provinces at Alexander's death and governed them for many years afterwards.

15. Arr. VI.29.4–30.2; Strabo 15.3.7; Plut. 69.3. The tomb is often photographed; see, e.g. Green, *Alexander the Great*, 170, or Schachermeyr, *Alexander*, Tafel XII.

16. Badian, *CQ* N.S. **8** (1958), 147ff.

17. For Harpalus' story see Badian, *JHS*, **81**, 1961, 16ff. (=Griffith, *Main Problems*, 206ff.), especially 23ff., 31ff.

18. Athenaeus 12.537d–540a =Chares (*F.Gr.Hist.* no. 125), Fr. 4. See also Arr. VII.4.4ff., Plut. 70, Diod. 17.107.6.

19. On the evidence for this date Hamilton, *Commentary*, 128–9.

20. Arr. VII.6.3–4. For the emendation of his text see Badian, 'Orientals in Alexander's army', *JHS*, **85** (1965), 160f.

On the reorganization of the Companion cavalry see Brunt, *JHS*, **83** (1963), 42ff., and Griffith, *JHS*, **83** (1963), 68ff.

Chapter 13: Alexander and the Greeks

1. See the speech 'On the Treaty with Alexander' (Pseudo-Demosthenes 17), especially paras. 4, 7, 10, 16. On the circumstances see G. L. Cawkwell, 'A Note on Ps. Demosthenes 17.20', *Phoenix*, **15** (1961), 74ff.

2. For the announcement at Susa see Dittenberger, *SIG*³ i.312; U. Wilcken, *SPAW*, 1922, 112ff.; A. Heuss, 'Antigonos Monopthalmos und die griechische Städte', *Hermes*, **73** (1938), 134ff. See also Diod. 17.109.2, 18.8.1–7.

3. Tarn, *Alexander*, I.112 and Wilcken, *Alexander*, 214 regard the Decree as 'an act of wise statesmanship'. Badian's more realistic view (*JHS*, **81** (1961), 25ff.) is adopted here.

4. Curt. IX.7.1–11.

5. Diod. 18.8.2ff., cf. id. 17.109.1; Curt. X.2.4–7; Just. XIII.5.2–5. For the date of the Olympic Games see R. Sealey, 'The Olympic Festival of 324 B.C.', *CR* N.S. **10** (1960), 185f.

6. Tod, *GHI*, nos. 201, 202.

7. e.g. by Wilcken, *Alexander*, 214f.

8. Plut. *Moralia* 219e; Aelian, *Varia Historia* II.19.

The best case for the negative is made by Balsdon, *Historia* 1 (1950), 383ff. (=Griffith, *Main Problems*, 199ff.), who gives all references. See, also, E. Bickerman, *Athenaeum*, **41** (1963), 70ff. For acceptance see Wilcken, *Alexander*, 209ff., Brunt, *G & R* **12** (1965), 210ff., and, especially, Habicht, *Gottmenschentum* 28ff., and, especially, 246ff.

9. VII.23.2. On this passage Habicht's arguments (Gottmenschentum, 247f.) are decisive.

10. See Hamilton, *Commentary*, 73 (on ch. XXVIII).

11. It is advanced by Tarn (*Alexander*, II.370ff.), who cites Eduard Meyer and W. S. Ferguson. His arguments are refuted by Balsdon, op. cit., 386f.

12. So Wilcken, *Alexander*, 209ff. Rejected by Tarn, *Alexander*, II.372f.

13. Suidas (s.v. *Antipatros*) states that Antipater, alone of Alexander's Successors, refused to call him a god; but he clearly refers to a time after Alexander's death and it would be rash to assert that the originator of the statement referred to an earlier period. For the Ionian League see Habicht, *Gottmenschentum*, 17ff., 245ff.

14. On the 'Porus' decadrachms see, especially, W. B. Kaiser, 'Ein Meister der Glyptik aus dem Umkreis Alexanders des Grossen', *JDAI*, **77** (1962), 227ff. cf. C. Seltman, *Greek Coins*, 213f. On Apelles see Pliny, *NH* 35.92.

15. Lysander: Plut. *Lysander*, 18; see Habicht, *Gottmenschentum*, 3ff., 243f. Philip at Aegae: Diod. 16.92.5; 95.1. For the altars of Zeus Philippius at Eresus and the statue of Philip at Ephesus (probably *not* a cult statue) see Habicht, op. cit., 14ff., 245.

16. Plut. 28. See Hamilton, *CQ* (1953), 151ff. (=Griffith, *Main Problems*, 235ff.), whose interpretation is, however, contested by Kraft, *Alexander*, 43–7.

17. For discussions of the religious position of the Persian king see the works cited by Balsdon, *Historia*, **1** (1950), 375 (=Griffith, *Main Problems*, 191), n. 66, and H. Bengtson, *Gr. Gesch.*⁴ (1969), 357, n. 5.

Chapter 14: The last twelve months

1. Pliny, *NH* 6.138 (Charax); Arr. VII.7.7; Strabo 16.1.9.

2. For the 'Successors' see p. 134. The sources for the mutiny are Arr. VII.8.1–11.9; Diod. 17.108.1–3; Curt. X.2.12–4.4; Plut. 71. Arrian alone correctly places it at Opis.
On Alexander's speech see my remarks on p. 26 and, further, F. R. Wüst, 'Die Rede Alexanders des Grossen in Opis', *Historia*, **2** (1953–4), 177ff. The details of the speech are not to be relied on. Tarn (*Alexander*, I.116f., II.434ff.) is confuted by Badian, *Historia*, **7** (1958), 428ff. (=Griffith, *Main Problems*, 290ff.). cf. Wilcken, *Alexander*, 221.

3. See Plut. 39.7.

4. VII.12.6.

5. Tarn, *Alexander*, I.112, Wilcken, *Alexander*, 222.

6. *JHS*, **81** (1961), 36ff.

7. *PACA*, **8** (1965), 12ff. Aetolians: Plut. 49.14–5; Cassander: Plut. 74.2–3.

8. See Arrian's remarks at VII.14.2ff.

9. On the position of *chiliarch* see Schachermeyr's remarks in *Alexander in Babylon*, 31ff. On Perdiccas' position after Hephaestion's death see H. Strasburger, *Ptolemaios und Alexander* (Leipzig, 1934), 47, and Bosworth, *CQ* (1971), 131f.

10. Plut. 72.6.

11. It is discussed by Schachermeyr, *JOEAI* (1954), 127f. (=Griffith, *Main Problems*, 331f.), and Wilcken, *Alexander*, 234f.

12. Plut. 72.4. On the cities see Arrian, *Indica* 40.6–8.

13. See Arr. VII.15.4–6; Diod. 17.113.1–4.

14. Cleitarchus (*F.Gr.Hist.* no. 137), Fr. 31 (=Pliny, *Nat. Hist.* 3.57). On this fragment see Badian, *PACA*, **8** (1965), 5ff., Hamilton, *Historia*, **10** (1961), 452ff., and, especially, Schachermeyr, *Alexander in Babylon*, 217ff.
Decisive: e.g. Tarn, *Alexander*, II.21ff., Bengtson, *Gr. Gesch*[4]., 357, n. 1.

15. Arr. VII.22.2–5; Diod. 17.116.5–7. Aristobulus characteristically states that the sailor was only flogged.

16. Arr. VII. 24.1–3; Diod. 17.116.2–4; Plut. 72.5–73.1.

17. See Tarn, *JEA*, **15** (1929), 13f., who combines the evidence of Arrian, *Indica* 43.7, Strabo, 16.4.4, and Theophrastus, *Hist. Plant.* 9.4.2–4.

18. Sources: Arr. VII.19.6–20.2; Strabo 16.1.11. Exploration: Tarn, *Alexander*, I.119, II.394f.; cf. Wilcken, *Alexander*, 229.

19. Heracleides: Arr. VII.16.1 (=Aristobulus Fr. 54). Patrocles: Strabo 11.6.1.

20. See Brunt, *JHS*, **83** (1963), 39.

21. Arr. VII.19.1; cf. VII.23.2. Diod. 17.113 appears to combine the embassies mentioned by Arrian at VII.15.4ff., and VII.19.1.

22. For discussion of this letter see Hamilton, *CQ* N.S. **3** (1953), 151ff. (=Griffith, *Main Problems*, 235ff.).

23. E. J. Bickerman, *Athenaeum*, **41** (1963), 70ff. Diod. 17.115.6 says that the reply of Ammon was that Hephaestion should be honoured as a *god*. For the letter to Cleomenes see p. 129.

24. Diod. 17.114.4; 115.1,5. Arr. VII.14.9. On Hephaestion's relations with Craterus see Plut. 47.9, and for those with Eumenes see Plut. *Eum.* 2, Arr. VII. 13.1, 14.9.

25. For this date see A. E. Samuel, *Historia*, **14** (1965), 8. On the evidence of Pseudo-Callisthenes see now D. M. Lewis, *CR* N.S. **19** (1969), 272.

26. Plut. 76–7; Arr. VII.25.1–26.3. On the *Diary* see ch. 1, n. 8. Leukemia: Schachermeyr, *Alexander in Babylon*, 68, n. 120.

27. Arr. VII.27; Diod. 17.118; Curt. X.10.14ff.; Plut 77.2ff. Strychnine: R. D. Milns, *Alexander the Great*, 255ff.

28. Argued by A. B. Bosworth, *CQ* N.S. **21** (1971), 112ff. An important article, but, as the author realizes, necessarily inconclusive.

Notes

Notes 183

Chapter 15: Alexander's plans

1. Arr. VII.1.2–3; Plut. 68.1; Curt. X.1.17–9.
2. Diod. 18.4.4ff. On Hieronymus of Cardia see T. S. Brown, *AHR*, **52** (1946–7), 684ff.
3. The best case for acceptance is made by Schachermeyr, *JOEAI*, **41** (1954), 118 (=Griffith, *Main Problems*, 322ff.); cf. id., *Alexander in Babylon*, 187ff.
4. Tarn, *Alexander*, II.378ff., Hampl, *Studies Robinson* 816ff. (=Griffith, *Main Problems*, 307ff.), cf. Andreotti, *Saeculum*, **8** (1957), 133ff.
5. Arr. VII.19.4.
6. Strabo 13.1.26.
7. As Schachermeyr does, *JOEAI* (1954), 129 (=Griffith, *Main Problems*, 333).
8. Badian, *HSCP*, **72** (1968), 183ff., at p. 201.
9. Rejected, however, by Schachermeyr, *Alexander in Babylon*, 193—wrongly, in my opinion.
10. Curt. IV.4.18.

Chapter 16: Looking back

1. Plutarch, *Agesilaus* 15.
2. Alexander himself had acted in accordance with the decree after the battle of the River Granicus. That it had not been rescinded is clear from his treatment of the mercenaries who surrendered in Hyrcania; see Arr. III.24.5.
3. See p. 75.
4. *Moralia* 328e.
5. See Tarn, *Alexander*, II.237f.
6. C. B. Welles, *G & R*, **12** (1965), 225.
7. On Isocrates see Tarn, *Alexander*, II.403; on Aristotle see Badian, *Historia*, **7** (1958), 440 (=Griffith, *Main Problems*, 302).
8. On Achaemenid policy see Polycleitus (Jacoby, *F.Gr.Hist.*, no. 128), Fr. 3, and Olmstead, *Persian Empire*, 189. How much of the treasure was in coin is not known; see table in Bellinger, *Coinage*, 68, n. 148.
For the view that most of the treasure was put into circulation see, e.g. Wilcken, *Alexander*, 148, 254f. It seems quite improper to reduce the figure of 30,000 talents to 15,000 while retaining the figure of 50,000, as Tarn (*Alexander*, I.132) does (following Beloch and others).
9. Bellinger, *Coinage* 72ff., suggests that the traditional Persian darics may have been struck from the treasure, but this theory is as yet untested.
10. Gorgus: Strabo 15.1.30. Crates: Strabo 9.2.18.
11. See Brunt, *JHS*, **83** (1963), 36ff.
12. See his article in *AUMLA* (1962) (=*Studies in Greek and Roman History*, Blackwell, Oxford 1964, 192ff.).
13. *Alexander* 26.14.

BIBLIOGRAPHY

The best starting-point for further study of Alexander is E. Badian's survey, 'Alexander the Great, 1948–67', in *Classical World*, vol. 65, nos. 2–3 (October–November, 1971), 37ff., 77ff. Although this is restricted to the most important aspects of Alexander-studies, it provides a virtually complete list of books and articles on these topics together with brief comment on many items. A short discussion of source problems and selected topics precedes the bibliography, and an appendix contains works published in 1968.

Books and articles appearing between 1940 and 1950 are reviewed by R. Andreotti, 'Il problema di Alessandro Magno nella storiografia dell' ultimo decennio', *Historia*, 1 (1950), 583–600, while G. Walser, 'Zur neueren Forschung über Alexander den Grossen' (published in 1956 and reprinted in Griffith, *Main Problems*, 345–79), deals with a slightly longer period.

Two important collections of articles must be mentioned. In *Alexander the Great: the Main Problems* (Heffer, Cambridge, 1966) G. T. Griffith has assembled sixteen important studies, five in German, bearing on 'the essential Alexander', while the 'Alexander number' of *Greece and Rome* (vol. 12, no. 2, October 1965) contains nine articles on topics ranging from 'Alexander's Early Life' to 'Alexander's Historical Achievement'.

Those who wish for further information, especially on older work, should consult the *Cambridge Ancient History*, vol. 6 (1926), G. Glotz and R. Cohen, *Histoire Grecque* IV.1, 2nd ed. (Paris, 1945), or H. Bengtson, *Griechische Geschichte*, 4th ed. (Munich, 1969). The most recent and most comprehensive collection of material is Jakob Seibert's *Alexander der Grosse* (Darmstadt, 1972); arranged chronologically by topics (from about 1877), it provides excellent surveys of particular problems, but unfortunately it (intentionally) excludes the contributions of general works to such problems.

I have included in the list of Modern Works only those books and articles I have cited several times; those dealing with particular points are not included, but their titles are given in full in the appropriate notes. I have also excluded work on the sources, reference to which is made in the notes to Chapter 1.

ANCIENT SOURCES

For text and translation of the 'fragments' see note 2 to Chapter 1.

Arrian

A. G. Roos' Teubner text in 2 vols. (I. Anabasis, II. Scripta Minora, including the Indica) has been reissued with additions and corrections and bibliographies by G. Wirth (1967, 68). Aubrey de Sélincourt's translation, *The Life of Alexander*, has been reissued by Penguin Books as *The Campaigns of Alexander* with a revised translation, introduction and notes by J. R. Hamilton (1971).

Diodorus

C. Th. Fischer's Teubner text (3rd ed., 1906) has been reprinted (1964) without change. C. Bradford Welles has edited volume 8 (containing Bk. 16.66–95 and Bk. 17) for the Loeb series; in addition to an excellent translation he has provided a useful introduction and notes.

Curtius

J. C. Rolfe's Loeb edition in 2 vols. (1946) is based on the Teubner text by E. Hedicke (1908), but contains a number of serious errors in the translation. More reliable is the Budé edition in 2 vols. by H. Bardon (2nd ed., Paris, 1961).

Plutarch

The best text is Konrat Ziegler's revised Teubner text (1968), included in vol. II.2 of the complete *Lives*. J. R. Hamilton, *Plutarch*, Alexander: *A Commentary* is mainly a historical commentary. The most recent translation of the *Alexander* is by Ian Scott-Kilvert in *The Age of Alexander* (Penguin Books).

MODERN WORKS

(Articles reprinted in Griffith: *Alexander the Great. The Main Problems* are marked with an asterisk)

Adcock, Sir Frank, *The Greek and Macedonian Art of War* (Berkeley, 1957).
Andreotti, R., 'Die Weltmonarchie Alexanders des Grossen', *Saeculum*, 8 (1957), 120–66 (with extensive bibliography).
Badian, E., 'The Eunuch Bagoas, A Study in method', *CQ*, 8 (1958), 144–57.
* —— 'Alexander the Great and the Unity of Mankind', *Historia*, 7 (1958), 425–44.
—— 'The Death of Parmenio', *TAPA*, 91 (1960), 324–38.
* —— 'Harpalus', *JHS*, 81 (1961), 16–43.
—— 'The Death of Philip II', *Phoenix*, 17 (1963), 244–50.
—— 'The Administration of the Empire', *G & R*, 12 (1965), 166–82.
—— 'Alexander the Great and the Greek Cities of Asia Minor', *Ancient Societies and Institutions: Studies presented to Victor Ehrenberg on his 75th birthday* (Oxford, Blackwell, 1966), 37–69.
—— 'Agis III', *Hermes*, 95 (1967), 170–92.
—— 'A King's Notebooks', *HSCP*, 72 (1968), 183–204.
* Balsdon, J. P. V. D., 'The "Divinity" of Alexander the Great', *Historia*, 1 (1950), 363–88.
Bellinger, A. R., *Essays on the Coinage of Alexander the Great* (Numismatic Studies 11, The American Numismatic Society), New York, 1963.
Bengtson, H., *Griechische Geschichte*, 4th ed. (Munich, 1969).
Berve, H., *Das Alexanderreich auf prosopographischer Grundlage*, 2 vols. (Munich, 1926).
* —— 'Die Verschmelzungspolitik Alexanders des Grossen', *Klio*, 31 (1938), 135–68.

Bickerman, E. J., 'Sur un passage d'Hypéride, *Epitaphios*, col. VIII', *Athenaeum*, **41** (1963), 70–85.

Bosworth, A. B., 'The Death of Alexander the Great: Rumour and Propaganda', *CQ*, **21** (1971), 112–36.

Brown, T. S., 'Hieronymus of Cardia', *AHR*, **52** (1946–7), 684–96.

* —— 'Callisthenes and Alexander', *AJP*, **70** (1949), 225–48.

Brunt, P. A., 'Alexander's Macedonian Cavalry', *JHS*, **83** (1963), 27–46.

—— 'The Aims of Alexander', *G & R*, **12** (1965), 205–15.

Burn, A. R., *Alexander the Great and the Hellenistic World*, 2nd ed. (New York, 1962).

—— 'Notes on Alexander's Campaigns', *JHS*, **72** (1952), 81–91.

—— 'The Generalship of Alexander the Great', *G & R*, **12** (1965), 140–54.

Dittenberger, W., *Sylloge Inscriptionum Graecarum*, 3rd ed., 4 vols. (Leipzig, 1915–24).

Edmunds, Lowell, 'The Religiosity of Alexander', *GRBS*, **12** (1971), 363–91.

* Ehrenberg, V., Alexander and the Greeks (Oxford, Blackwell, 1938). Ch. 2, *'Pothos'*, is reprinted in Griffith, *Main Problems*.

Fredricksmeyer, E. A., 'Alexander, Midas, and the Oracle at Gordium', *CP*, **56** (1961), 160–8.

Fuller, J. F. C., *The Generalship of Alexander the Great* (London, 1958).

Green, Peter, *Alexander the Great* (London, 1970).

Griffith, G. T., *'Makedonika*. Notes on the Macedonians of Philip and Alexander', *PCPhS*, N.S. **4** (1956), 3–10.

—— 'A Note on the Hipparchies of Alexander', *JHS*, **83** (1963), 68–74.

—— 'Alexander the Great and an Experiment in Government', *PCPhS*, N.S. **10** (1964), 23–39.

—— 'Alexander and Antipater in 323 B.C.', *PACA*, **8** (1965), 12–17.

—— 'The Macedonian Background', *G & R*, **12** (1965), 125–39.

—— (Ed.) *Alexander the Great: The Main Problems* (Heffer, Cambridge, 1966).

Habicht, C., Gottmenschentum und griechische Städte, 2nd ed. (Munich, 1970).

* Hamilton, J. R., 'Alexander and his "So-called" Father', *CQ*, **3** (1953), 151–7.

—— 'Three Passages in Arrian', *CQ*, **5** (1955), 217–21.

—— 'The Letters in Plutarch's *Alexander*', *PACA*, **4** (1961), 12–20.

—— *Plutarch*, Alexander: *a Commentary* (Oxford, 1969).

Hampl, F. 'Alexander der Grosse und die Beurteilung geschichtlicher Persönlichkeiten in der modernen Historiographie', *La Nouvelle Clio* 6 (1954), 91–135.

* —— 'Alexanders des Grossen Hypomnemata und letzte Pläne', *D. M. Robinson Studies* (St Louis, Mo., 1953), 2. 16–29.

Jacoby, F., *Die Fragmente der griechischen Historiker*, vols. B, BD (Berlin, 1927–30).

Kraft, Konrad, *Der 'Rationale' Alexander*. Frankfurter Althistorische Studien, Heft 5 (Kallmünzen, 1972).

Marsden, E. W., *The Campaign of Gaugamela* (Liverpool University Press, 1964).

Milns, R. D., 'The Hypaspists of Alexander III—Some Problems', *Historia*, **20** (1971), 186–95.

—— 'Alexander's Seventh Phalanx Battalion', *GRBS*, **7** (1966), 159–66.

—— *Alexander the Great* (London, 1968).

Narain, A. K., 'Alexander and India', *G & R*, **12** (1965), 155–65.

Olmstead, A. T., *A History of the Persian Empire* (Chicago, 1948).

* Pearson, Lionel, 'The Diaries and Letters of Alexander the Great', *Historia*, **3** (1954–5), 429–55.

Pearson, Lionel, *The Lost Histories of Alexander the Great* (Philological Monographs 20), New York, 1960.

Schachermeyr, Fritz, *Alexander der Grosse* (Vienna, 1949).

* —— 'Die letzten Pläne Alexanders des Grossen', *JDAI*, **41** (1954), 118–40.

* —— 'Alexander und die Ganges-Länder', *Natalicium Carolo Jax . . . oblatum*, vol. 1, 123–35, *Innsbrucker Beiträge zur Kulturgeschichte*, **3** (1955).

—— *Alexander in Babylon und die Reichsordnung nach seinen Tode* (Vienna, 1970).

Seltman, C., *Greek Coins*, 2nd ed. (London, 1955).

Stein, Sir Aurel, *On Alexander's Track to the Indus* (London, 1929).

Tarn, Sir William, *Alexander the Great*, 2 vols. (Cambridge, 1948).

Tod, M. N., *A Selection of Greek Historical Inscriptions*, vol. 2 (Oxford, 1948).

Welles, C. B., 'The Discovery of Sarapis and the Foundation of Alexandria', *Historia*, **11** (1962), 271–98.

—— 'Alexander's Historical Achievement', *G & R*, **12** (1965), 216–28.

Wilcken, Ulrich, *Alexander the Great*, trans. G. C. Richards (London, 1932). Reprinted with a new introduction, notes, and bibliography by Eugene Borza (New York, 1967).

Wheeler, Sir Mortimer, *Flames over Persepolis* (London, 1968).

Wirth, G., 'Nearchos, der Flottenchef', *Acta Conventus XI 'Eirene'* (1971), 615–39.

—— 'Alexander zwischen Gaugamela und Persepolis', *Historia*, **20** (1971), 617–32.

INDEX

339   Philip campaigns in Scythia. Alexander summoned to join him.

338   Battle of Chaeroneia (2 August). Alexander among the Macedonian
       envoys to Athens.
       Philip summons Peace Congress at Corinth.
       Death of Artaxerxes III.

337   Spring: First meeting of Council of Corinthian League. Philip appointed
       Hegemon. Subsequently Philip reveals plan for attack on Persian
       Empire and is chosen *strategos autokrator*.
       Philip marries Cleopatra, niece of Attalus. Alexander and Olympias go
       into exile. Alexander returns to Pella.

336   Spring: Parmenio and Attalus begin hostilities in Asia Minor.
       Accession of Darius III to Persian throne.
       Marriage of Alexander of Epirus to Philip's daughter, Cleopatra.
       Philip murdered at Aegae by Pausanias; Alexander succeeds him as
       Alexander III.
       Alexander succeeds to his father's position as *Hegemon* and *strategos
       autokrator* of Corinthian League.

335   Alexander subdues tribes on Lower Danube and Illyrians. Recalled
       by news of Theban revolt. Destruction of Thebes.

334   Spring: Alexander crosses into Asia Minor at head of allied army,
       leaving Antipater in charge of Macedonia and Greece.
       Battle of River Granicus (?May). Democracies established in Asia
       Minor. Miletus and Halicarnassus alone resist.
       Alexander disbands fleet.

334–333 Alexander winters at Gordium.

333   Spring: Death of Memnon during siege of Mytilene, but Persian naval
       offensive in Aegean continues until Issus.
       Alexander marches through Cilician Gates to Tarsus, where he falls ill.
       November: Battle of Issus.

333–332 Submission of Phoenician cities. Persian envoys reach Alexander at
       Marathus with first peace offer.
       Agis III, King of Sparta, hires Greek mercenaries who survive Issus.

332   January–August: Siege of Tyre. Second Persian peace offer reaches
       Alexander.
       Agis collects more mercenaries in Crete.
       September–October: Siege of Gaza.
       Persian satrap surrenders Egypt. Alexander crowned Pharaoh at
       Memphis.
       Macedonians regain control of the Aegean and recover Chios,
       Lesbos, etc.

331   Beginning: Expedition to oracle of Ammon at Siwah.
       Foundation of Alexandria (?7 April).
       Alexander returns to Tyre. News arrives of revolt of Agis.
       Battle of Gaugamela (1 October).

CHRONOLOGICAL TABLE

359   Philip becomes regent of Macedon, and (within a few years) king, as Philip II.

?357   Marriage of Philip and Olympias.

356   Philip founds Philippi, gains goldmines of Mt Pangaeum, and captures Potidaea. His horse wins at Olympia.
Birth of Alexander at Pella about 20 July.
Parmenio defeats Paeonians and Illyrians.

353–352 After initial loss Philip defeats Phocians in Thessaly.

?352   Philip appointed *archon* of Thessaly for life.

?350   Demosthenes' *First Philippic*.

349   Demosthenes' *Olynthiac* speeches (August–September?).

349–348 Philip besieges Olynthus, which falls in September or October 348.

346   End of Third Sacred War. Peace of Philocrates.
Isocrates in his *Philippus* urges Philip to lead 'crusade' of Greek states against Persia.

343–342 Aristotle invited to Macedonia to become Alexander's tutor.
Artaxerxes III of Persia recovers Egypt.

342   Philip founds Philippopolis (Plovdiv) in Thrace, which becomes a Macedonian province.
Olympias' brother, Alexander, becomes King of Epirus with Philip's backing.

340   Philip besieges Byzantium and Perinthus. Athens declares war on Macedon.
Alexander left in Pella as regent: Campaigns against the Maedi and founds Alexandropolis.